DISABILITY, CULTURE, AND EQUITY SERIES

Alfredo J. Artiles, *Series Editor*

D1526113

Equity Expansive Technical Assistance for Schools

Educational Partnerships to Reverse Racial Disproportionality

Kathleen A. King Thorius

TEACHERS COLLEGE PRESS

TEACHERS COLLEGE | COLUMBIA UNIVERSITY
NEW YORK AND LONDON

For John and Mae, who keep me grounded, loved, and looking forward to what's next.

Published by Teachers College Press,® 1234 Amsterdam Avenue, New York, NY 10027

Copyright © 2023 by Teachers College, Columbia University

Front cover design by Edwin Kuo. Image by Evannovostro / Shutterstock.

Library of Congress Cataloging-in-Publication Data

Names: Thorius, Kathleen King, author.
Title: Equity expansive technical assistance for schools : education partnerships
    to reverse racial disproportionality / Kathleen A. King Thorius.
Description: New York : Teachers College Press, [2023] | Series: Disability, culture,
    and equity series | Includes bibliographical references and index.
Identifiers: LCCN 2023003922 (print) | LCCN 2023003923 (ebook) |
    ISBN 9780807768242 (paper : acid-free paper) | ISBN 9780807768259
    (hardcover : acid-free paper) | ISBN 9780807781678 (ebook)
Subjects: LCSH: Special education—Computer network resources. |
    Technical assistance—United States. | Minority people with disabilities—
    Education—United States. | Education and state—United States. |
    Discrimination in education—United States.
Classification: LCC LC3969 .T46 2023 (print) | LCC LC3969 (ebook) |
    DDC 371.9—dc23/eng/20230313
LC record available at https://lccn.loc.gov/2023003922
LC ebook record available at https://lccn.loc.gov/2023003923

ISBN 978-0-8077-6824-2 (paper)
ISBN 978-0-8077-6825-9 (hardcover)
ISBN 978-0-8077-8167-8 (ebook)

Printed on acid-free paper
Manufactured in the United States of America

Contents

Acknowledgments

The people and organizations that have contributed to this book—through their ideas, their support, and their critical and nurturing partnership over the years—are too many to mention, yet I will try my best. To Seena Skelton, for 12 years you have been my constant companion in this work. With you and because of you I have grown and learned more than I ever would have on my own. To my parents, who have always loved me unconditionally and supported my path, even when it took me far away from home. To my early career mother-mentors, especially Samara Way, you continue to model collaborative consultation and the pursuit of excellence and equity in education for all students. To Susan Scharoun and Reverend Vincent Hevern, your teaching led me to graduate school and you both made it clear that sharing and examining the role of one's identity is a crucial part of our responsibility for supporting one another along our journeys. To Elizabeth Kozleski, you are a grand visionary and systems thinker who pushed me with the highest of expectations; you seemed to know just when I needed those pushes and that I would reach those expectations as well. To Alfredo Artiles, you gave me both the space to figure out who I was in this work and gentle critique and example as a scholar. You continue to shape my trajectory. Finally, I share my deepest gratitude to all those at the Great Lakes Equity Center, past and present, including Tiffany Kyser, Robin Jackson, Katy Rusnak, Erin Sanborn, Crystal Morton, Paulo Tan, Ruthie Payno-Simmons, Cynthia Mruczek, Angelina Castagno, Tammera Moore, Sophie Richardson, and many others who have led and joined in solidarity with our intersectional coalition toward equitable and just schools for all.

Introduction and Overview of the Book

A few months ago, I was searching for citations of my technical assistance–related scholarship as I addressed reviewer comments on a manuscript for which I received a "revise and resubmit" decision. The manuscript detailed a research study on the theory, process, and outcomes of a partnership between one of four regional Equity Assistance Centers (EACs) funded by the U.S. Department of Education's Office of Elementary and Secondary Education—where I serve as executive director—and a midwestern State Education Agency (SEA). The partnership focused on literacy achievement of students with disabilities, and the manuscript was coauthored by three agency administrators. During my citation search, I came across the recently published dissertation of one of the agency administrators. In the dedication section she had written: "To Dr. Kathleen King Thorius and Dr. Seena Skelton of the Great Lakes Equity Center. Learning with you about special education and equity helped me see that there is a place for my thinking about literacy within the special education world" (Novak, 2021 p. ii).

Reading Novak's dedication was a powerful moment for me, and I am extremely grateful to have been in partnership with her and her SEA colleagues. In that moment, I reflected on the essence of the theory and practice of technical assistance I have been developing over the past 2 decades, together with many colleagues and mentors. I also considered the stark contrast between what I believe, know, and do now, and how I thought about and practiced my work for a significant portion of my professional career. But I also recognized that I still struggle to resist the status quo of the expert/novice paradigm of technical assistance.

I entered the world of technical assistance practice and scholarship mostly by accident. In 2005, after 6 years as a school psychologist in a southwestern border state preceded by 1 year practicing on the east coast, I decided to pursue a doctoral degree in curriculum and instruction with a concentration in special education. I sought this path because of my dissatisfaction with how my role and my work appeared to be contributing to the placement of students of color, immigrant students, and English learners in special education, along with the pressure I had felt from educators and administrators to

1

do so. Further, I had become disheartened by the inadequacy of educational services and student outcomes prior to and because of special education. As a white nondisabled woman, I was growing more and more troubled with practices and language that felt (and were) racist and ableist toward the students we taught, and whom we were identifying as disabled and placing into special education.

But I did not know the history of these practices, or that they were being replicated all over the United States, particularly in educational settings that served high populations of students of color. In 2005, I was unaware of the phenomenon of racial disproportionality: the over- or underrepresentation of students of color in special and gifted education and in more restrictive educational settings relative to their white counterparts (Gabel et al., 2009). However, disproportionality was the exact phenomenon to which I had been contributing. Albeit unwittingly at times, at other times I participated with deep tensions and frustrations as I worked with primarily white educators whose beliefs about Brown, Black, and Indigenous students, their families, and their communities, were laced with ideologies of white nationalism, ableism, xenophobia, and racism: ideologies I will connect to racial disproportionality throughout this book.

School psychologists, the reader may know, typically are positioned as boundary role professionals (Illback & Maher, 1984), powerful gatekeepers of special education, as Mehan (1993) found in his study of the discourses of various team members involved in special education decision-making meetings. More recently, Walcott and colleagues (2016) found in their survey of members of the National Association of School Psychologists that special education evaluations remain the primary professional responsibility for most in that profession, situating this activity as the linchpin of special education eligibility decision-making processes. Moreover, school psychologists (e.g., Morgan & Farkas, 2016) spearheaded the 2016 emergence of a debate regarding whether disproportionality was indeed a problem; school psychologists historically have been recognized as the most highly influential practitioners in school processes for evaluating students' eligibility for special education and, ultimately, school-based teams' decisions to identify students as disabled (e.g., Becker et al., 2014; Knoff, 1983; Yoshida et al., 1978). As some researchers who study racial disproportionality have demonstrated, one of the main reasons school psychologists have long held privileged status in decision-making processes relates to their administration of intelligence assessments and their use of scientific language to communicate such test results in ways that leave little room for dispute in the construction of the disabled student (e.g., Harry & Klingner, 2006). This privilege exists despite the school psychologist, among members of decision-making teams, which include the students' parents or caregivers, and the teacher of record (Bradley-Johnson et al., 1995), typically having spent the least amount of time with the student being considered for special education eligibility, as was the case in my own practice.

The centrality of the school psychologist's assessment and judgment of a student's status as disabled (Love, 2009) underscores the ways in which disability is defined and responded to in schools. The medical model of disability at the heart of special education processes (Triano, 2000) asserts that disability is located within the body-mind of the student being identified (Mehan, 1993) and that disability can be confirmed or ruled out objectively through standardized clinical and academic assessments (McDermott & Varenne, 1998). Yet, the origins and functions of such assessments throughout history warrant closer and critical scrutiny. Throughout this book, I will reflect on these issues and their relationship to histories of eugenics and other efforts to stratify society along racial and ability hierarchies.

Moreover, because of their roles as special education *influencers*, school psychologists and those in similar positions, such as psychometricians, are often on the receiving end of pressure from those who are making the case behind the scenes for a student's disabled status and, relatedly, their belonging in special education. In the southwestern border state district where I worked, I experienced this case-making constantly as educators and administrators asserted their beliefs that students were "so special ed," or in relation to my role in the district's selected assessment process for identifying and placing students in gifted and talented education programming, as they used it as justification for referring white students only. In some cases, I experienced pressure from administrators and other educators to engage in unethical practice, which has been well documented in the school psychology literature as a cause of professional burnout (e.g., Boccio et al., 2016). For instance, one day I was standing on the playground for recess duty, when out of the blue, a white nondisabled educator defiantly told me, "I don't refer Hispanics for gifted testing because they get extra points for speaking Spanish and that's not fair." Throughout this book I will share several exchanges that remain with me from the years I practiced as a school psychologist and that corroborate the research base on the root causes of disproportionality as tied to systemic and individual racism and ableism. Also through these real-life examples, I offer myself to the reader as an object of critique because in many instances, like this one, I said nothing to express my disagreement, my tensions, or my disgust. My silence was complicity.

As I transitioned from school psychologist to PhD student not yet knowing of the phenomenon of disproportionality, I had no awareness of technical assistance either: not as a concept, or as a network of centers funded by the U.S. Department of Education's various offices to work with state and local education agencies (i.e., school districts) on matters of policy and practice-related capacity building and implementation. Nonetheless, after meeting with my future doctoral chair, Dr. Alfredo Artiles, I began a 5-year journey as a graduate research assistant in the National Center for Culturally Responsive Education Systems (NCCRESt). NCCRESt was a technical assistance center funded by the Office of Special Education Programs (OSEP) and charged with partnering with state education agencies to eliminate patterns of racial disproportionality in special education.

During this time, Artiles and colleagues from another state university had been awarded a personnel preparation grant from the OSEP as well. I joined a small cohort of doctoral fellows in this dual-university, interdisciplinary program to prepare culturally responsive special education professors. I took courses in qualitative and quantitative research methods, visual anthropology, language policy, curriculum foundations, comparative education, bilingual literacy, and special education, and was exposed deeply to sociocultural theory by the faculty who mentored me through my coursework and dissertation, including, in addition to Artiles, Drs. Elizabeth Kozleski, Terri McCarty, and Norma González. Kozleski was NCCRESt's project director as well as principal investigator with Artiles and Drs. Janette Klingner, and Beth Harry and William Tate were coprincipal investigators. As I will share in subsequent chapters, it was through my experience with NCCRESt and with these individuals that I was immersed and first mentored in the development and practice of technical assistance toward addressing racial disproportionality in special education.

However, as I embarked on this journey, my initial understandings of technical assistance were closely connected with a major responsibility I enacted as a school psychologist: functioning as a consultant to educators and families on appropriate prevention, intervention, and treatment of students' academic, behavioral, and social challenges leading to or related to their identification for special education eligibility. My job was to know the research about "what worked" (e.g., Vaughn et al., 2022), although at the time some educational researchers were beginning to raise questions about an evidence base that had largely ignored students of color, English learners, and Indigenous students, as well as the lack of opportunities to learn they and those with similar identity markers had experienced in their schooling (Artiles et al., 1997; Donovan & Cross, 2002; Klingner & Harry, 2006). Accordingly, part of NCCRESt's (2009) approach to technical assistance was the development of open access resources that described the inadequacies of the research and practice base related to educating "culturally and linguistically diverse learners" (p. 17) and offered research-based policy and practice solutions (e.g., Garcia & Ortiz, 2004). I provide more detail on NCCRESt's approaches to technical assistance in subsequent chapters.

During the 7 years NCCRESt was funded (2002–2009), the prevailing responsibilities of technical assistance providers were characterized in existing research as top-down approaches to consulting with partner agencies on evidence-based practical interventions and improvements to existing operations (McInerney & Hamilton, 2007). However, I would come to learn from my mentors, in particular, Kozleski, Artiles, and Klingner, that as much as these approaches prevailed, they were insufficient to effect the systemic change necessary to reverse deep inequities in operations, belief systems, and policies at the root of pernicious issues like racial disproportionality and other systemic equity challenges related to school discipline (Skiba et al., 2016). Feedback I received from Klingner on a professional development resource I developed as an NCCRESt graduate researcher (King et al., 2008) on how Response to Intervention (RTI) (D. Fuchs & Fuchs, 2006) could be designed and leveraged to prevent and address disproportionality, illustrates my lack of these systemic understandings, along with my culture-neutral focus on the technical aspects of RTI.

> Kathleen, you hit the mark on module 1, in which you set the stage for understanding the concept of opportunity to learn and lack thereof as foundational to why RTI is promising approach for CLD (culturally and linguistically diverse) students. But you missed it in this second module. Here, you spend more time rearticulating the technicalities of readings intervention research with English Language Learners, but neglect to account for how culture and context does (or more often does not) inform how these interventions are developed in the first place. I'm happy to look at another version once you've had a chance to consider and revise based on this feedback. (J. Klingner, personal communication, February 10, 2007)

Although Janette passed away in 2014, she continues to teach the next generation of scholars who work to address educational inequities and develop policy and practice innovations toward inclusive, just, and equitable educational systems. I am grateful for her wisdom and that she took such care in teaching and supporting me and so many of my colleagues and friends in our personal and professional growth.

With lots to look back upon and, hopefully, much more on the path ahead, I offer this book for technical assistance practitioners and those in similar roles who partner with educators and other stakeholders across local, state, and federal arenas. I also offer it for teacher education and education leadership and policy faculty who prepare educators in colleges and schools of education. This book is as much a critical personal journey as it is a theoretical and practical guide for what I term *equity expansive technical assistance* (Tan & Thorius, 2019; Thorius, 2019; Thorius & Kyser, 2021), and it is full of examples that illustrate the approach as praxis: scholarly activity "explicitly committed to critiquing the status quo and building a more just society" (Lather, 2017, p. 72).

Given that racial disproportionality in special education has been a common thread through my practical, scholarly, and technical assistance activities, I situate disproportionality as the central issue to be addressed through the approaches I describe. However, as racial disproportionality has been described as a "miner's canary"—a phenomenon that signals pervasive and widespread danger within the ecosystems of our schools and classrooms (Waitoller et al., 2010)—the examples I share will illustrate a variety of educational contexts, beliefs, practices, policies, and relationships that may be addressed through equity expansive technical assistance. Accordingly, the purpose of the book is spurred by the larger context of historical and current construction and treatment in schools of race and racism, and disability and ableism, by past and current efforts, via policy, practice, and partnerships with technical assistance centers and educational agencies, to address these issues.

The book has two parts: The first describes the quest for equity and theory in partnerships to eliminate racial disproportionality in special education, and the second deals with facilitating critical en/counters: the application of equity expansive technical assistance partnerships to reverse racial disproportionality in special education. In Part I, I do some case-making of my own; I justify the need for equity expansive technical assistance, and for applying the framework to the elimination of racial disproportionality in special education.

I begin Chapter 1 with a discussion of the history and complexity of disproportionality (Artiles, 2009): an issue that has reemerged as a hot-button topic in scholarly communities and popular media (e.g., Samuels, 2016). I highlight previous reviews of U.S. special education disproportionality literature, which have found that most extant research has emphasized practice-based explanations and/or aimed to measure the quantitative extent of the issue (e.g., Cruz & Rodl, 2018; Waitoller et al., 2010). Then, I describe the necessity of disproportionality research to move beyond suggestions of technical and piecemeal operational improvements, to account for the complex history and relationship between race, racism, disability, and ableism that mediate current manifestations of systemic educational inequities in the form of racial disproportionality. I acknowledge scholarship that has extended disproportionality research through more intentional theoretical grounding, systemic focus, and explicit attention to the intersection of racism and ableism (Sullivan & Artiles, 2011; Thorius, 2019; Voulgarides et al., 2017). Next, I detail research on policy approaches to remediating disproportionality that have favored special education process improvements and increased governmental monitoring, and summarize research that has shown little impact of such efforts (Albrecht et al., 2012; VanDerHeyden et al., 2007; Wanzek & Vaughn, 2011). I close with a brief discussion of researcher-documented attempts to address disproportionality: brief, because of the dearth of research on the subject.

In Chapter 2, I detail the history of U.S. technical assistance research and practice, and technical assistance's movement into the educational sphere largely via efforts funded to improve state and local educational agencies' special education policies and practices. In short, education technical assistance emerged in the 1980s, drawing from public health prevention models (Schalock et al., 1994; Senge, 1990; Trohanis, 1982), and today continues to rely on a public health model of universal prevention and targeted and intensive intervention (Datnow & Stringfield, 2000; Fixsen et al., 2005). I also document that the bulk of technical assistance research has been self-published by technical assistance centers led by the researchers (e.g., Blase, 2009; Fixsen et al., 2005) rather than peer-reviewed studies and that the majority of this research details two common approaches (McInerney & Hamilton, 2007): a top-down approach for shepherding policy from federal to local systems, and a bottom-up approach for developing local interventions and scaling them up. Both rely on an expert/novice paradigm (Sawyer, 2005) characterized by providers' consultation on programs, policies, or practices to build organizational capacity (Fixsen & Blase, 2009; Katz & Wandersman, 2016; Trohanis, 1982).

Commenting on this research, Kozleski and Artiles (2012) asserted that technical assistance must stimulate complex solutions to historical issues undergirded by systemic oppressions. Technical assistance needs to remediate how *systems* facilitate equity rather than simply consulting on technical improvements to existing operations, since technical assistance has largely failed to redress educational inequities across and between student groups, according to these former NCCRESt leaders. Relatedly, in the second part of Chapter 2, I describe the relationship between federal and state policy meant to address disproportionality, and technical assistance designed to facilitate the elimination of disproportionality, with an emphasis on the technical assistance designed and carried out under the auspices of NCCRESt.

In Chapter 3, I describe the foundational theory and conceptual tools contributing to the framework of equity expansive technical assistance. Namely, I detail activity theory (Vygotsky, 1978b), including second-, third-, and a developing fourth-generation cultural–historical activity theory (Cole, 1996), or CHAT, and its accompanying theory of expansive learning that contributes to this framework.

In Part II, I describe the processes, features, and impacts of the development and application of equity expansive technical assistance. I introduce the framework in Chapter 4, a framework characterized by four related elements: (1) shifts from top-down, expert/novice knowledge transfer to a relational partnership in which the technical assistance provider is a critical friend, thought partner, and bearer of expertise—but not an expert—who supports partners in examining and disrupting inequities in the status quo; (2) shifts from primary concerns with technical improvements in isolated policies and practices, to systemic transformation of educational policy, practices, and belief systems; (3) process-based theorization of systemic transformation; and (4) explicit engagement with historical and current sociocultural beliefs, relationships, practices, policies, and other contextual factors related to the manifestations of (in)equities in the education system(s) of concern.

In Chapter 5, I connect the elements of equity expansive technical assistance to partnership features and processes for eliminating disproportionality. Elsewhere, I have published research on the power of artifacts (e.g., history of eugenics and traces in modern special education policies and practices) that support cultural–historical analyses of social and political forces contributing to inequities and bring educators in contact with contradictions between their expressed goals of eliminating disproportionality and their pathologization of children's differences at the intersection of race and disability (e.g., Thorius, 2016, 2019). To illustrate this connection more concretely, in Chapter 6, I present a vignette comprising elements of technical assistance partnerships between our EAC and school districts working to redress disproportionality as part of systemic transformation efforts. In this vignette, situated in the fictitious Florence Unified School District, I detail real scenarios that emerge within partnerships to illustrate the pervasive yet varied nature of disproportionality, and the complexity of technical assistance efforts to address any entrenched and systemic inequity such as disproportionality.

In Chapter 7, I describe an in-depth example of the design and implementation of a technical assistance partnership between our EAC and an SEA toward remediating racial disproportionality in special education, in the form of findings from a related research study. This chapter illustrates in closer detail our process of formative intervention methodology (see Bal et al., 2012; Engeström, 2011; Thorius, 2016) wherein technical assistance providers introduce mediating artifacts into the partnership activity system to stimulate: (1) contradictions between practice and policy inequities that manifest as disproportionality, and partners' goals for equitable education; (2) examination of the extent of and underlying contributors to disproportionality; and (3) development, enactment, and assessment of the impact of locally relevant innovations. The book wraps up in Chapter 8 with a conclusion and discussion of implications for future policy, practice, and partnerships.

Before I move on to Chapter 1, I imagine the various reasons you, the reader, may have chosen to read this book; you may be a principal of a school in which special education disproportionality has been an issue of concern and about which you have received directives from the school district to eliminate the problem. It is my intent that readers with similar concerns will learn systemic ways of addressing disproportionality that unearth and address underlying conditions of inequities, not simply reduce numbers of students of color who are eligible for special education and placed in more restrictive settings compared with their white counterparts. This will require a whole-team effort where inquiries and solutions are generated in partnership with those who are most impacted by disproportionality.

You may be a new technical assistance provider who is looking to learn about the history of our collective work and the impact it has made on systemic improvements. I hope that you are supported and further compelled to learn more about the groundbreaking work of those who have come before us, along with the possibilities for the future of technical assistance that is both ground-up and acknowledges the knowledges and experiences of those who have led and participated in small- and large-scale partnerships for systemic transformation.

You may be a policymaker, or perhaps someone who develops calls for proposals or notices inviting applications for U.S. Department of Education technical assistance centers that reflect the legislative requirements of existing federal law. I hope you are galvanized in your considerations of the ways in which such centers may be legislated, resourced, and structured to make the most of the opportunities afforded through their funding and legislated focus.

You may be a state- or district-level administrator seeking external guidance or partnership in addressing long-standing inequities in your respective systems. I hope you find useful the theoretical and practical framing of such partnerships in your search for "critical friends." These types of friends bring core assertions regarding the importance of equity in this work, challenge assumptions, clarify language, identify contradictions, and develop an atmosphere of trust (Sachs, 2000; Swaffield & MacBeath, 2005) by honoring and respecting the knowledges and experiences of those within your systems as you build capacity together.

Whatever your roles and reasons for reading, the urgency of our work together to create conditions for belonging and success for all of our students cannot be understated. Our nation is more deeply divided than at any time over my 25-year career as a public educator. Among the many sources of unrest, political operatives are carrying out coordinated strategies to create distrust of public education as a means for maintaining and redistributing material wealth and power to those who have always had such capital. We must continue to build coalitions toward realizing public education's continued promise: the creation of a nation where our differences and similarities are equally appreciated, in which decision-making and resources are shared, and where outcomes are favorable for all.

THE QUEST FOR EQUITY AND THEORY IN PARTNERSHIPS TO ELIMINATE RACIAL DISPROPORTIONALITY IN SPECIAL EDUCATION

Disproportionality— A Cultural-Historical Problem in Search of a Cultural-Historical Solution

MEETING THE MOMENT WITH EQUITY ASSISTANCE

The injustices of the past several years at the intersection of systemic racism and the deadly COVID-19 pandemic, which have impacted communities of color disproportionally, including children with disabilities (Houtrow et al., 2020), accentuate the urgency of equity-focused transformation in our communities and schools. As our nation continues to respond to these injustices, students, families, and educators grapple with recovery from the most widespread disruption of public education in history. Yet, many injustices are deeply woven into the fabric of U.S. history as overt and nuanced forms of exclusion, marginalization, and segregation. Moreover, our nation remains deeply divided about the necessity of work to address systemic inequities in the form of racism, sexism, ableism, xenophobia, homophobia, and religious discrimination. This division impacts public schools nationwide, while educators, families, students, and policymakers contend with widespread misinformation about and backlash against advancements in educational equity and strive to stay the course by ensuring academic progress and social–emotional well-being of our youth.

Within this complex and intense moment, U.S. Secretary of Education Miguel Cardona has renewed the federal government's commitment to monitor state legislation that may pose threats to students' civil rights, and President Biden and the secretary have articulated across multiple outlets their pursuit of a comprehensive approach to advancing equity for all. The Equity Assistance Center program has been an exemplar of this pursuit as a federal resource for public education agencies navigating and responding to inequities since it was authorized under Title IV of the Civil Rights Act as the first federally funded educational technical assistance program. As the largest project of the Great Lakes Equity Center in the Indiana University School of Education–IUPUI, for almost 7 years the Midwest and Plains EAC has served the 13 states in our region by responding to over 1,000 requests for assistance, almost half of them since the start of the COVID-19 pandemic. Prior to that, for 5 years we effectively served six states as a different regional EAC. Throughout this time, we have served with deep respect for EAC program legacy, which seeks to remediate the injustices woven into the fabrics of our schools and society, and their impact on students' educational access, participation, and outcomes.

The mission of the Midwest and Plains Equity Assistance Center (MAP Center) is to ensure equitable educational access, participation, and outcomes by expanding state and local education agencies' capacities to provide robust, effective opportunities to learn for all students, regardless of and responsive to race, sex, national origin, and religion, as well as language, disability, and income, and to eliminate inequities among and between groups. More specifically, we partner with educators across public pre-K–12 education systems to

1. promote and ensure students' civil rights and integration in relation to race, sex, national origin, religion (Coomer et al., 2017a; Venzant Chambers, 2019), income (Diem, 2017), and disability (Skelton, 2019a);
2. build and sustain supports for students' and educators' mental and social health and well-being, especially in the context of social unrest and widespread illness and loss, and in underserved communities, including tribal and rural communities (Vigil-Hayes et al., 2021);
3. improve school culture and climate through prevention of and response to instances of sexual, racial, and other forms of bullying and harassment, including in online learning environments, which proliferated during COVID-19 (Lazzell et al., 2020), and in the context of state bills targeting LGBTQIA+ students with the potential to violate students' civil rights (Cardona, 2022);
4. improve recruitment, retention, and distribution of effective and diverse educators (Jackson et al., 2017), including addressing teacher shortages significantly exacerbated by COVID-19 (Giffin et al., 2021);
5. improve education leaders' capacity to develop and implement evidence-based systemic innovations (Chen et al., 2014);
6. build and facilitate agency, family, and community partnerships and networks (Morton, 2017), including those that create safe and welcoming environments for newcomer students who are refugees and English learners;
7. develop and facilitate effective approaches to dropout prevention and reentry (Mackey, 2018);

8. support local education agencies (LEAs) transitioning to unitary status in desegregation cases and restructuring for racial and socioeconomic diversity (Diem & Pinto, 2017);
9. support data-based decision-making on research-based, culturally responsive, and universally designed policies and practices (Waitoller & Thorius, 2016; Weeks & Sullivan, 2019);
10. ensure appropriate placement and integration of students with disabilities at race, sex, national origin, and religion identity intersections (Cavendish et al., 2014; Shealey et al., 2005); and
11. address disproportionate discipline and exclusionary policies, practices, representation, and programmatic segregation (Khalifa & Briscoe, 2015).

Although all of the aforementioned goals are interrelated, it is the last two that align most closely with those approaches to technical assistance that I describe in this book. Throughout my time as executive director of the MAP Center and a previous regional EAC, and as codirector of another EAC situated in the southwest region of the United States, center personnel and I have encountered time and again the issue of students' disproportionate identification for special education eligibility, placement into more restrictive settings, and exclusionary discipline in relation to their racial background as manifestations of the complex injustices experienced by our students and common reasons that educators seek our partnerships. The pervasiveness and persistence of racial disproportionality in special education identification, placement, and school discipline are well documented in educational research, and in what follows I provide a synthesis of this research, which informs how we design technical assistance partnerships and activities to address these inequities.

SORTING THROUGH THE RESEARCH: AN INTRODUCTION TO THE PROBLEM OF DISPROPORTIONALITY

Scholars and practitioners alike have discussed the overrepresentation of students of color in special education programs since the enactment of federal law P.L. 94–142, the Education for All Handicapped Children Act of 1975 (Dunn, 1968; Johnson, 1969). For many, P.L. 94–142 was hailed as a civil rights victory that promised to address decades of exclusion and institutionalization of students with disabilities in state-run "idiot asylums," with histories of maltreatment and where students died as a result (P. M. Ferguson, 2008). Indeed, this groundbreaking civil rights law led to the integration of students with disabilities into public education systems in myriad ways, albeit with marked variation across locations, communities, and student identities. Despite its promise, however, special education has operated un/intentionally to further marginalize students of color, including/as well as those who are immigrants and from low-income households and communities. Prevailing notions continue to apply special education incorrectly as a "place" (Danforth et al., 2006; Zigmond et al., 2009), which Ferri and Connor (2005) have criticized as a "tool of exclusion" (p. 453), where children and particularly children of color can be put to remove them from the responsibility of general education and educators.

Forty plus years of large-scale analyses have illustrated persistent racial/ethnic disparities in special education identification and placement patterns (Skiba et al., 2016). Nationally, students of color continue to be disproportionately represented in special education classifications, with American Indian or Alaskan Native students and African American students being numerically overrepresented and Asian American students, underrepresented (U.S. Department of Education, 2020). Underrepresentation is also of concern due to the possibility of denial of access to services for students who would benefit from them, and who historically have been underserved in relation to race, ethnicity, language, and national origin (Skiba et al., 2016). Disproportionality, therefore, is complex, multidimensional, and highly consequential for educational opportunity, particularly for learners who have been systematically marginalized over time.

Special education disproportionality is quantitatively defined as a group's over- or underrepresentation in a special educational category, program, or service as compared with the group's proportion in the overall population (Donovan & Cross, 2002). It typically is calculated through one of three measures: as a composition index (Donovan & Cross, 2002), risk index, or relative risk ratio (Parrish, 2002). Composition index compares the proportion of students in special education from one racial or ethnic group with the proportion of students in that group in the school population. The formula for calculating a composition index is: (Number of students from racial/ethnic group in disability category or placement environment / Total number of students in disability category or placement category) * 100. Risk index calculates the percentage of students from a specific racial/ethnic group, and in a particular educational setting (e.g., school, district, state), who receive special education and related services for a particular disability. The formula for calculating risk index is: (Number of students from racial/ethnic group in disability category / Number of enrolled students from racial/ethnic group) * 100. Finally, one may compare the risk index calculated for a particular racial or ethnic group with another group's risk index to determine a relative risk ratio: the risk that one racial or ethnic group is placed in special education as compared with another group, or with all other racial or ethnic groups combined. The formula to determine relative risk ratio is: Risk index for racial/ethnic group for disability category / Risk index for comparison group (or all other groups combined) for disability category.

In 2019, 6,561,998 students ages 5 (school age) through 21 were served under the Individuals With Disabilities Education Act (IDEA), Part B. That year, for all disabilities, American Indian or Alaska Native students, Black or African American students, Hispanic/Latinx students, Native Hawaiian or Other Pacific Islander students, and students associated with two or more races, with risk ratios of 1.6, 1.4, 1.1, 1.5, and 1.1, respectively, were more likely to be served under IDEA, Part B, than were students in all other racial/ethnic groups combined. During this time, Black or African American school-age students were more likely to be served under IDEA than students in all other racial/ethnic groups combined for the following disability categories: autism (1.1), developmental delay (1.5), emotional disturbance (1.8), intellectual disability (2.2), multiple disabilities (1.3), other health impairment (1.4), specific learning disability (1.4), traumatic brain injury (1.1), and visual impairment (1.1). Further, American Indian or Alaska Native students ages 5 through 21 were almost four times as likely to be served under IDEA, Part B, for developmental delay than were students ages 5 through 21 in all other racial/ethnic groups combined (risk ratio of 3.8) (U.S. Department of Education [USDOE], 2021).

Beyond these quantitative indicators of risk, qualitative approaches to measuring and understanding disproportionality account also for the historical, political, and social contexts that shape the educational practice of labeling students of color (most often Black and African American, as well as Indigenous, students) as intellectually, socially, and behaviorally inferior to white students, even as compared with white students with the same disability labels, through educational segregation. In the National Research Council's *Minority Students in Special and Gifted Education* report, Donovan and Cross (2002) described the issue of overrepresentation as a "paradox of special education." That is, although special education placement is meant to allocate appropriate services and additional resources for children with disabilities, it also stigmatizes students, segregates them from their peers, exposes them to low expectations and a weak curriculum, and limits postschool outcomes such as employment options, income level, and access to higher education (Klingner et al., 2005; Losen & Orfield, 2002). This paradox is an impetus to address equity concerns like overrepresentation in special education, a field in which social, racial, and disability inequalities are alive and well, and to provide opportunities for critically examining U.S. educational systems (Artiles, 2003; Losen & Orfield, 2002).

It is no accident that historically disproportionality has occurred most commonly in relation to those disability categories that rely on the highest degrees of professional judgment, such as specific learning disability, emotional disturbance, and speech and language impairment (Zhang et al., 2014). This relationship reveals that when educators have avenues to offer their judgment on the appropriateness of special education labels and placements for students of color and, in tandem, to remove some or all the responsibility for labeled students' learning and progress through special education eligibility determination, they indeed may go down those roads. Drawing from my background as a school psychologist in a southwestern urban elementary school district, I never knew of a special education self-contained classroom that was not full, and moreover, full of students of color, when the more inclusive settings (physically inclusive, anyway) tended to be where white students with disability labels received most of their instruction and related services.

In 2019, a total of 6,237,889, or 95.1%, of the 6,561,998 students ages 5 through 21 served under IDEA, Part B, were educated in general education classrooms for at least some portion of the school day. At that time, 68% of white students, as compared with 60% of Black students and 63.4% of Latino students, spent more than 80% of the day in the general education classroom. Further, while 16.3% of Black students spent less than 40% of the day in the general education classroom, the corresponding rate for students who were white was only 10% (USDOE, 2021).

READING THE RESEARCH: A SYNOPSIS OF WHAT WE KNOW ABOUT DISPROPORTIONALITY'S ROOT CAUSES

The bulk of disproportionality research has focused on documenting the existence of the phenomenon, as well as personal, practical, and political contributing factors. In our 2017 review of disproportionality literature, for example, Voulgarides, Fergus, and I grouped research studies that sought to understand the roots of disproportionality into two main categories: those focused on practice-based factors and those focused on sociodemographic-based factors. We identified two main theoretical arguments researchers used to frame their findings on practice-based factors:

(a) a cultural mismatch between middle class, white teachers and school administrators with low-income and/or racial and ethnic minority student populations and (b) gaps in the development and implementation of interventions and other referral systems, which cause disproportionate outcomes. (p. 64)

With regard to the former explanation, this was a common theme I observed during my time as a school psychologist in that southwestern urban elementary district, and which contributed to teachers' decisions to refer children for prereferral interventions, leading most often to special education eligibility determination. In a 2nd-grade classroom where a white educator recently had referred three Latino students to the school's "teacher assistance team," I observed the teacher writing English/Spanish code-switching phrases on the board. After she completed her writing, she read the phrases aloud, and then asked the class, "Why shouldn't we talk this way?" And the group of about 30 seven-year-olds, mostly Mexican immigrant students, who spoke Spanish as their primary language and code-switched commonly in their academic and social communication, responded in a chorus, "because it sounds like we're uneducated." It was apparent *they had been taught to say that* (!) by their teacher, despite the importance of code switching in biliteracy development (Escamilla et al., 2014). Despite these and other contexts within which emerging English learners were denied opportunities to learn in ways that developed their biliteracy practices, the three students from this classroom eventually were referred for special education eligibility determination by the teacher.

The latter explanation framed by disproportionality researchers—gaps in development and implementation of interventions and other referral systems—is characteristic of this exchange among a group of educators from a study I conducted on special education prereferral practices in an urban elementary school. In this interaction, educators were discussing a student about whom the teacher of record (TOR) had leveled concerns to the school's prereferral intervention team. Such teams are common within most special education referral systems (VanDerHayden et al., 2007). Excerpts in italics are from my own fieldnotes.

> *TOR:* There is no motivation whatsoever. She is like a bump on a log. She just wants to sit there and do nothing. I cut spelling words down to 10. I have the data. 16, 32, 8, 24, 32, 12 out of 40.
>
> *Kate (the team leader) puts a chart labeled "Intervention Action Plan," transcribed from chart paper used at the initial intake on the table.* I taught her finger spelling. Did you ever see her doing (to TOR)?
>
> *TOR:* No.
>
> *Kate:* She does it for me.
>
> *Group hypothesizes the student does not retain information.*
>
> *TOR says she was from another district:* "Mom was adamant she was tested" and "they were ready to put her in special ed."
>
> *TOR says student has been referred to special education and is being evaluated. School Psychologist confirms.*
>
> *Teacher 2:* Is she pretty equally low in reading and math?
>
> *TOR:* Let me look what her SRI scores are real quick. Her grades are all Ds and Fs.
>
> *Kate:* We've got 10 to 15 more minutes to decide how we want to move forward.
>
> *TOR:* I don't see that she's made any gains. *A discussion about what more they can do ensues, including reading in a small group facilitated by 5th-grade readers. The TOR reminds them she has cut down the student's spelling words.*

School Psychologist: That's not really an intervention.

TOR: It's not?

Kate: My intervention is finger spelling and teaching lessons to get an idea of her retention.

Principal: Mom signed consent (for special education testing) at parent teacher night?

TOR: Yeah.

Kate: Let's continue 30 minutes small-group reading, but it's not all 30 with her.

School Psychologist: I'll document that. For intervention we think of things to improve skills. It's not . . . *TOR cuts off SP, reflecting back to an earlier question about how she grades the student's spelling, complaining that reducing the point value of each word "is a gimme." The group decides math intervention is no longer necessary. Kate asks TOR about how she monitors progress.*

TOR: I take grades . . . Do we need to meet again if she's going through testing?

School Psychologist: We could even do it informally in a month or so. I just need to get all the data. *School psychologist reiterates she needs to know every intervention.*

TOR (whispering): She's not motivated. She is not a happy child. She's a miserable little person. (Thorius et al., 2014, p. 292)

In this example, so-called interventions were described as teaching the student finger spelling—the process of spelling out words by using hand shapes that correspond to the letters of the word associated with American Sign Language—and limiting the student's number of spelling words. Regardless of the inadequacy of these approaches for supporting a learner who is exhibiting the performance and social–emotional well-being these educators describe, and the school psychologist's mild protestations, consent for special education eligibility determination had already been obtained from the child's mother, at parent–teacher conference night no less, where 10-minute time slots were typical practice.

In another comprehensive review of disproportionality research, Waitoller and colleagues (2010) grouped researchers' framing of disproportionality research in three ways: (1) a sociodemographic perspective in which researchers examined characteristics of and relationships between individuals and contexts; (2) a critical perspective in which power issues related to race were examined; and (3) a practical explanation that linked the role of professionals' actions and behaviors to contributing to and maintaining overrepresentation. Underlying the explanations for student disabilities, characterized across all existing reviews of the disproportionality research, however, were racist ideologies tacitly acknowledged through cultural mismatch theories and having residue in current belief, practice, and policy systems.

With due respect to the many scholars who have dedicated significant portions of their careers to the study and the elimination of disproportionality, research on the roots of disproportionality must continue and more deeply account for this racism in individual beliefs as well as in context-based policies and practices. Special education scholars who have studied special education eligibility evaluation processes have argued that the ambiguity and the complexity of such processes make them susceptible to racial bias (Algozzine & Ysseldyke, 1983). Sullivan and colleagues, in their 2019 multistudy experimental investigation of bias in school psychologists' eligibility decisions, reported that an extensive body of experimental and quasi-experimental research in clinical settings showed that demographics frequently influence diagnosis (e.g., López, 1989; Neighbors et al., 2003). Accordingly, they sought to study whether similar bias in 302 school psychologists' professional judgment could explain in part special education disproportionality in the high-incidence categories of autism, emotional disturbance, and intellectual disability.

As rationale for their study of these three categories in particular, Sullivan and colleagues noted that all have ambiguous definitions, which in the case of the emotional disturbance (ED) label include elements unsupported by the research. Sullivan and her colleagues noted that ED has been a condition verified through research to be "in the eye of the beholder" (Algozzine, 2017, p. 138) and based largely on culturally loaded perceptions of "troubling" behavior (Hart et al., 2010, p. 149). Although Sullivan and colleagues found little evidence of racial disproportionality in this particular study, they noted participants' tendencies to make eligibility decisions unsupported by and even contrary to evaluation data. The authors connected these decisions to the influence of confirmation bias: seeking data to affirm and confirm the reason for special education referral, rather than more objectively and systematically evaluating students' eligibility (e.g., Algozzine & Ysseldyke, 1981; Fish, 2017; O'Reilly et al., 1989; Ysseldyke et al., 1981).

In Harry and Klingner's 2006 book-length study of disproportionality in one western school district over a 3-year period, they examined opportunities to learn, routine discourse interactions between students and teachers, and normalized practices in schools related to special education referral, assessment, decision-making, and placement (i.e., school culture around special education). Their key findings indicated that school structure, individual and structural racial biases toward students of color and their families, cultural dissonance, racism, and placement processes contributed to disproportionality. Harry and Klingner also found that the culture of referral in a specific school was more powerful than evaluation results in determining special education eligibility. That is, regardless of the schools' "rational" models for determining eligibility, these processes were influenced greatly by institutional and political agendas and perspectives of professionals, much more than the procedures as written. "In reality," the authors concluded, "institutional and personal biases and beliefs combined with political pressures" (p. 92) to produce overrepresentation.

To illustrate this combination of institutional, political, and personal factors in action, I share more examples from our 2014 study on the implementation of multitiered systems of support (MTSS) in an urban elementary school where students of color made up about 63% of the school population and were taught by an 88% white female teaching population. Each week, members of our research team observed three simultaneous discussions of students referred by their teachers to the MTSS team. Our data collection and analysis over one school year involved multiple methods, at the heart of which were weekly participant observations of meetings within which the MTSS educator team engaged in decision-making processes to address teacher reports of a student's academic and/or behavioral difficulties. We spent time with the team as they determined student placement in educational intervention cycles, selected and designed these interventions, monitored learner progress, and determined the appropriateness of student referrals for special education eligibility consideration.

Overwhelmingly, we found that teacher assumptions and beliefs about students and families shaped how MTSS was applied, including in educator decisions to eventually recommend most MTSS-referred students for special education eligibility determination. Also appearing to contribute to their practice, educators were under heavy systemic pressure for students to perform well on standardized assessments in an accountability-focused environment where their pay and school resources were tied to test scores. In this context, teachers, the principal, and the school psychologist shared in interviews and in meetings their assumptions that families were to blame for students' academics and behavior. We saw this overtly in MTSS meetings where educators repeated deficit-laden descriptions of students and families, who were primarily people of color and lived in lower socioeconomic households, as justification for why students were disabled and needed to receive special education services. During one meeting, several white teachers conversed about a Black student who recently had been suspended. The teacher of record exclaimed, "Was supposed to bring a parent when came back. Didn't. Just sat in ISS." A different teacher added, "A man came in with mom and did the talking." The teacher of record responded: "He's probably her pimp" (Thorius et al., 2014, p. 291). And the group laughed. This racist conversation occurred in front of two members of our research team, including me. Several times, I wondered what might have been said if we had not been there observing.

On another day, another member of the research team and I walked into the teachers' lounge where the MTSS meetings were held. Someone had taped a photocopy of a letter to the editor of a local paper on the lounge refrigerator where many teachers stored their lunches each day. Across the top "FYI" had been written in red marker. The letter read:

Rating teachers on the basis of pupil progress is foolish and unfair in the cases of kids who never get cognitive training in poor homes. No matter how good the first grade teacher, teaching essentially falls on deaf ears. There can be no progress when there is not much to start with. So you can congratulate, in advance, teachers of kids from educated homes and say "tough luck" to the ones who deal with products of ignorant homes. How about cognitive pre-school for them? As the twig is bent, so grows the tree. (Thorius et al., 2014, p. 294)

During another meeting, a teacher commented, "They're all thieves. I have a bunch of thieves in my room." A colleague concurred with concerns about leaving her purse in her classroom. The conversation concluded with one educator's comment that while students at the school were smart enough to steal, they were not smart enough for academic work.

Across these racist comments and exchanges, we found that educators believed their students were poorly supervised at home, and that the parents refused to comply with school requests to support student learning and could not care less about their children's education. Juxtaposed against these representations, schooling and the teachers themselves were portrayed as students' and families' saviors. That is, educators positioned themselves as helpers by referring and placing students in special education. Elsewhere, I have referred to this phenomenon as a *cloak of benevolence* under which educator and systemic ableism and racism intersect and hide (Thorius, 2019). The following comment by one of the MTSS team leaders illustrates this concept, in response to a question I asked her about family participation in the MTSS process:

When parents come to school, they look uneasy. I attempt to explain, just to let you know your child is in trouble and we want to help. When parents come we learn more about the home. Death, jail, things we kind of knew already, but we hear more of the details. (Thorius et al., 2014, p. 294)

Yet, refuting educators' deficit-laden characterization of families, our research team often observed family members in attendance at these early morning meetings, in many instances arriving before teachers and waiting in the hallway. Of 22 sessions, families attended 11, yet the team leader reported to us in an interview that there was only a 10% family participation rate. At the same time, educators asked questions at the beginning of meetings like, "Did we call his mom?" Moreover, during the meetings family members often demonstrated their understandings of teacher expectations and shared some concerns about their children's opportunities to learn in this elementary school. For example, three different parents asked why their children were being pulled out of their general education classroom for interventions during instruction, and why interventions had not been fully implemented. We also observed family members promising to implement home interventions and talking about their engagement with artifacts, such as alphabet flashcard checklists with known letter sounds checked off.

Several parents also expressed worry about whether it was healthy to medicate their children for ADHD, which was a common educator recommendation. In response, however, teachers encouraged family members to keep students on medication or were dismissive of their concerns. For example, a mother shared her worry that her child was experiencing a decrease in appetite as a side effect of taking Adderall, and a teacher who was not even the child's teacher of record told the child, who was present, "take two bites of everything," then continued talking about the child's difficulties. Comments about whether and why students should be on medication occurred during just over half of our weekly observations. Many of these students ended up referred for special education eligibility determination due to suspected emotional disturbance, yet the educators' minds had already been made up prior to the eligibility determination process, as indicated by educators handing to parents already-completed ADHD checklists and giving them instructions to take their children to the doctor for a diagnosis.

In the midst of their time leading NCCRESt, Artiles, Kozleski, and colleagues (2010) analyzed how disproportionality had been explained in the research since Lloyd Dunn (1968) argued in the flagship special education journal *Exceptional Children* for the cessation of labeling children from minority groups as mentally retarded on the basis of slightly low scores on intelligence tests. Grounded in the rationale that culture seldom is acknowledged explicitly in disproportionality research, the authors illuminated three ways of framing culture embedded in these explanations, drawing from Waitoller and colleagues' 2010 review, and their own analysis of existing research, including Harry and Klingner's 2006 study. Artiles and colleagues noted that in many studies, culture was applied as a regulative frame; culture regulates the behavioral and value norms—the "way-of-life" (p. 288)—shared by members of a demographic group or environmental setting and thus are linked to prescriptions for that group's treatment. The authors linked this explanation to disproportionality remedy efforts focused on educators' familiarity with students' family and community cultural practices in order to inform instruction, as recommended in Donovan and Cross's (2002) National Research Council report on disproportionality.

The second way of framing culture was a subframe of the regulative view and one that is generally static: culture as a marker. In this framing of culture, it is assumed that one's culture is defined by normative routines of individuals within one's identity group(s). Disproportionality research framed in this way has sought to examine the relationship between educators' or students' race and their behaviors or experiences, such as special education referral or likelihood of being labeled as disabled. In these studies, remedies for disproportionality are focused on educators' confrontation of their biases about certain groups of students, typically related to teacher and student racial identity.

The third frame of culture was "virtually nonexistent" (Artiles et al., 2010, p. 289) in disproportionality scholarship: the interpretive frame. This approach accounts for how culture affords and constrains groups' sense-making of everyday events, and the psychological and material tools groups and individuals use to think, act, and connect with one another, including understandings of rights and responsibilities. The authors called for more disproportionality scholarship to be framed in this way, including how individuals and groups create new and novel interpretations of social events (Erickson, 2001), as well as historical and structural aspects of culture. In their discussion, the authors quoted from earlier work by Artiles and Dyson (2005), who captured the historical, structural, and dynamic aspects of culture, and how such dynamics are shaped by local context:

> As people navigate the regularities of a cultural community, tensions arise between the traditional cultural practices and the emergent goals that are shaped by the specific circumstances surrounding local events. Individuals negotiate these tensions by using their agency (use cultural resources) to adapt to ecological factors, resist local demands, or renew cultural legacies. It is important, therefore, to understand people's use of cultural rules and meaning-making processes as always mediated, not only by their individual tool kits and the cultural norms of their community, but also *by the immediate contexts and ecological circumstances in which events take place* [emphasis added]. This is how the dialectic of cultural stability is crafted, how cultural production and reproduction co-exist. (p. 48)

In their suggestions for future disproportionality research, Artiles and colleagues (2010) focused primarily on analysis of the phenomenon and its root causes as connected with this third framing of culture. In this book, I attempt to apply their suggestions to the development and provision of technical assistance that accounts for the roles of history, structure, and local context as contributing to disproportionality.

Sullivan and Artiles (2011) continued the NCCRESt principal investigators' work by applying structural theory to study how disproportionality functions as a feature of a hierarchical racialized social system rather than simply as a result of individuals' beliefs and practices. They examined statewide and within-district disproportionality patterns in 183 Arizona local education agencies using 2004–2005 school year data. For each district, Sullivan and Artiles computed disproportionality risk indexes and relative risk ratios for each racial group's special education representation across all disability categories. They used these to generate relative risk ratios for each group in each disability category and compared these ratios against five potential predictors of disproportionality that had been studied in existing research: (1) proportion of students of color, (2) proportion of teachers of color, (3) proportion of students receiving free or reduced-price lunch, (4) district size, and (5) student–teacher ratio. Although the authors were not able to confirm their hypotheses about proportion of teachers of color having negative relationships with disproportionality, or student–teacher ratios having a positive relationship with disproportionality, a few other key findings underscore the importance of their analysis.

First, over a third of LEAs demonstrated substantial over- or underrepresentation in 43 of 56 examined disability/race pairings. Second, statewide, 11.5% of students were identified for special education, and risk of identification was greatest for African American and Native American students, of whom 13.95% and 14.43%, respectively, were identified. Third, overrepresentation was most prevalent in groups that constituted the smallest proportion of the overall student population. This pattern also held for Latino students but to a lesser extent, likely due to broader representation as 40% of the total Arizona student population. Sullivan and Artiles's findings point to the importance of disproportionality analyses across multiple scales, including state, district, and local community, as well as the relationship between variables across these scales and predictors of disproportionality.

An important insight from almost all research analyses of disproportionality is that special education embodies a paradox in which resources, access, and opportunities are made available to disabled individuals, while barriers, discrimination, and marginalization also may arise for those identified with disability labels (Tefera et al., 2013). In their discussion of disproportionality, the importance of creating culturally responsive educational systems, and the impact of interpretive frames of culture on disproportionality, Klingner et al. (2005) asserted, "It is imperative to understand the ideological premises and histories leading to the ratification of the policies that guide educators' work," (p. 10) including those premises and histories that lead to discrimination and other negative consequences of disproportionate special education identification and placement. The existing research on the roots of disproportionality has contributed important knowledge about origins and solutions to this complex issue, including the influence of student, school, and community sociodemographic factors on risk for special education placement (e.g., Skiba et al., 2008). Research has also illuminated how professionals' practices ranging from prereferral, referral, assessment, and teams' diagnostic decisions, influence or mediate disproportionality: the focus of two-thirds of the empirical studies published in scientific journals between 1968 and 2006 (Waitoller et al., 2010). However, as Sullivan and Artiles (2011) pointed out, most studies focused on the latter, meaning that most research has failed to account for the sociopolitical context within which educators operate and have been socialized, as well as the impact of history on these contexts. It is this view of culture that guides traditional approaches to technical assistance I describe in this book.

As Tefera and colleagues (2013) assert in their review of teacher influences in the racialization of disability, "teacher decisions to refer students to special education is a phenomenon that should be studied as shaped by individual, historical, and institutional forces" (p. 262). We must consider those cultural practices and processes engaged by individual educators, as well as those accepted as cultural norms and parameters of education systems, yes, but it remains necessary to deepen our understanding of the historical ideologies educators have adopted regarding disability, race, and their intersections that shape current policy and practice.

DISPROPORTIONALITY AS A CONTESTED PHENOMENON: ILLUMINATING AND OBSCURING SYSTEMIC RACISM AND ABLEISM

Despite the hundreds of studies regarding disproportionality's existence as a phenomenon, including those noted above, after almost 5 decades the issue is still a "hot" topic. In a 2006 *Educational Researcher* special issue on disproportionality guest edited by Artiles, authors O'Connor and DeLuca Fernandez criticized some of the findings of the National Research Council disproportionality report (Donovan & Cross, 2002) on the basis that portions of the report perpetuated a "Theory of Compromised Development" about students of color and their families. O'Connor and DeLuca Fernandez asserted that the report oversimplified the concept of development and misspecified poverty as "that which places minority students at heightened 'risk' for special education placement" by situating "middle-class (white) children as the unmarked norm against which the development of 'other' children is evaluated" (p. 6). In doing so, O'Connor and DeLuca Fernandez argued that the report underanalyzed how this norm is constructed within "the culture and organization of schools and how it increases the likelihood that minority children will be evaluated as academically and behaviorally deficient and in need of special services" (p. 6). Grounding their arguments in research demonstrating that organically caused disabilities were distributed across racial groups at proportionate rates, O'Connor and DeLuca Fernandez rejected the logic that children of color enter schools more at risk for disability due to impoverished homes and communities, and asserted instead that "schools determine who is more likely to be designated as disabled" (p. 6; see also McDermott et al., 2006) on the basis of white-developmental referents and the structuring of educational opportunity in relation to student race.

However, in 2015, the notion of the predisposition of students of color to be disabled reemerged in the research. Replicating and extending elements from their earlier work, Paul Morgan and several colleagues sent shock waves through the special education community via an article, also in *Educational Researcher*, in which they concluded that students of color who had been found to be overrepresented in special education through decades of research, in fact had been underrepresented. Accordingly, they took aim at the purpose and function of federal disproportionality policy under the Individuals With Disabilities Education Improvement Act of 2004 (IDEA): "Our results suggest that current federal educational legislation and policy-making designed to minimize overidentification of minorities in special education may be misdirected" (p. 288). The American Educational Research Association issued a national press release on their study, and the piece was further launched into the public media limelight via an op-ed by Morgan and Farkas in *The New York Times* (2015), provocatively entitled: "Is Special Education Racist?" Several scholars with expertise on disproportionality were quick to counter the study on the grounds that "much research, even that published in good journals, is not good research" (Keith, 2008, p. 2167). In the National Association of School Psychologists' newsletter *Communique*, school psychology scholars Cohen et al. (2015) urged school psychologists to apply their understandings of research methods to critique Morgan and colleagues' work:

> School psychologists should be expert consumers of research. We have a responsibility to help other school personnel understand research findings. We should provide the cynical voice in any euphoric conversation about the next big thing, and analyzing research methods could be a powerful tool in that discussion. (p. 22)

Cohen and colleagues further commented that the key to interpreting Morgan et al.'s findings cynically could be found in the authors' own language: "Our results indicate that racial- and ethnic-minority children who are otherwise similar to white children are consistently less likely to be identified as disabled" (p. 287). Cohen and colleagues suggested, rather:

> With respect to the authors' statistical models, this statement appears to be true, but can it be applied in practice? In the case of ED and ID, probably not because many of the factors that the authors control for cannot actually be separated from the experience of being an African American in the United States, in the early 21st century. At the present time, minority status in American cannot be separated from risk that arises from a history of segregation, oppression, low expectations, and differential educational experiences (Wiggan, 2007), all of which have significant impact on behavior and academic performance. Couple that with the prominent role that educator perceptions play in educational decisions (Hosp & Reschly, 2003; Mehan et al., 1986), and a different picture emerges. (p. 22)

Various media outlets continued to question Morgan and colleagues' findings from this and subsequent studies. However, other scholars applied Morgan et al.'s findings to critique decades of previous disproportionality research (importantly, led by scholars of color) on the basis of "less convincing methods" as asserted by Nora Gordon (2017), a professor of public policy writing for the increasingly conservative Brookings Institution, who also noted that Morgan and colleagues' findings were "by now well established" (n.p.).

But those whose research was being dismissed as "less convincing" would not be dismissed. In 2016, Skiba, along with Artiles, Kozleski, and Harry (former NCCRESt leaders) and Losen (leader with the Harvard/UCLA Civil Rights Project and author with Gary Orfield of *Racial Inequity in Special Education* [2002]), critiqued Morgan and Farkas's 2016 study as erroneous for several reasons. For one thing, there were issues with sampling. The central dependent variable in Morgan and Farkas's study was derived from survey data included in a much larger early childhood national database in which special education teachers reported on fewer than 5,000 students' primary disability categories. In this same year, 5,536,150 students were served under IDEA based on actual IDEA child count data collected systematically and published by the U.S. Department of Education's Office of Special Education Programs (2001). Skiba and colleagues (2016) also noted inadequate analysis and failure to account for disproportionality's complexity in Morgan and colleagues' research.

Beth Harry, whose groundbreaking 3-year situated study of disproportionality with Janette Klingner contributed extensively to the field's understandings of the phenomenon's complexity, wrote a scathing critique of Morgan and colleagues' research as a set of "overloaded academic arguments designed by elites to obfuscate and confuse" (2017, n.p.). Further, Harry described the title that Morgan and Farkas chose for their *New York Times* op-ed article, "Is Special Education Racist?" as tapping into readers' fears and suspicions, and the subsequent text as relying on complicated statistics that the vast majority of the readership would not understand. She concluded that, due to their "final uncomprehending analysis, those [readers] who want to believe it will, and those who don't won't" (n.p.) Harry noted that Morgan and Farkas's work had refuted the "everyday information that can be gleaned from a quick walk through the special education classrooms of typical school districts in the United States," (n.p.) and therefore she questioned why the authors chose to study a sample of children who were not representative of the population of students who actually were being served in special education programs, among other sampling concerns. Methodological concerns aside, however, she also wondered why in the face of a study that sought to refute all existing disproportionality knowledge, the authors chose to go to *The New York Times* without waiting to engage in academic discourse, as is so often the case when new research contradicts what is already understood about a topic.

Reading Harry's critique of Morgan and colleagues' work, I cannot help but see its relevance to so much of our discourse about education today. That special education disproportionality continues to evoke emotional and intellectual arguments on the basis of a set of studies by one group of lead researchers, in spite of decades of research by others, many of whom have found individual and systemic racism as significantly contributing to disproportionality, reflects the backlash that happens when research implicates individuals' and systems' racist behaviors, beliefs, and policies. This also occurs when white and white nondisabled individuals refute experiences of racism of people of color, and discredit and misrepresent, for political and social gain, the efforts of people of color and others to address systemic oppression at various intersections.

One needs to consider no further than the disinformed fervor with which political operatives, and increasingly white suburban parents, are asserting that critical race theory (Delgado & Stefancic, 2017) is being taught in public schools, along with widespread state legislation effectively banning focus on equity, inclusion, diversity, race and racism, sex, and gender in curriculum or instruction (Leadership Conference on Civil and Human Rights, 2020). A common talking point on the subject is that education about systemic racism (what some are blanketly calling "CRT") is itself racist. It creates for white youth, they argue, a risk of discomfort and sense of being blamed for racist systems such as slavery that occurred in the past and for which contemporary white people bear no responsibility. Just last night, I heard Ron DeSantis exclaim in his 2022 gubernatorial victory speech, "Florida is where WOKE goes to die!"

These strategic and coordinated attacks on public education and efforts to surface and remedy systemic oppressions such as racism and ableism through representative curriculum and social recognition of children for all of who they are, is the approach de jure for maintaining a ruling white wealthy class by attempting to dismantle the federal government through public policy and powerful social campaigns to undermine trust in public institutions (e.g., journalism, education, the Environmental Protection Agency, the FBI). The goal is to constrain the will and the power of the majority of citizens to influence policies and practices for the common good (MacLean, 2017).

POLICY AND PRACTICE APPROACHES TO ELIMINATING DISPROPORTIONALITY

Just as research and politics are fraught with tensions over the recognition of and attempts to remediate educational inequities, so too are federal and state disproportionality policies. The most wide-sweeping policy related to disproportionality, of course, is the federal law that governs special education. P.L. 94–142 was reauthorized in 1990, changing its name from the Education of All Handicapped Children Act to the Individuals With Disabilities Education Act. IDEA was reauthorized again in 1997 to include several regulations directly aimed at redressing disproportionality, including requirements that states: (a) collect and report data on special education representation disaggregated by race, (b) analyze data to "determine if significant disproportionality based on race is occurring in the state or schools," and (c) revise "policies, procedures, and practices used in the identification and placement" if it is determined that significant disproportionality exists. By the early 2000s, disproportionality was prioritized as one of the top three enforcement concerns of the federal government (Albrecht et al., 2011). Accordingly, developments in IDEA's (2004) reauthorization to align with the 2001 No Child Left Behind Act included prioritization of greater accountability and improved educational outcomes for children in special education, along with disproportionality monitoring and enforcement. Monitoring focused on the provision of a free appropriate public education in the least restrictive environment (LRE) and disproportionate representation of racial and ethnic groups in special education and related services. These indicators were scrutinized by requiring that states submit State Performance Plans (SPPs) and Annual Performance Reports (APRs) under the SPPs to the U.S. Secretary of Education; OSEP placed three disproportionality indicators in the SPPs. However, although these regulations emphasized SEAs' responsibility to monitor and address disproportionality in local education agencies (i.e., districts), SEAs were permitted to define their own thresholds for what constituted, and the methods used to calculate, significant disproportionality.

IDEA (2004) also introduced enforcement provisions to the definition of significant disproportionality by requiring LEAs with significant disproportionality on any of the indicators to spend 15% of their IDEA, Part B (i.e., Services for School-Aged Children) funds on coordinated early intervening services for students not yet identified as needing special education but who would benefit from increased academic and behavioral support to succeed in general education.

A relatively small but sound body of scholarship has analyzed the impacts and limitations of federal and state policy on eliminating disproportionality. Albrecht and colleagues (2012) detailed how federal interpretations of IDEA's 2004 requirements allowed SEAs to conclude that even when an LEA's quantitative indicators of disproportionality were high, these numbers did not need to be addressed if the LEA determined that they were not the result of inappropriate special education identification processes. In these instances, and due to the fact that IDEA also allowed states to set their own thresholds for levels at which disproportionality was significant and thus must be addressed, states could and did rationalize disproportionality as stemming from issues out of educator control (i.e., students' learning deficits) or not serious enough to warrant remediation. Albrecht and colleagues concluded that federal law and regulatory guidelines had not been effective in addressing disproportionality. Similarly, writing the position summary on federal disproportionality policy for the Executive Committee of the Council of Children with Behavioral Disorders (a division of the special education professional organization Council for Exceptional Children), this same group of authors (Skiba et al., 2013) detailed three issues with federal disproportionality policy interpretation. First, the federal government allowed states to use several different disproportionality definitions, even in the same state. Second, the federal government failed to monitor disproportionality in schools' discipline practices, particularly the application of suspension and expulsion in relation to student race and disability. Finally, it required states to engage in two distinct inquiries into disproportionality, which led to confusion among practitioners: *significant disproportionality* under Section 618 and *disproportionate representation* under Section 616 of IDEA 2004. There were several differences in how these two concepts were defined in statute. The authors summarized:

> Significant disproportionality is viewed as a simple numerical criteria that may be defined by each state, but triggers the use of funds for prevention without qualitative considerations or a finding of non-compliance with the Act. In contrast, disproportionate representation is dependent on first finding that the disparity in question was caused by *inappropriate identification*, determined through the qualitative review of LEA policies, practices, and procedures. As a result, the review of policies, practices, and procedures at the LEA level becomes a *consequence* of identification for significant disproportionality, but part of the *criteria* needed to establish disproportionate representation as a result of inappropriate identification. (p. 112, emphasis in original)

The key phrase here is "as a result of inappropriate identification." Despite a large body of research demonstrating how disproportionality is implicated by policies, practices, and beliefs across the time and space of educational contexts, Skiba and colleagues contended that this narrow focus on identification processes alone for determining whether numerical disproportionality (i.e., significant disproportionality) was indeed *disproportionate representation* ignored this research. As a result of this phrase, and of IDEA leaving the metrics for determining significant disproportionality up to the states, far fewer LEAs had been identified with significant disproportionality than the disparities in rates of identification, placement, and disciplinary removal across racial and ethnic groups suggested (Government Accountability Office [GAO], 2013; Sullivan & Osher, 2019).

Confirming Skiba et al.'s conclusion, the GAO found that in 2010, states required about 2% (n = 356) of all LEAs nationwide to use IDEA funds for early intervening services to address disproportionality. Half of these districts were concentrated in five states, including 73 LEAs in Louisiana. The GAO's analysis found extensive variability in how states were defining overrepresentation, including some ways in which it was highly unlikely that any LEAs would be identified through SEA metrics. The GAO (2013) concluded:

> Education's oversight of racial and ethnic groups' overrepresentation in special education is hampered by the flexibility states have to define significant disproportionality. Specifically, Education periodically reviews states' definitions as part of its onsite monitoring under IDEA, but the department has not required a state to change its definition when it makes it unlikely that overrepresentation will be identified. States in turn are required to identify districts and ensure that these districts reserve the required amount for early intervening services. (n.p.)

In addition to issues with determining disproportionality in the first place, including differences in the ways disproportionate representation and significant disproportionality were defined, Skiba and colleagues summarized other key issues of interpretation within federal disproportionality policy. For one, connecting the determination of disproportionality with special education procedure noncompliance did not account for overwhelming research that it was *general* education practices that appeared to contribute most to these disparities. Next, despite the inclusion of attention to LRE in the definition of significant disproportionality, OSEP did not include educational environment as an area to be monitored and enforced.

In February 2014, President Barack Obama launched the My Brother's Keeper initiative to address persistent opportunity gaps faced by boys and young men of color. In a report to President Obama published in May 2014, the My Brother's Keeper Task Force identified disparities in special education as a significant challenge that should be addressed under his administration. Consequently, that June the USDOE published a request for information inviting public comment on the GAO's 2013 report and recommendation that a standard methodology for determining significant disproportionality be adopted. In the same year, under the Obama administration, USDOE sought to address these ambiguities by proposing a new rule that would require states to use a standardized approach to assess significant disproportionality across all LEAs, including disproportionality in educational placement (i.e., LRE). The new rule also would require addressing disproportionality in discipline using the same remedies required to address disproportionality in special education identification and placement. In addition, disproportionate districts would be expected to extend their use of 15% of IDEA, Part B, funds marked for early intervening, to students in preschool (not kindergarten, as had been the previous requirement). Finally, the new rule clarified requirements for reviewing and revising policies, procedures, and practices when significant disproportionality was determined to be occurring. In December 2016, USDOE issued its final regulations establishing a standard methodology that each state would have to use in its annual determination of whether significant disproportionality based on race and ethnicity was occurring in the state. Those 2016 final regulations were set to go into effect on July 1, 2018, remedying the inadequacy of states' definitions or findings of significant disproportionality across states that meant individual claimants had to rely on litigation to show intentional discrimination (Strassfeld, 2017). However, these regulations were released around the same time that Morgan and Farkas had their *New York Times* op-ed published in which they presented their own research findings as a challenge to almost all previous disproportionality research and in which they suggested that federal disproportionality policy had been misguided.

Someone appeared to be listening to their challenges. The 2016 "Equity in IDEA" became one of many Obama-era regulations aimed at protecting students' rights that the Trump administration sought to roll back. In February 2018 under Secretary of Education Betsy DeVos, the USDOE proposed to postpone by 2 years the date for states to comply with the "significant disproportionality" regulations, as well as the inclusion of children ages 3 through 5 in the analysis of significant disproportionality. Central to their rationale was the body of research conducted by Morgan, Farkas, and their colleagues: the body of research that had been disputed and critiqued by dozens of disproportionality researchers, including Skiba and Albrecht, who led the critique of IDEA's disproportionality provisions based on their knowledge of and contributions to disproportionality scholarship. The government's justification included for the proposed delay included the following statement:

> The Department also believes that the racial disparities in the identification, placement, or discipline of children with disabilities are not necessarily evidence of, or primarily caused by, discrimination, as some research indicates. See, e.g., Paul L. Morgan, et al, "Are Minority Children Disproportionately Represented in Early Intervention and Early Childhood Special Education?", 41 Educational Researcher 339 (2012) (that higher minority identification and placement rates reflect higher minority need, not racism); John Paul Wright, et al, "Prior problem behavior accounts for the racial gap in suspensions," 42 Journal of Criminal Justice 257 (2014) (racial gap in suspensions is not due to racism)." (31306 Federal Register / Vol. 83, No. 128 / Tuesday, July 3, 2018 / Rules and Regulations)

Three years before Gordon dismissed all disproportionality research prior to Morgan and colleagues' work as "less convincing," other researchers (Galston & Davis, 2014) with the Brookings Institution released a public policy report asserting that U.S. education was in great need of "a reformed federalism" that reflected "a more appropriate division of responsibility between the federal government and other jurisdictions" in the wake of controversy over No Child Left Behind. The authors concluded:

State and local governments, which provide the lion's share of funding and administration for elementary and secondary education, will have to take the lead in making desired educational improvements a reality. The only coherent alternative—a centralized system along European lines—goes against the grain of our history and institutional arrangements and is entirely infeasible. (p. 15)

The USDOE's next set of justifications for the delay of the proposed rules centered around concerns that a federally set standard calculation of disproportionality would lead to "quotas" for identifying students for special education by race or ethnicity. They argued that such calculations could result in states' and districts' production of equal rates of identification across racial groups, thus denying services to students (of color) who needed them.

In the text of their justification for finalizing the delay of the proposed rules, the DeVos-led USDOE overemphasized public comments regarding concerns with a standard disproportionality calculation quota. The USDOE received comments from 390 individuals and organizations, with more than 85% opposing the delay, yet they pushed ahead to finalize the delay of the Equity in IDEA regulation. Yet, the USDOE presented only a few opposing comments, and only those comments that provided alternative suggestions for mitigating quotas through compliance monitoring.

Indeed, many opponents of the proposed delay submitted public comments during the 90-day period set by the USDOE prior to finalizing the proposed regulation. Many opposition comments, including those by the American Civil Liberties Union (2018) and National Council for Learning Disabilities (n.d.), noted the harm that would be caused by delaying the extension of early intervening services to students in need or by continuing to unfairly suspend or expel students. Other opposition comments took issue with the research being used to justify the delay. Prominent disproportionality researcher Voulgarides criticized the USDOE's decision on the basis that it minimized civil rights concerns at the heart of the matter, instead emphasizing the federalist commitment to "states' rights" that was characteristic of the Trump administration.

In her 2019 chapter, "Civil Rights Remedies and Persistent Inequities: The Case of Racial Disproportionality in Special Education," Voulgarides argues that eliminating disproportionality will be incredibly difficult to achieve under the current legislative framework of IDEA. Critical policy analysis approaches provide some insight into why and how federal and state policy has been ineffective in eliminating disproportionality. In 2015, coauthor Brendan Maxcy and I applied such analysis to appropriation of Response to Intervention, also included in IDEA 2004 as an approach to eliminating disproportionality. In our article, we suggested that although 1997 revisions to the Individuals With Disabilities Education Act showed promise for addressing special education equity concerns, including disproportionality, research on policy implementation was necessary to build understandings of why inequities persisted despite such policy.

Focusing on implementation as a process whereby policy is appropriated by local actors, we proposed a framework for study of special education policy appropriation that included four contextual forces drawn from Welner's (2001) work on zones of mediation. The first two of these are *inertial* forces related to the deeply embedded cultural practices of schooling in a local site, and *normative* forces that include educators' beliefs about their students, including students' capacity for learning and student identity markers. Related to disproportionality, normative and inertial forces intersect as widely held belief systems and practices related to teaching, learning, and students, and related local daily or routine practices that reinforce these beliefs, including, for example:

> grouping students according to ability and age, practices associated with delivering instructional services to students with special needs in or away from the general education classroom, as well as organizational arrangements that shape the physical and professional interactions of special education teachers with their peers. (Thorius & Maxcy, 2015, p. 120)

Further, *technical* forces shape a local site's zone of policy mediation and include organizational capacities and functions connected with how resources are developed and distributed (Welner, 2001). Finally, *political* forces mediate policy appropriation as related to how certain group and individual power, privilege, and marginalization shape policy responses.

Taken together, the foci of inertial, normative, technical, and political forces provide a frame for examining local environments where disproportionality policy is enacted, including the pressures and expectations experienced by educators and other local actors who prioritize, interpret, and respond to such policy. Like expanding technical assistance beyond the *implementation* of evidence-based practices, this framework has relevance for enriching technical assistance to account for the influence of practitioners and of local context in shaping the interpretation and appropriation of policies and practices promoted by technical assistance providers. Finally, exploring the local manifestations of these forces can provide insight into the successes and limits of federal disproportionality policy.

RESEARCHER-LED/RESEARCH ON APPROACHES TO ELIMINATING DISPROPORTIONALITY

Despite the vast number of studies that document and examine disproportionality's root causes, there have been very few studies on researcher-facilitated efforts to partner with educators toward its elimination. These few studies include a body of work led by Bal and colleagues (e.g., 2012, 2014) with local education agencies in a midwestern state focused on eliminating racial disproportionality in school discipline. Research has demonstrated that school discipline disproportionality is closely connected to special education eligibility patterns, particularly related to the category of emotional disturbance (Bal et al., 2019). Bal, also an NCCRESt doctoral student alumnus, drew from cultural–historical activity theory, and more specifically Engeström's (2001) theory of expansive learning and formative intervention, to develop collaborative approaches to addressing disproportionate school discipline with educators and families.

Another study about researcher-facilitated efforts to remediate disproportionality was one conducted by Ahram and colleagues (2011). The study was a statewide project funded by the New York State Education Department (NYSED) (2004–2009). Ahram and Fergus held leadership roles with the Technical Assistance Center on Disproportionality (TACD) at New York University's Metropolitan Center for Urban Education (aka Metro Center) directed by Noguera. At that time, a large number of New York State districts had been identified as having disproportionality through the SPP process, and the NYSED began to cite districts for overrepresentation under Chapter 405 Laws of 1999. Cited districts were offered the opportunity to participate in a 5-year project facilitated by the TACD, which would provide intensive technical assistance in three ways: (1) classroom observations in the school district, (2) root cause analyses of disproportionality, conducted over 1 year in six sessions with the district, and (3) development and implementation within the district of a 3-year plan for culturally responsive professional development to build educators' capacities to eliminate disproportionality.

Ahram and colleagues documented root causes of disproportionality in two suburban school districts in different regions of the state, as well as their technical assistance with these districts to eliminate disproportionality. To my knowledge, it is the only peer-reviewed study on disproportionality-related technical assistance; therefore, I describe this study in some detail. Both the Carroll and the Hannover districts participating in the study were suburban and comprised a majority of white students (75% and 50%, respectively). Carroll's next largest racial group was Black students, at 20%, while Hannover's was Latino, at 35%. Over the course of 5 years, both districts decreased identification of students of color in special education; Carroll had a modest decrease in classification of Black students (−14.46%) and a significant decrease in classification of Latino students (−25.33%). Hannover had a significant decrease in classification of Black students (−29.64%) and Latino students (−23.86%). Although root cause analysis revealed some differences between the districts, both districts demonstrated root causes as follows:

(1) Deficit thinking related to conceptions of race and socioeconomic status serves as a driving force behind the decision to refer. In many cases, disability is a socially constructed category, and the decision to refer to special education is informed by biases related to race and class (i.e., racism and classism). (2) [Another root cause is associated with] inadequate institutional safeguards to prevent referrals and to provide teachers with assistance in meeting the needs of struggling learners. (Ahram et al., 2011, p. 2245)

Through their analysis of educators' explanations, or "hunches" (p. 2246) about why disproportionality existed in their respective districts, the authors found that educators noted deficit-based explanations of student and family poverty, and parents' failure to support their children's academic and intellectual development, although these explanations often appeared conflated with explanations at the intersection of race (e.g., "They bring ghetto to the school" [p. 2246]). The authors concluded that an avoidance to name race appeared connected to fear of being considered as racist. One Carroll staff member noted that many of the barriers in recognizing and addressing disproportionality were related to educator resistance to "acknowledging that there was a race issue" (p. 2247). Yet, across both districts, educators shared perspectives that they feared Black students, particularly in the face of increases in the Black student population. The authors also found that student performance on state assessments was linked to educators' decisions to refer students to special education as a way of "gaming the system" (p. 2252) by lessening accountability for these students' progress in general education in the wake of No Child Left Behind (Figlio & Getzler, 2002).

As the researchers moved toward the design and implementation of each district's professional development plan based on root cause analyses, they documented the considerable emphasis on technical "institutional fixes" (p. 2254) to existing policies and procedures for referral to special education, including changes to referral forms and application of schoolwide multitiered systems of support (formerly known as Response to Intervention). The authors noted, however, that such changes functioned as an "equity safeguard" (p. 2254) for students at risk of classification. The authors concluded that although educators' deficit beliefs about students are resistant and slow to change, explicit changes in school practices appear to have some impact on the ways in which these beliefs contribute directly to disproportionality.

IMPLICATIONS OF EXISTING RESEARCH ON TECHNICAL ASSISTANCE APPROACHES TO REMEDIATING DISPROPORTIONALITY

In consideration of the whole of the body of disproportionality research, it is apparent that remedies for addressing disproportionality must mirror the complexity of the phenomenon itself (Tefera & Fischman, 2020). Sociocultural and sociohistorical analyses have been helpful in gaining understanding of this complexity, as have analyses that study various patterns of sociodemographic variables and their relationship to the occurrence of disproportionality. However, the research body has demonstrated that the problem does not emerge out of a single predictor variable or only in specific settings. Disproportionality occurs within local and broader sociohistorical and cultural contexts that vary across sites (Cruz & Rodl, 2018). As such, disproportionality will be experienced differently in each context, demonstrating the need for technical assistance approaches that account for the existing research on disproportionality but also incorporate attention to sociocultural and sociohistorical contexts to support the development of complex and locally relevant solutions.

I close this chapter with another story about my time as a school psychologist in the Southwest. In many ways it is a worst-case scenario of the intersections of ableism, racism, xenophobia, inappropriate and invalid assessment processes, and inadequacy of systemic resources. It was 1999, and I was fresh out of graduate school on the east coast. I made the move to the Southwest from the Northeast where I had worked in a city high school, and where the majority of students were Black, and more specifically, African American, Cape Verdean, and Haitian. When I got to my new school in the Southwest, I was in a very unfamiliar context. Almost 90% of the students were immigrants from Mexico, many of them undocumented, and it quickly became apparent to me that the Spanish I learned in school from 7th to 12th grades and for one semester in college was grossly inadequate. Yet, there I was, the only school psychologist in a school of 1,500 students, about 15% of whom had disability labels and received some form of special education services. This school, like almost all others in the district, had one self-contained classroom where primarily students labeled with intellectual disabilities (albeit using the former ableist category of mild mental retardation [MIMR]) spent more than 80% of their school day. Very early on, the teacher of this classroom, who was a 1st-year professional fresh out of her undergraduate program, and I sat down to familiarize ourselves with the 10 students' individualized education programs, present levels of educational performance, education goals, and dates for what we short-handed as "3-year re-evals." The first student up for reconsideration of special education eligibility was a 7th-grade boy I'll call José. José and his family spoke Spanish as their home language and emigrated from Mexico when José was about 4 years old. José had been identified for special education in 1st grade under the category of MIMR and placed in a self-contained classroom where he had been educated ever since. This was José's third school in 6 years, because the district had a history of moving self-contained classrooms from school to school as total district enrollment increased.

When it came time to review his file more closely, I began with the former school psychologist's psychoeducational evaluation report and my stomach dropped. José had been assessed using the Wechsler Intelligence Scale for Children, in English, in 1st grade. A Vineland Adaptive Behavior Scale had been completed by his 1st-grade teacher as the second required measurement for determining eligibility under the MIMR category. On both measures, José received a score just under two standard deviations from the middle of the bell curve—68 and 69, respectively. I quickly thumbed through the rest of the report, looking for evidence of classroom observations, family interview and developmental history data, anything to support the eligibility decision. I found very little.

The original concern was that José had not been learning his letter sounds as quickly as his peers, was often silent in class, sometimes appeared confused when the teacher provided instructions, and relied too much on his peers for assistance. Ok, I reassured myself, let me take a look at the 3-year reevaluation report from 4th grade. All I found was a brief report and signature page that the team had concluded that no new assessments were needed to determine José's continuing eligibility for special education under his current category, or to determine the appropriateness of his educational placement. That is, it had been determined that no new assessments were needed for a now-7th-grade young man who had been labeled with MIMR since he was 6, relying solely on an assessment administered in English and an adaptive measure completed by his teacher. I was sick to my stomach at this point. All we could do, I thought, was reconvene the team and recommend assessment in English and Spanish and ask José's mother to complete the Spanish version of the adaptive behavior scale. So that is what we did, and José scored in the so-called average range on both. Now the team was faced with exiting from special education a 7th-grader who had been in a self-contained classroom since 1st grade and having him reenter general education where he would switch classrooms and teachers for all his content areas.

Here I ask the reader to pause to engage in a reflection activity I have used with educators with whom I have shared the same story in the context of technical assistance partnerships to address disproportionality and other systemic inequities related to student access, participation, and outcomes. As disturbing and challenging as these real-life stories may be, and as much as they may connect with similar instances we have engaged or observed in our experiences, the opportunity to examine the ideological, historical, and systemic roots of these occurrences provides another opportunity for locating and disrupting these scenarios in our own contexts.

1. What assumptions about intelligence informed what happened to José?
2. What assumptions about language mediated what happened to José?

3. What assumptions about (immigrant) families (of color) shaped what happened to José?
4. What procedural factors contributed to what happened to José?
5. What structural factors (in the school or district) contributed to what happened to José?
6. What features of time and place contributed to what happened to José?
7. What public policies may have contributed to what happened to José?

With this brief exercise as a preview of deeper and more systemic approaches to come, I move to the next chapter to provide a history of the development of technical assistance as a federal approach to influencing policy implementation near and far, before connecting this history to our current efforts to remediate disproportionality through equity expansive technical assistance partnerships.

CHAPTER 2

Technical Assistance as Cultural-Historical Activity

One of the central purposes of this book is to present a theory for equity expansive technical assistance, based in part on the need for research on the subject in general, as well as on the need for such research that is grounded in theory. The state of the research base is unsurprising, however, when we trace the origins and roots of technical assistance in foreign and domestic policymaking and enactment, and movement into educational contexts such as special education where the research base has been largely atheoretical (Artiles, 1998). We must study and understand our cultural histories, so we are not condemned to repeat (Santayana, 1906) those aspects that have contributed to deep societal and educational inequities; this assertion also applies to studying and understanding the cultural history of technical assistance.

In his 1949 inaugural address, President Harry Truman announced a program to "mak[e] the benefits of our scientific advances and industrial progress available for the improvement and growth of underdeveloped areas." Truman's early "technical assistance" efforts sought to win hearts and minds of the developing world.

> For the first time in history, humanity possesses the knowledge and skill to relieve suffering of these people. The United States is pre-eminent among nations in the development of industrial and scientific techniques. The material resources which we can afford to use for assistance of other peoples is limited. But our imponderable resources in technical knowledge are constantly growing and are inexhaustible.

Congress approved Truman's Point Four Program in 1950, establishing the Technical Cooperation Administration (Macekura, 2013). Four years later, in *Brown v. Board of Education of Topeka, Kansas* (1954), the Supreme Court ruled that separating public school children on the basis of race was unconstitutional. The Court's decision signaled the end of legalized racial segregation in U.S. public schools and overruled the "separate but equal" principle set forth in the 1896 *Plessy v. Ferguson* case. Over the next decade, intensive social–political tension and activism led by African American, Black, and other people of color, along with President Kennedy's proposal that Congress pass sweeping civil rights legislation that would address voting rights, public accommodations, school desegregation, and nondiscrimination in federally assisted programs, culminated in President Johnson signing the Civil Rights Act of 1964 into law just hours after Congress passed it on July 2, 1964. The Act's Title IV—Desegregation of Public Education, Section 403—Technical Assistance, authorized the Commissioner of Education

> upon the application of any school board, State, municipality, school district, or other governmental unit legally responsible for operating a public school or schools, to render technical assistance to such applicant in the preparation, adoption, and implementation of plans for the desegregation of public schools. Such technical assistance may, among other activities, include making available to such agencies information regarding effective methods of coping with special educational problems occasioned by desegregation, and making available to such agencies personnel of the Office of Education or other persons specially equipped to advise and assist them in coping with such problems.

Thus, the Desegregation Assistance Centers were born as the first educational technical assistance centers, and the only technical assistance centers with origins connected to issues of nondiscriminatory treatment, equal access and opportunity under the law, and protection from isolation by identifiable characteristics.

When originally enacted, Title IV was concerned with desegregation based on race, color, religion, or national origin; in 1972, Title IV was amended to add desegregation based on sex. Over the past 50 years, the original Desegregation Assistance Centers evolved into the network of 10 federally funded regional Equity Assistance Centers; in 2016, acting Secretary of Education King reduced the number of centers to four, which now focus on equity in relation to religion as well as race, sex, and national origin.

In the current day, the U.S. Department of Education funds technical assistance centers to support educators with reshaping systemic policy and practice. Technical assistance is a broad term for nonfinancial services aimed at professional and organizational capacity development. Technical assistance is carried out in various forms, including research and experiential information and knowledge sharing, instruction, consulting, and program and policy review. The Equity Assistance Centers are part of a much larger network of technical assistance centers funded by USDOE and its Offices of Elementary and Secondary Education (OESE) and Special Education and Rehabilitation Services. The 2022 fiscal year budget included $102.8 billion in new discretionary budget authority for USDOE, a 41% increase above fiscal year 2021 appropriation. Within the technical assistance network, three types of centers are managed by OESE: (1) Equity Assistance Centers, which received $6.6 million in funding; (2) Statewide Family Engagement Centers, which received $12.5 million to "promote parent and family engagement in education or provide comprehensive training and technical assistance to SEAs, LEAs, schools, and organizations that support partnerships between families and schools," and (3) one national and 19 regional Comprehensive Centers, which received $52 million to provide technical assistance to SEAs and other recipients to "implement, and sustain effective evidence-based practices that improve instruction and student outcomes" (USDOE, 2022, p. 22).

Along with OESE, the Office of Special Education Programs oversees $49.3 million in competitive grants for technical assistance and dissemination of materials based on knowledge gained through research and practice. Recipients include the National Center for Systemic Improvement; the National Center on Intensive Intervention; projects associated with the Schoolwide Integrated Framework for Transformation, or SWIFT Schools; the IRIS Center, the Center on Positive Behavioral Intervention and Supports; and the What Works Clearinghouse. OSEP also funds 94 Parent Information Centers (PICs), along with five centers that provide technical assistance to the PICs. Notably, in 2022 the OSEP education budget included a $40.8 million request for Demonstration and Training Programs (an increase of $35.0 million from fiscal year 2021) to support model demonstration projects and technical assistance focused on competitive integrated employment, and supplements for the PICs to provide additional support needed because of the COVID-19 pandemic. Additionally, the USDOE's Institute of Education Sciences funds four national research centers and a network of 10 Regional Education Laboratories that provide technical assistance to "school districts, state departments of education, and other education stakeholders to help generate and apply evidence, with the goal of improving learner outcomes" (USDOE, 2022, p. 60).

For such a large fiscal and human investment in technical assistance by the USDOE, there has been relatively little research that documents its theory, process, and impact, particularly in the field of education (Thorius, 2019). Of the research that exists, a good portion is published by technical assistance centers themselves (e.g., Blase, 2009; Fixsen et al., 2005), rather than peer-reviewed (for an exception, see Thomas et al., 1997). Other existing research has been conducted and published in related, but non-education fields, such as community psychology (e.g., Chinman et al., 2008; Hunter et al., 2009). As Katz and Wandersman (2016) noted in their review of existing research across fields that was largely concentrated in community psychology, public health, and medicine,

> The review of articles found very few instances in which an explicit model or organizing framework was used to plan, implement, and/or evaluate TA [technical assistance]. Thus, although TA is widely practiced, it is not well defined or

clearly operationalized into a series or sequence of tasks. It appears that the world of TA is like the early days of psychotherapy; there are inconsistencies in the literature, no agreement on the necessary ingredients, and relatively little use of systematic empirical evidence. (p. 424)

I admire and appreciate the work of many education technical assistance center leaders and personnel who have written and self-published on the features of their work. It has contributed to my understandings and shaped the structure and goals of technical assistance across educational fields and foci. Likely, a reason for the prominence of self-publication stems from the demand for assistance and a minimal emphasis by the federal government on peer-reviewed research activities by such centers. At the same time, the centrality of evidence-based practices from which education technical assistance draws requires that we have a robust evidence base on such technical assistance itself. The peer review process is an important aspect of developing research evidence. Complementing this perspective by arguing for educators' access to educational research, and particularly research related to the education of students with disabilities, OSEP leaders published in the academic journal *Remedial and Special Education* on the dangers of publishing *only* in peer-reviewed journals. Without naming technical assistance specifically, they described what many in the field define as a central purpose of technical assistance, along with shepherding federal policy to more localized settings (McInerney & Hamilton, 2007): translating research into educational practice through communication and partnership. Schiller et al. (1995) asked and answered, "So, how can research make a difference in the classroom, and help teachers help children?"

> The Division of Innovation and Development, Office of Special Education Programs, believes that the answer is through communication and cooperation. This partnership is needed now more than ever because of shrinking resources, increasing diversity, and school reform efforts aimed at altering traditional teaching practices and school organization. As a community, the challenge for the Division of Innovation and Development and for the special education research is threefold: (1) The community must continue to build a knowledge base that addresses the vital problems for children, educators, and families. (2) Researchers must communicate findings to families, teachers, and policymakers in a way that fosters improved special education practices. (3) Links must be fostered between practitioners and researchers to develop and implement the knowledge base. (p. 372)

Most modern-day technical assistance centers emerged in the 1980s, and their services over time increasingly have been organized in ways that parallel public health prevention models (Schalock et al., 1994; Senge, 1990; Trohanis, 1982). These services, framed by these models, typically are structured as universal prevention, and targeted and intensive interventions (Datnow & Stringfield, 2000; Fixsen et al., 2005). Technical assistance has been defined in various ways in educational research, which McInerney and Hamilton (2007) summarized as top-down and bottom-up approaches. In top-down approaches, technical assistance providers facilitate research to practice translation and/or federal or state policy interpretation and implementation within more localized education systems, including districts and schools. Within bottom-up approaches, technical assistance providers respond to systems' identification of policy or practice issues, and requests for support to develop local solutions that can be scaled up across larger systemic contexts. Whichever the approach, however, both rely on an expert/novice paradigm. That is, an external expert provides technical assistance to a novice recipient (Sawyer, 2005). Technical assistance services usually are carried out through the provider's consultation on "programs, policies, or practices" (Katz & Wandersman, 2016, p. 417), with an overarching goal of building organizational capacity (Trohanis, 1982) (e.g., aligning state or local education agency infrastructure, supporting personnel development [Fixsen & Blase, 2009]).

In more depth, within top-down approaches to technical assistance, providers communicate to the recipient information on evidence-based interventions to improve policy or practice. In such cases, the partner is expected to implement such interventions in ways that are technically sound and with fidelity (McInerney & Hamilton, 2007). Research on top-down technical assistance has mixed reviews, with some research documenting that the competing policy and practice demands of local contexts, as well as personal and systemic capacities, can lead partners to adopt such interventions inappropriately or incompletely (Fullan & Miles, 1992). Successful top-down approaches, defined as those that achieve desired outcomes, require that the interventions communicated, modeled, and taught by the technical assistance provider are both considerate of and appropriate to the local content *and* that the partner enacts the intervention with accuracy. Research has linked poor administrative support and ecologically invalid interventions to the failure of top-down approaches (Loucks-Horsley & Roody, 1990; Schein, 1992).

Bottom-up approaches also have been classified as developmental technical assistance. In such approaches, providers typically communicate with individuals and groups in a particular education agency or agencies to identify issues of policy and practice that indicate a need for improvement. Next the partnership typically revolves around designing and/or building locally relevant interventions and then implementing them. Fullan (1991) and other researchers and technical assistance providers note the importance of job-embedded professional development, teacher study groups, and peer coaching to the success of developmental technical assistance (Osher & Kane, 1993).

Research on the success of bottom-up approaches also has demonstrated mixed success, with the most common reasons being lack of access to research on interventions, misinterpretations of research data (Guskey & Huberman, 1995), and limitations on time and resources (Huberman, 1983). Schiller and colleagues (1995) described the role of educators in partnerships geared toward translating research into practice along a continuum, which provides some possible explanations for this limited success, as has been demonstrated in the research on education systems' change (e.g., Sashkin & Egermeier, 1993). Teacher roles, they suggest, can be arranged developmentally as "applying," "translating," and "creating" knowledge (p. 373).

Further, research has shown that bottom-up technical assistance rarely leads to sustained impact on teaching and learning (Crandall et al., 1982). This has been attributed to the strong pull of the status quo, or the history of knowledge and activity: Educators' existing knowledge and routine practices tend to reemerge when they experience challenges implementing change beyond the scope of a particular technical assistance partnership (Fullan, 1991). Successful bottom-up approaches require effective leadership, cross-system and stakeholder buy-in, along with educators' access to resources and related capacity to identify, access, and evaluate interventions (Little, 1993; Louis & Rosenblum, 1981).

ENHANCING TECHNICAL IMPROVEMENTS WITH CONTEXTUAL ANALYSIS AND APPLICATION

Both top-down and bottom-up technical assistance approaches have received substantial criticism for inadequate consideration of local context when disseminating or developing interventions to be enacted as policy and practice improvements (Kane & Kocher, 1980; McLaughlin, 1990). Moreover, the research base from which technical assistance providers have been encouraged to draw to inform their suggestions of policy and practice improvements has been criticized for its rigidity in scope and application, and incompatibility with the dynamic and social nature of educational contexts (Erickson & Gutiérrez, 2002).

Representing a major contribution to the understanding of contextual importance for technical assistance is the field of implementation science, including its conceptualization of the evidence base with which such implementation is concerned. Attention to context is important, because research across fields from education to public health has found similar issues: Successful impact of an innovation does not guarantee its incorporation into routine practice (e.g., Bauer & Kirchner, 2020). The overarching goal of implementation science is the development of generalizable knowledge to be applied beyond individual systems of concern (Bauer et al., 2015). In a 2013 special issue of the special education field's flagship journal, *Exceptional Children*, B. G. Cook and Odom described the history and application of implementation science to reduce well-documented gaps between knowledge of evidence-based practices and their implementation in schools (e.g., Mostert & Crockett, 1999–2000), including through technical assistance.

The conceptualization of evidence-based practices emerged from the field of medicine and psychology in the 1990s (American Psychological Association, 2006; Guyatt et al., 1992). The movement of implementation science into the field of special education occurred concomitantly, in the late 1990s and early 2000s, with the field's efforts to set the standard for evidence-based education practices, including Response to Intervention models for universal instruction, early intervening, and special education eligibility determination. At this time, developments in special education relating to what counted as "evidence-based" meant that practices had to meet a set of prescribed standards (B. G. Cook et al., 2009; Odom et al., 2005) for research design, quality, and quantity; and had to be validated by "multiple, high-quality, experimental or quasi-experimental (often including single-case research) studies" (B. G. Cook & Odom, 2013, p. 136) and show favorable student outcomes (Slavin, 2002).

There were 111 mentions of scientifically based or evidence-based practice included in the 2001 reauthorization of the Elementary and Secondary Education Act (ESEA) as the No Child Left Behind Act, including the following criterion for supporting research: "uses every opportunity to conduct experimental or quasi-experimental designs in which individuals, entities, programs, or activities are assigned to different conditions and with appropriate controls to evaluate the effects of the condition of interest" (§9101(37)). This conceptualization of what counts as evidence-based practice was further codified in the reauthorization of ESEA, defined as statistically significant findings at three levels based on "at least one well-designed and well-implemented" experimental, quasi-experimental, or correlational study, respectively (§8002.21.A). In the 5 years that followed, the vast majority of federal research funding was awarded for the development of evidence-based practices, with very little invested toward implementation approaches (Clancy, 2006; Institute of Education Sciences, 2010, as cited in Fixsen et al., 2013).

Greenhalgh and colleagues' (2004) in-depth analysis of research on the dissemination of evidence-based practices categorized researchers' efforts in two ways: "letting it happen" or "making it happen" (p. 593). Accordingly, implementation science provided a path for "making it happen" in the form of a process-oriented outcome: bridging the gap between research on evidence-based practices and their application, with fidelity. Fidelity here refers to both the stickiness of these practices that had been so elusive in previous attempts to bring research knowledge into local settings, given the many contextual factors that afforded and constrained their application, and the scaling up of evidence-based practices across local and state-level systems, defined by Fixsen et al. (2013) as "the point at which at least 60% of the service units in a system are using the program with fidelity and good outcomes" (p. 214). Accordingly, implementation science processes informed researchers' achievement of these outcomes with local and state education agency partners, with technical assistance playing the crucial role of mediator between research and practice. The OSEP funded the first national technical assistance center focused on implementation science in 2007: the State Implementation and Scaling Up of Evidence Based Practices, or SISEP, Center. Moreover, across most USDOE offices' notices inviting applications for technical assistance centers over the past 15 years or so, grantees' understanding of and facility with implementation science has been emphasized, as it has been in the past two notices inviting applications for the Equity Assistance Center program.

Fixsen and colleagues with the National Implementation Research Network (NINR) at the University of North Carolina, Chapel Hill, defined a state-level implementation science process that included "developing a planning team at the state policy level, selecting a team or teams for providing technical assistance and coaching, providing training to practitioners and technical assistance providers together, and transferring control from professional development projects . . . to state providers" (B. G. Cook & Odom, 2013, p. 142). Accounting for weaknesses researchers identified in previous approaches to technical assistance, the NINR process was conceived as a simultaneously bottom-up and top-down approach for implementing evidence-based practices and the creation of systems in which these practices could be sustained. Crucial to this process is the role of technical assistance providers as external facilitators who, based on research by Nord and Tucker (1987), are able to support systemic change in the context of existing organizational culture, disposition toward change, and staff members' professional knowledge and capacities. Over the past 15 years, the NINR, the OSEP-funded SISEP Center (2007–present), the OESE-funded National Center on Innovation and Improvement (2007–2012), and the OESE/OSEP-funded Technical Assistance Center on Positive Behavioral Interventions and Supports have modeled the relationship between development of research knowledge and application of evidence-based practices.

CONSIDERING CONTEXT IN THE DEVELOPMENT AND DESIGN OF EVIDENCE-BASED PRACTICES: EQUITY CANNOT BE "IMPLEMENTED"

As valuable as the development and application of implementation science processes are, along with the evidence-based practices such processes seek to bring into and scale up across education systems, the complexity of factors contributing to disproportionality requires technical assistance that is equally complex. Here, I am not arguing against the complexity of implementation science or evidence-based practices, per se, but rather raising questions about ways in which context is accounted for and the evidence base defined. Context, for example, includes educators' belief systems and orientations to race and disability, school cultural practices related to special education referrals, along with histories of oppression spanning decades of inequities in student access, participation, and outcomes (Kozleski & Artiles, 2014) when disaggregated by race, disability, and other demographics.

In 2012, drawing from their work leading NCCRESt's efforts to eliminate disproportionality and applying it to their more recent roles as principal investigators with the Region IX EAC from 2008 to 2011, Kozleski and Artiles asserted that technical assistance must stimulate development of complex solutions to contextual issues rooted in racism, ableism, and other systemic oppressions. Such complexity and attention to context, they argued, were necessary if technical assistance was to play a key role in remediating how systems facilitate equity in opportunities, rather than simply consult on technical improvements to existing operations:

> TA [technical assistance] is often prized when it avoids critiquing equity outcomes and focuses on improving operational aspects of education systems such as improved scientific rigor in assessment, identification, and intervention. This focus, we argue, deflects attention from equity as a core value of a public education system within a democracy, and therefore, the recipients of TA learn to view their work in terms of operational tasks while outcomes that benefit the most oppressed groups of students can become tangential to technical improvements to the system. (p. 433)

Thus, although some contextual factors contributing to disproportionality as found in the research may be alleviated through the implementation and scaling up of evidence-based practices through technical assistance informed by implementation science processes, some factors are so entrenched and multilayered that they do not fit neatly into the ways in which implementation science and related evidence-based practices have been conceptualized. Simply put, there is no evidence-based practice for addressing systemic oppression, particularly when evidence-based practice is defined in the ways in which it has been in the special education and implementation science literature. The characteristics of research on evidence-based practices to be applied and scaled up through implementation science warrant careful, critical examination.

In 2022, our EAC published a research brief authored by equity fellow Amanda Sullivan and school psychology doctoral student researchers in which they questioned the research base of evidence-based practices and offered ways for altering such practices to support social justice in education. Sullivan, a school psychologist by training and coordinator of the School Psychology Department at the University of Minnesota, is widely considered an expert on disproportionality and has applied complex quantitative research methodologies to examining the phenomenon in local and state settings (e.g., Kinkaid & Sullivan, 2017; Sullivan, 2011). In their brief,

Sullivan and her colleagues remind us of the substantial concerns scholars and practitioners—particularly scholars of color and from other minoritized communities—have raised about the "narrow, and often exclusionary nature of the evidence on which such practices are based (Cohen et al., 2004; Kaplan et al., 2020; Lilienfeld et al., 2013; Wells et al., 2009)" (p. 1). First, they note that prominent sociocultural researchers have critiqued evidence-based practices for their rigid scope and application only to the contexts under study in the research base; just because an evidence-based practice is successful in a research context, does not mean it will have similar success in the day-to-day dynamic contexts of districts, schools, and classrooms (e.g., Berliner, 2002; Erickson & Gutiérrez, 2002). Although to some extent this understanding was an impetus for implementation research (Gamoran & Dibner, 2022) and the growth of the field of implementation science, the contexts surrounding deep equity issues such as disproportionality are social, historical, political, spatial, and cultural; accordingly, first the contexts with which implementation science must be concerned—those that promote the bridging and scaling up of evidence-based practices—must be explicitly and holistically conceptualized.

Second, and of equal importance, are the narrow definitions of research applied to identify an evidence-based practice. Given that the evidence-based practice movement in special education relies on medical models of disability and intervention, most evidence-based practices are concerned with improving students' academic and behavior performance (B. G. Cook et al., 2020). Evidence-based practices, at least the ways in which they have been defined in the special education literature and federal legislation, do not address the low expectations of teachers for students of color (belief systems), or stigmatizing impacts of disciplinary actions in the classroom, for example, both of which have been identified in disproportionality literature as contextual factors contributing to the phenomenon. Relatedly, the research designs privileged in the definition of evidence-based practices in the literature itself, and in the federal regulations and notices inviting applications for technical assistance, minimize and discount the importance of qualitative research and associated findings, favoring "scientific research, such as that used in medical research and other 'hard' sciences," that "offers rigorous methodologies for studying what works, for determining whether a particular curriculum or instructional technique will result in improved academic performance . . . for a majority of the children for whom it was designed" (Wilde, 2004, p. 1).

In contrast, qualitative research, which by nature can account for the complexity of context beyond a set of predetermined dependent and independent variables, has been described in a publication disseminated by federally funded National Clearinghouse for English Language Acquisition and Language Instruction Educational Programs as having the potential to meet "*nearly* all of the statutory provisions of the NCLB legislation" (Wilde,

2004, p. 17, emphasis in original). At the same time, within the limited space dedicated to the contributions of qualitative research to evidence-based practice, the author described such research as potentially compromised by the researcher "who collects, filters, and organizes the information; this person's biases (both for and against the program) can have an impact on the outcome(s) of the study," and who can "become so intimately involved in the community that they virtually loses [sic] their identity" (p. 17).

CHAPTER 3

Theoretical and Conceptual Foundations of Equity Expansive Technical Assistance

In the previous chapters, I have laid out several key aspects contributing to disproportionality, and indeed many education inequities experienced by students at various marginalized identity intersections. I also have detailed past and current approaches to technical assistance and accompanying critiques that technical assistance must more purposefully account for advanced understandings of culture, context, history, and theory in systemic approaches to addressing educational inequities.

In recognition of these factors, equity expansive technical assistance is informed by several interconnected sociocultural and critical theories, which I unify under the umbrella of cultural–historical activity theory (CHAT; Cole, 1996; Engeström, 1987). In this chapter, I detail these theories to demonstrate the adequacy of their complexity to account for multiple contextual factors in the design and facilitation of technical assistance partnerships that can and do improve conditions for and outcomes of equity in a given educational system.

First and foremost, CHAT provides a way for organizing interdisciplinary approaches to studying human learning and development. Given that educator learning is central to the development of the capacity to effect change in policy and practice through technical assistance, I start with how CHAT accounts for the nature of human learning and development. In acknowledgment of the utmost importance of how cultural contexts, past and present, contribute to and sustain educational inequities, CHAT provides the overarching framework for equity expansive technical assistance because of its concern with individuals' *mediated learning within a given cultural context*, or *activity system* (Engeström, 1987), along with transformative impacts on systemic outcomes. CHAT is also concerned with the relationships between activity system participants' learning and the ways in which their collective activities across various contexts interact across time and space, including the ways in which rules, divisions of labor, and communities associated with these contexts mediate learning. Across all generations of CHAT, the transformative agency and purposeful action of those engaged in joint activity toward a shared object are central to understanding how activity, the object of activity, and the outcome of activity over time expand as new learning is produced in the context of activity.

CHAT is grounded in the work of L. S. Vygotsky, A. R. Luria, and A. N. Leontiev, and their focus on human cognition and behavior as mediated by cultural artifacts: tenets of what originally was conceptualized as activity theory (Vygotsky, 1978a). Drawing from Marx, Leontiev, Luria, and Vygotsky asserted that behaviorism and psychoanalysis were inadequate approaches to understanding why people acted in certain ways, and that human activity was more complex than responses to stimuli (Wertsch, 1981). Rather, following the Center for Research on Activity, Development and Learning (http://www.helsinki.fi/cradle/index.htm), they proposed that human activity is simultaneously artifact-mediated and object-oriented. Vygotsky linked this conceptualization of activity to development, by theorizing that learning is social and mediated through joint development of tools (i.e., artifacts) that allow humans to interact with, and therefore learn about, the world. Over time, this learning leads to social transformation. In essence, Vygotsky equated psychological development (i.e., learning) with development and use of artifacts to build human consciousness about the world.

Since its inception, there have been three generations of activity theory, although the first generation also is commonly known as Vygotsky's cultural–historical/sociocultural theory (Engeström, 2001). This theory is widely recognized as having redefined understandings of human development in connection with historical, social, and cultural contexts (Martin & Peim, 2009). First-generation activity theory includes three elements: human *subjects*, the *object* (i.e., motivation) for the activity, and the *artifacts* that mediate human activity toward this object (Vygotsky, 1978b). Mediation is a fundamental concept of first-generation activity theory, which posits that higher level cognition is mediated by signs, defined as "artificial, or self-generated, stimuli" (Vygotsky, 1978b, p. 39); the concept modifies what behaviorism theorizes as a direct relationship between stimulus and human response (Skinner, 1971; Watson, 1913) into a mediated relationship. Artifacts are both material and symbolic, and afford and constrain subjects' action. Material artifacts are tangible tools that individuals utilize in an activity (e.g., computers, pens), while symbolic artifacts are nontangible and have cultural meaning (e.g., language, theories, frameworks) (Lantolf, 2000; Vygotsky, 19878b).

Vygotsky often examined language as such a sign, particularly as related to child development, and its role in mediating how children plan how to solve a problem as well as their actions associated with problem solving. Two more concepts central to Vygotsky's first-generation activity theory are *internalization* and *perezhivanie*. Internalization refers to an individual's reorganization of their cognition to assimilate new signs (Vygotsky, 1997), whereby individuals transform "means of social behavior into means of individual psychological organization" (Vygotsky & Luria, 1994, p. 138). Perezhivanie in effect is the *prism* that refracts the impact of one's environment on the development of the individual (Veresov, 2020). Vygotsky (1994) elaborates, "It is not any of the factors in themselves (if taken without reference to the child) which determines how they will influence the future course of his development, but the same factors refracted through the prism of the child's perezhivanie" (p. 340).

The last concept central to first-generation activity theory is that of the zone of proximal development, which Vygotsky (1978a) defined as the difference between a child's level of actual development, or the tasks a child is able to accomplish independently, and their potential for development, which he defined in line with the tasks a child is able to accomplish under adult guidance and "in cooperation with more competent peers" (Vygotsky, 1935, p. 35, as cited in Kostogriz & Veresov, 2021).

Taken together, these four concepts associated with first-generation activity theory reflect that development is neither linear nor cumulative. Rather, development involves individuals' reorganization of their internal psychological processes and "development, as often happens, proceeds here not in a circle but in a spiral, passing through the same point at each new revolution while advancing to a higher level" (Vygotsky, 1978b, p. 56). Studies applying first-generation activity theory typically have been concerned with "mediated work action" (Engeström & Sannino, 2021, p. 7), including the social history of such action that affords and constrains subjects' current activities.

Adding to the elevating, spiraling, and reorganizational nature of human development theorized by Vygotsky, other activity theorists more explicitly accounted for the cultural–historical nature of human development. Leontiev expanded first-generation activity theory from an individual to a collective activity by adding several elements related to the systems within which human activity is undertaken, namely, the community, rules, and the division of labor. *Community* refers to social and/or cultural groups of people involved in the activity and that bring with them *rules*: social norms that afford, constrain, and otherwise inform and influence behavior. *Division of labor* indicates how responsibilities are distributed across community members within the activity (Cole & Engeström, 1993). Leontiev also broke down further the concept of activity, separating it into actions and operations, the latter of which are automatic, unconscious, and determined by the conditions under which human action is undertaken (Engeström & Miettinen, 1999). Said differently, an activity is the overarching system in which an individual acts to realize an object; an action is goal-oriented and contributes to the overarching activity, although it may or may not align with the overall object of activity. Lastly, an operation is an automatic process that contributes to the actions contributing to the activity (Kuutti, 1996).

Leontiev also defined further the concept of the object—the shared motive or the motivating force for participants' engagement in activity—which also influences the structure of the activity and, in turn, transforms both the object and the subject in the process. Leontiev's additions to activity theory have implications for the development of technical assistance approaches that mediate educators' development while accounting for the systems within which they work, as well as the unconscious and automatic operations that contribute to educators' learning within these systems of activity.

Engeström (1987, 2001) played a crucial role in further developing CHAT with applicability to studying organizational change in work settings, including teaching and teacher education (Roth et al., 2009; Wilson, 2014). He did so by adding several elements related to the *systems* and *contexts* within which human activity is undertaken, namely, the community, rules, and the division of labor. This expanded framework allowed for examination of the "interrelationships between activities, actions, operations and artifacts, subjects' motives and goals, and aspects of the social, organizational, and societal contexts within which these activities are framed" (Batiibwe, 2019, p. 6). Studies applying second-generation CHAT commonly have been applied to include a researcher-interventionist along with practitioners to understand work activity and organizational change over time (Engeström & Sannino, 2021).

In third-generation CHAT, Engeström (2001) also specified that the unit of analysis include at least two interacting activity systems with a shared object between them. Engeström identified several grounding principles of third-generation CHAT, which allowed for the study of, as well as research interventionist approaches to studying, systemic change:

1. "A collective, artifact-mediated and object-oriented activity system, seen in its network relations to other activity systems" as the primary unit of analysis (p. 136).
2. The multivoicedness of the activity system, meaning that participants' varied perspectives and histories are sources of both tension and possibility.
3. Historicity of the activity system, which requires that any analysis of the activity system account for the local history of that activity, its objects, and mediating artifacts or tools.
4. The centrality of systemic contradictions as the force for development and transformation. Contradictions are defined as "historically accumulating structural tensions within and between activity systems" (p. 137) that stimulate participants' own self-reflection as well as collective change efforts, which ultimately change and expand the original object or motivation of activity and open doors to innovations to resolve contradictions. In future work, Engeström and Sannino (2011) clarified that by studying observable tensions

and conflicts, researchers can extrapolate the systemic contradictions that underlie activity systems.

5. Concern with transformation of the activity system, defined in Engeström's reconceptualization of Vygotsky's zone of proximal development as "the distance between the present everyday actions of the individuals and the historically new form of the societal activity that can be collectively generated as a solution to the double bind potentially embedded in the everyday actions" (p. 174).

Our equity expansive technical assistance and associated research is concerned with those involved in, and the elements of joint activity within, technical assistance partnerships, including the object and outcomes, mediating artifacts, community members, division of labor, and rules that shape how educators work toward partnership outcomes, that is, the elements of an activity system (Engeström, 1987). Given our understandings of CHAT, we know that these elements interact and influence one another, and are shaped by cultural and historical factors that include socialization into education professions, personal biases, and experiences with privilege and oppression connected with identity and role: the cultural–historical aspects of CHAT (Koszalka & Wu, 2004). Moreover, CHAT's principle of contradictions allows for critical analysis and identifies opportunities for systemic transformation, and the method of expansive learning can move abstract ideas to concrete practice (Miles, 2020). Thus, CHAT holds potential for "new ways of theorizing phenomena that emphasize relations and histories" (Roth, 2012, p. 101) and rests on the idea that systemic change occurs through goal-oriented, tool-mediated cultural practices (Engeström & Sannino, 2010). CHAT informs our approach to the study and the design of technical assistance as a mediating structure (González & Artiles, 2020) with the purpose of facilitating educational organizations' expansion of existing equity-related goals: a process of formative intervention (Engeström et al., 2014). In Part II, I connect these theoretical tools and processes more explicitly to the theory of equity expansive learning we have developed over time through our work with hundreds of school districts and several state departments of education around the country seeking to address educational inequities in their own local settings.

FACILITATING CRITICAL EN/COUNTERS: THE APPLICATION OF EQUITY EXPANSIVE TECHNICAL ASSISTANCE PARTNERSHIPS TO REVERSE RACIAL DISPROPORTIONALITY IN SPECIAL EDUCATION

CHAPTER 4

Equity Expansive Technical Assistance

Above all, equity expansive technical assistance is concerned with persistent systemic change that disrupts and dismantles historical legacies of normative assumptions, beliefs, and practices about individual characteristics and cultural identities that marginalize and disenfranchise people and groups of people. Addressing these concerns requires coordinated efforts that build human and system capacities for policy and practice improvements through collaborative consultation, professional learning, and contextual analysis supported by theory-grounded, research-based resources. In the first part of this chapter, I describe the ways we organize our work, including how we enter into partnership with organizations and agencies, before detailing and providing examples of the four elements central to the framing of equity expansive technical assistance.

TECHNICAL ASSISTANCE ORGANIZED BY DURATION AND INTENSITY

We coordinate our technical assistance efforts across three tiers that vary in terms of scope, intensity, and duration. By organizing our universal, targeted, and intensive services, we ensure that our doors are always open and there is always space at our table; to date, we have partnered with 100% of eligible agencies that have requested our assistance. This is a crucial aspect of equity expansive technical assistance; we must be there when the need arises and be accessible to all.

Our tier one *equity research and resources* technical assistance services are research-based, data-driven, and results-focused, and exist in many formats, including cross-stakeholder vodcasts, and policy and practice review rubrics. Under the auspices of our current EAC, the MAP Center, we have made available via our website over 700 digital print, video, and audio resources, almost 200 of which we have authored and produced ourselves. The remaining have undergone rigorous vetting prior to posting on our website's Equity Resource Library. Center resources have been accessed via our website over 50,000 times in the past 6 years, and we have been able to determine impact of these resources on policies, practices, and knowledge, which is a project-specific performance measure defined and tracked by the federal government.

Based on survey data from our MAP Center Annual Partner Questionnaire sent to more than 1,000 subscribers, 90% of respondents reported our equity research and resource services were of high quality and useful for building knowledge, and 30% reported that they contributed to tangible policy and practice changes. This latter point is important in that it suggests that even our least intensive technical assistance has led to tangible improvements in local settings. The following partner comment speaks to the impact of tier one TA on policy and practice improvements: "We were able to use the tools from MAP [Center] to create protocols around adoption of content area standards . . . we've incorporated several resources into our trainings . . . and use your one-pager 'Reframing the Achievement Gap' often."

Although those who interact with and apply our resources to their own contexts may never initiate direct contact with our center staff, we purposefully design equity research and resources so that, at the very least, users/readers will encounter a primary stimulus designed to evoke a contradiction in their daily activities as an educator, along with a secondary stimulus that may support them in resolving the contradiction. An example of such a resource is the MAP Center's *Equity Express*, which is a "choose your own adventure" style (Packard, 1969) interactive media resource linked to a regular newsletter coming out of our center that aims to represent pressing equity dilemmas facing educators, based on regional needs-sensing activities. Our center's most recent *Equity Express* editions feature primary contradictions regarding (1) teaching about and acknowledging race and racism in classroom instruction; (2) including transgender athletes on sports teams; and (3) acknowledging same-sex parent family structure in elementary school curriculum.

In the second *Equity Express* example (see Figure 4.1), we presented a scenario in which a parent/caregiver of a cisgender girl swimmer confronts a coach about a transgender student's participation on the team. In this edition of *Equity Express* (Rusnak et al., 2022), we explored the different ways in which coaches may respond to negative pushback about transgender students' participation in school sports, and the intents and impacts different responses may illicit. As secondary stimulus to resolve contradictions connected with how educators may choose to respond to this parent, we embedded associated resources to assist educators in navigating these types of conversations, toward the object of cultivating critical consciousness and inclusivity in school sports.

Of medium intensity, shorter-term and fixed or cyclical duration, our tier two *equity learning networks* are diverse professional and community learning opportunities. These networks have been valuable change levers for LEA/

Figure 4.1. Transgender Awareness in Sports

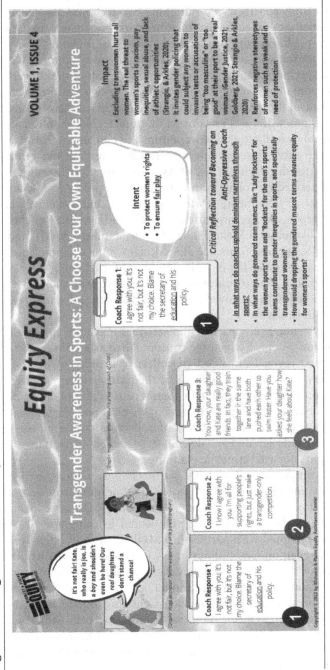

Source: Rusnak et al., 2022.

SEA stakeholders, reaching over 10,000 individual project participants over the past 6 years. Over 92% of survey respondents reported an increase in knowledge and capacity as a result of tier two technical assistance. A participant comment on an equity learning network postevent questionnaire illustrates how the knowledge was applied in the local context: "The information from this session was shared with our district equity council. We developed goals and specific action steps to be taken as a result of the conversations and guidance from this session." During another tier two learning event, administrators from an Illinois school district shared details of their LEA's Climate for Learning Framework and recognized that our technical assistance had been instrumental in facilitating district culture and climate improvements.

Our tier three *systemic equity partnerships* are our most intensive, sustained relationships with SEAs, LEAs, and other government agencies, and are characterized by collaborative consultation, policy review and revision, professional development, strategic planning, and systemic analysis and planning processes. We organize the goals and activities of these partnerships in individualized Memoranda of Understanding (MOU) and Technical Assistance Scope and Sequence (TASS) plans. Our systemic equity partnerships have resulted in the most in-depth and far-reaching impacts for partnering agencies. Due to duration and intensity, over the past 6 years, we have partnered with just over 100 school districts and state departments of education in this way.

Our systemic equity partnership activities may take any or all of the following forms, each of which we conceptualize as a connected activity system oriented toward an object of collective activity, which is to address the inequity that led to the genesis of the partnership: regularly scheduled consultation calls; participation in a series or selection of online professional learning network events; participation in systemic partnership academies; engagement in a customized process of collecting data and analyzing local context with a designated and diverse set of stakeholders, paired with a process of equity-focused strategic planning.

For example, in our *systemic partnership academies*, partners participate in existing center-designed professional development sessions that incorporate formative intervention methodology. These academies involve at least 8 full days of dynamic professional learning spread over several months and aligned with partnership MOU goals and objectives. Therein, partners deepen understandings of essential equity constructs and increase capacities to dislodge oppressive deficit ideologies, policies, and practices, and to promote asset-based educational practices. Examples of existing systemic partnership academies include Centering Equity in Evaluation and Continuous Improvement, Leading Equity-Focused Initiatives, Equity-Oriented Strategic Planning, Equity-Oriented Educators, Centering Equity in Teaching, and Increasing and Sustaining Culturally Responsive and Diverse Educators.

Systemic equity partnerships also may include participants' engagement in our center's Equity Context Analysis Process (ECAP) (which we often pair with our Equity-Oriented Strategic Planning Partnership Academy). The ECAP enables LEAs to inclusively, comprehensively assess equitable practices at classroom (face-to-face and online), school, and district levels. The ECAP differs from traditional equity audits in that it involves the whole school community in data collection, analysis, and setting equity priorities. About 2 years ago, Community Unit School District 308 (CUSD 308; IL) requested support to develop their Diversity, Equity, and Inclusion (DEI) plan. Guided by our staff and ECAP protocols, staff administrators and community members surveyed 40 administrators, 424 staff, and 661 parents/caregivers (reporting data for 791 students). Also, school leaders conducted 29 teacher interviews and completed 45 classroom observations across grades, content areas, and eight schools, for a total of 675 minutes. After an analysis session with the district's 40-member ECAP review team, CUSD 308 utilized a decision rubric and determined equity priorities to incorporate into a DEI plan. One priority was student involvement in policy decisions, leading to an MOU addendum and to center and district leaders cofacilitating a related session with students and educators. The next year, district leaders designed and facilitated their own districtwide session: Students and Adults: Partners in Creating Systemic Equitable Practices.

Another example of a systemic equity partnership demonstrating significant impact is our longstanding collaboration with the Minnesota Department of Education (MDE) wherein our center facilitated MDE's implementation of Minnesota Statutes, Section 124D.861, and the School Desegregation/Integration rules, through the MDE Achievement and Integration program. A third example of our systemic equity partnerships is that with the Nebraska Department of Education (NDE), wherein department staff increased their capacity to refine and implement a statewide equity plan required by the federal government as an accountability structure tied to the Every Student Succeeds Act (2015). Our technical assistance included customized professional development and collaborative consultation sessions with NDE administrators, and resources related to review and revision of NDE's social studies standards to eliminate bias affecting 22,988 teachers and 315,542 students.

Organizing our technical assistance across tiers allows for fluidity in service intensity and duration; as partners' capacity increases in relation to an intensive systemic equity partnership, we are able to revise MOUs to decrease service intensity. If more critical and urgent equity issues emerge for partners who have already accessed equity research and resources, and our equity learning networks, we are able to increase service intensity. Although a tiered model such as this has become commonplace for organizing USDOE-funded technical assistance center services, we know that such frameworks at times have neglected, or even perpetuated, concerns with equity. Our current and previous key personnel have published extensively on equity considerations in and absent from multitiered systems of support (e.g., Artiles et al., 2010; Thorius & Maxcy, 2015); thus, we strategically engage diverse stakeholders and multiple forms of data to inform service tiers.

All of our MAP Center partnerships are initiated by the partnering agency, per the regulations that govern EAC project activity, while projects falling outside the scope of EAC work may be initiated through our Great Lakes Equity Center reaching out directly to a potential partner, or through the partnering agency reaching out to us. Most typically, however, our technical assistance partnerships are initiated via one of three pathways. The first is that an educator or other member of an educational community finds out about our center through word of mouth or a digital product created by our center that they have come across. Many of these partners already have engaged with our equity research and resources, which are available universally to all, at no cost, through our center's social media channels and website. Another pathway is a critical incident, often involving an acute instance of racial or sex-based bullying, harassment, or discrimination, that serves as the primary stimulus for the educator or educators seeking out direct technical assistance. In most of these instances, those responsible for initiating the partnership come with some level of willingness to examine the contributions of local contexts to the issues at hand, and to engage in remediation efforts.

Finally, some partners come to our center after having been investigated by the Office of Civil Rights (OCR) and/or the U.S. Department of Justice and found to have violated a student's or students' civil rights. In several of these instances, our EAC has been named directly within the public education agency's resolution agreement or consent decree with the federal government as a required support for remediation of policies and practices found through the government's investigation to have contributed to the violation. Within this context, there are varying degrees of openness or willingness of the partner to engage with our center; at times, district or school educators position themselves as unfairly targeted or suggest that findings are inaccurate or not the fault of agency educators. I revisit these pathways, and their implications, in subsequent chapters as I detail activities related to partnerships to eliminate disproportionality.

THE DEFINING ELEMENTS OF EQUITY EXPANSIVE
TECHNICAL ASSISTANCE

In the previous section, I detailed the ways in which our technical assistance services are organized by tiers of duration and intensity, with some examples of activities within each tier. However, it is the underlying conceptual and theoretical framework of the equity expansive approach to technical assistance that is most relevant for understanding and adapting our approaches elsewhere. It is this framework that informs the *why*, *how*, and *what* for of any technical assistance endeavor, and indeed any professional learning effort aimed at addressing educational inequities.

I define and frame equity expansive technical assistance through four interlocking elements: (1) shift from top-down, expert/novice knowledge transfer to a relational partnership in which the technical assistance provider is a critically conscious friend, thought partner, and bearer of expertise—but not an expert—who supports partners in examining and disrupting inequities in the status quo; (2) shifts from primary concerns with technical improvements in isolated policies and practices, to systemic transformation of policy, practices, and belief systems; (3) process-based conceptualization of systemic transformation informed by a theory of expansive learning (Engeström, 2001); and (4) explicit engagement with historical and current sociocultural beliefs, relationships, practices, policies, and other contextual factors related to the manifestations of (in)equities in the education system at the heart of the technical assistance partnership. Next, I detail each feature, focusing on how they play out in our partnerships.

FROM TOP-DOWN EXPERT TO CRITICALLY CONSCIOUS PARTNER

Since the core assertion of equity expansive technical assistance is that interlocking forms of oppression must be disrupted and remediated such that all systemic stakeholders experience equity, technical assistance providers themselves must develop dispositions, thought patterns, and actions that support the realization of racial equity and social justice (Brooks & Miles, 2010; Brooks & Witherspoon Arnold, 2013; Marshall & Oliva, 2006). This requires *redistribution* of traditional power dynamics connected with top-down, expert/novice technical assistance paradigms, as well as of unequal power differentials between researchers and practitioners, a core element of educational equity (Great Lakes Equity Center, 2012).

All of us come to our professional roles with our own histories of socialization into our fields; the field of technical assistance is no different. Moreover, our identities "are not located solely in the individual, but, rather are negotiated in social interactions that take form in cultural spaces" (Nasir & Saxe, 2003, pp. 15–16). Accordingly, technical assistance providers make meaning of their professional identities through participation in multiple worlds in and outside the context of technical assistance partnerships: worlds in which ideologies and hegemony interact to limit people's access, participation, and outcomes. Brookfield (2005) defined ideology as a:

> broadly accepted set of values, beliefs, myths, explanations, and justifications
> that appears self-evidently true, empirically accurate, personally relevant, and

morally desirable to a majority of the populace. The function of this ideology is to maintain an unjust social and political order. Ideology does this by convincing people that existing social arrangements are naturally ordained and obviously work for the good of all. (p. 41)

Hegemony, although related, is broader than ideology and captures the ways in which social constructions mediate and sustain dominant ideologies such that oppressed people and groups unconsciously consent to, or even uphold, systemic inequalities and injustices because of their belief in the status quo ideology (Radd & Kramer, 2016).

In the Introduction, I detailed some of my own socialization, particularly as related to my orientation to disability as a younger person, which led me into school psychology as a first-generation college graduate: a field full of ideologies and hegemony related to disability and competence. Across my personal and professional history, I was socialized and then intentionally prepared to engage in a top-down model of practice, including in my consultation with educators, and to approach my day-to-day role as a school psychologist from a problem-solving stance, which typically involved matching existing research on academic, social, or behavioral interventions with students perceived by educators to be struggling in school.

Rather, equity expansive technical assistance requires providers to unlearn these stances and practices, to engage in their own ongoing development of critical consciousness, and to adopt the disposition of a collaborative, critical friend who listens, learns, and reflects back educators' policies, beliefs, and practices that appear to constrain equitable conditions for teaching and learning. Critical friends ask questions; they (re)frame and challenge deficit-based assumptions, clarify language, and identify contradictions in and across people's goals and actions, which works best within an atmosphere of trust (Currie 1996). Critical friends also contribute to new insights and opportunities, and bring core assertions to their work (Swaffield & MacBeath, 2005).

Approaches for engaging in ongoing critical consciousness development are described in two of our center's open access research briefs (Radd, 2019; Radd & Macey, 2013). In short, critical consciousness was first introduced by Freire (1970), as the concept of conscientization: the process of growing awareness about and organizing against systems of power that constrain the freedom of oppressed groups. We apply the notion of conscientization to the dispositions and ongoing cycles of critical reflection and action required of equity leaders, including ourselves as technical assistance providers. Critical consciousness for equity leaders, according to Radd (2022), includes (1) the willingness and ability to attend to manifestations of power and privilege that systematically advantage some while disadvantaging others, and (2) transformation of this attention and related insight into beliefs and actions to "create more just action, processes, structures, and circumstances" (Radd & Kramer, 2016, p. 584).

As technical assistance providers who are critical friends, however, we also must continue to reflect on our *own* frames and beliefs about ourselves and our work, and the ideology and hegemony they contain. In a 2016 study with general and special educators involved in a center technical assistance partnership regarding inclusive mathematics instruction for students with significant disabilities, I drew from sociocultural identity theory (Holland et al., 1998) to explore how special education teachers cognitively and procedurally made sense of their identities based on their socialization into the profession. Specifically, I drew from the concept of a figured world: a "socially and culturally constructed realm[s] of interpretation in which particular characters and actors are recognized, significance is assigned to certain acts, and particular outcomes are valued over others" (p. 52). Within these realms, people *figure* their identities through participation in activities and social relationships. Such figuring is characterized by how people cognitively make sense of who they are as individuals, and how they procedurally perform these identities. Together, these characterizations account for the complex and fluid processes of identity production within figured worlds (Holland et al., 1998). As identity shifts, individuals also come to develop and recognize their capacity for agency within the figured worlds within which they participate, and in relation to how they may be positioned socially by others.

Throughout my 15 years as a technical assistance provider, and 25 years in public education, my cognitive and procedural identity has continued to change and expand in relation to those critical friends I mentioned in earlier chapters who have been my mentors and colleagues. At the start of my career, much about my figured world mirrored the cognitive and procedural sense-making I observed in the special education teachers from my 2016 study. Cognitively, whether I was fully aware of it or not, I figured myself as patient, intelligent, an expert and leader, a gatekeeper of special education, and, to some extent, a sort of missionary or savior in the racial, ethnic, linguistic, and socioeconomic communities where I worked. I performed this identity through daily routines that revolved around conducting assessments, observing and diagnosing, sorting, advising, deciding, and fixing students and their families. Rather, expansive technical assistance providers intentionally engage in reflection and activities that develop their critical consciousness of two key aspects about our histories as individuals and professionals, and seek to remediate these histories as they relate to power and oppression.

The first of these aspects is connected to our embodiment and positionality. Positionality refers to a person's sociocultural identities and how these identities mediate privilege or marginalization in a given context and as related to those of others who are present in that context. Taken together, positionality and embodiment mediate how we "show up" in the technical assistance relationship as raced, gendered, dis/abled, and otherwise-identified individuals, and how we relate to our partners in ways that create unique conditions for affiliation, privilege, and marginalization. That is, our *positionality* relates to how we are positioned in society (England, 1994) and in the technical assistance relationship based on our embodiment. As a white, cis-heterosexual, nondisabled upper middle-class woman who was born in the United States and who speaks English as my primary language, who has a PhD, and who holds leadership roles in the university and technical assistance settings, I almost always can expect the following when I enter into the technical assistance relationship:

1. I am welcomed into the space.
2. I most often look like most of the other leaders in the setting.
3. I am assumed by educators to know what I am talking about.
4. I receive prompt and positive responses to my communications.

Further, when I am situated alongside colleagues of color, with disabilities, who are LGBTQ+, and who are at these and other marginalized identity intersections:

5. I am assumed to be the one in charge.
6. I am referred or deferred to more often.
7. I am disproportionately thanked or recognized for my efforts.

In the rare instances when I do not receive this treatment or accompanying assumptions about my belonging and competence, it has always been from other white individuals, which has manifested in two ways. First, on occasion, my knowledge has been dismissed or minimized because it departs from and is critical of dominant framing of special education and/or technical assistance. In these cases, a few individuals, who, to this date, have been cisgender men, have framed my approaches to facilitating others in developing locally relevant solutions as inefficient; in other words, they have said they want to be told what to do from the start rather than waste time examining context and developing responses to inequities. In other instances, my work has been dismissed or criticized for breaking with white solidarity and disrupting white comfort zones (Delgado 2002) that enable white people to distance ourselves from race and racism (Leonardo & Zembylas, 2013) and prioritize white feelings (Matias, 2016; Matias & Mackey, 2016).

For example, while I was keynoting to a school district in which rampant racial disproportionality in school discipline led to an OCR investigation and resolution that involved developing culturally responsive, positive schoolwide discipline approaches, a white woman stormed out of the room of about 500 people, crying, "All you are doing is blaming white people!" To that point, less than 5 minutes into my hour-long talk, I had shared a slide that displayed the phrase "Black Lives Matter" and asked that we consider what the recent racial violence and murder on August 12, 2017, by white supremacists in Charlottesville, Virginia, meant for our own practice: what we needed to consider and do moving forward to address racial discrimination in the local setting.

To be clear, it is not always the case that I successfully break with white solidarity. In some instances, my own colleagues have pointed out my failure to interrupt my contributions to centering white people's feelings and comfort in technical assistance interactions, or my complicitly in allowing other white individuals to monopolize discussions or reframe the perspectives of people of color or those with intersecting or other marginalized identities. The equity expansive technical assistance practitioner engages in constant critical reflexivity about their practices and knows that they will continue to make mistakes and take missteps along their personal and professional journeys. To be a critical friend to others, we must receive critiques from our friends and colleagues and continue to incorporate those critiques into changes in our beliefs, dispositions, and practices.

Here, I offer an excerpt from one of our MAP Center *Equity by Design* practitioner briefs, developed by one of our equity fellows, Dr. Sharon Radd. In "Complexities of the Self: Inner Work for Equity Leaders," Radd (2022) reflects on her own positionality as it relates to her equity leadership.

> My primary positionality related to this brief is as a white cisgender female with a significant amount of formal education. This is important to note, because although (1) I have spent decades studying and leading for educational equity; (2) much of my scholarship and practice address the impact of whiteness; and (3) my personal and professional circles are multi-racial, I still see the world through a white-informed lens. Even when I am persistent in considering the influence of my view, as I am in writing this brief, I may not notice its impact. Thus, while I write this brief with the intent that it can be useful for equity-focused leaders with a wide-range of identities, both privileged and marginalized, I recognize that some principles may not extend effectively across identities and seek the reader's engagement in considering effective, equity-promoting modifications. (pp. 1–2)

In addition to the importance of technical assistance providers with dominant identities reflecting on their positionality, including how they are received and believed by those with whom they partner, we also must be intentional in our approaches to interacting within partners in individual, small-group, and large-group exchanges. In all instances, we aim to create environments wherein all participants are valued, and their presence and work are recognized as crucial to the success of the partnership. We strive to create contexts where we are expected to and do value and invest in one another's humanity. This means that we do our very best to show up for one another and ourselves. And this means that at times we must hold accountable partners whose words and actions have caused harm, either in the past or in the current moment. It can be a struggle to do this in a way that maximizes the chance for the partner to remain open to being part of the solution; however, we must not allow concerns with maintaining comfort for those who typically experience such comfort in relation to their identities, to derail the larger partnership goal. I provide a detailed and true example of this struggle in what follows.

In 2018, our center hosted a 2-day professional learning event where an identity-diverse group of educators from around the country came to Indianapolis to learn processes for collaborative inquiry toward setting goals of transforming their education systems. Our multiracial, -faith, -lingual, -national personnel, who also identify with disabilities and are LGBTQ+, share responsibility for planning and facilitating interactions and activities within all center learning events. On the second day of this intensive and intimate gathering, I was leading an activity regarding the necessity of seeking and affirming the personal narratives of those who have benefitted least from systemic practices as a source of inquiry and direction for systemic transformation. Andrea (pseudonym), a Black woman education agency leader who was nearing retirement, stood and shared her efforts throughout her career to lead inquiry processes related to disproportionality in student discipline. In particular, she homed in on her countless hours of intensive research about, and development of binders of print resources on, the best solutions to addressing disproportionality, and which she had engaged in community-based settings with much success. Despite her efforts and persistence, however, her acknowledgment of inequities and ideas for appropriate solutions in educational settings were dismissed by those with white male identities. She shared with our group that she had gone through her career feeling like these and other administrators did not believe her personal experiences with racism and sexism, or trust her professional capacities and history of success appraising and addressing systemic racism.

The equity expansive technical assistance provider recognizes that there are multiple pathways one might take in responding to Andrea's story. In this moment, I chose to direct the group back to one of the essential commitments for engaging in equity work, which had been introduced by a Black woman colleague at the beginning of the first day of the institute: receiving and believing the experiences of those who have been marginalized and recognizing these experiences as instrumental in setting goals and building solutions to transform systems. As much as I did this to reinforce the commitment itself, I also responded in this way to acknowledge the contribution of my colleague as relevant to the current interaction. Next, I spoke directly to Andrea, saying, "As a white woman, I am sorry. We believe you. I believe you." Andrea responded, "I have never heard that before from a white person."

Andrea was visibly emotional as her table mate, a Black male administrator from a different state, moved to sit next to her and placed a hand on her shoulder. The room sat in silent attentiveness, holding space for her and the group to feel the weight of what she had shared with us all. Then an early-career white female educator spoke up, directing her comment at Andrea, "I know just how you feel. I have had so many men who have not believed me in my life." It felt as if the air had been sucked out of the room. My colleagues and other participants looked at me, and in that moment I looked to one of my Black colleagues, who gave me an almost imperceptible nod. I responded with something to the effect of, "We are sitting with what Andrea has shared. Even though you have experienced sexism, as a white woman you cannot know how Andrea feels or the full impact of her experiences with racism and sexism. Let's talk at the next break." I am certain some readers have suggestions for what I could have done differently to either more strongly or more gently critique the white educator, to convey the impact and function of her statement as a point of comparison to Andrea's story, or to lessen the likelihood that this educator would shut down and close herself off from further discussion or learning, as what happened with the white woman who stomped out of my keynote. My decision to respond in that way, to apologize, to recognize, and to disrupt false equivalencies, was based on three things.

Regarding my apology to Andrea for the harms against her perpetuated by white male educators, I considered and claimed that I am a person with dominant racial identity. My apology was meant to communicate my acceptance of responsibility for the harms caused by other members of my identity group because certainly I have perpetuated similar harms or at the very least benefitted from those harms. For example, as a former school psychologist it is quite likely that my advice, opinion, and knowledge were sought after and believed by white males more frequently and with greater depth than the expertise of my colleagues of color. By stating my belief in Andrea's story, and speaking on behalf of the group gathered there—our collective belief in the accuracy and impact of her experiences—I considered that central to the concept of equity is the notion of representation, which according to Fraser (2008) includes opportunities for marginalized groups to represent themselves in decision-making processes that advance and define claims of exclusion and respective solutions.

Regarding my third action, to disrupt false equivalencies, this move reflects both my own identity as white and my experiences with whiteness and white womanhood, in which white women privilege their own experiences with sexism in the face of intersectional racism and sexism, or what Crenshaw (1991) calls intersectionality. Here, it was also important that I would hold this participant accountable not to refocus the concern of the conversation toward her or, in other words, to center whiteness in the conversation. The brief invitation to speak at the next break created a window into keeping the conversation going—to communicate to that participant her value—but without derailing or decentering our group's focus on the intersectional racism and sexism that Andrea had experienced and shared with us. Together, we value and invest in one another's humanity.

One final note about the above example: Radd (2022) reminds those of us with more access to power in relation to our positionality that while we may intend to be and believe we are redistributing that power to create equity-focused changes, we must reflect purposefully on the frames that motivate us to do so. Radd offers that a white education leader operating from a white savior framework (Hughey, 2014) to redistribute power, actually may reproduce and reinforce patterns of inequity and white supremacy in an organization. Any and all of my actions and interactions within the context of a technical assistance partnership are vulnerable to my operation from this frame. We must remain vigilant and committed to interrogating our motives for engaging in equity expansive technical assistance, part of what Radd and colleagues (2021) call conscious praxis.

MAP Center Director Dr. Seena Skelton (2019a) has written about how her positionality as a Black woman with a disability mediates the ways in which she performs her role, and how she positions herself and is positioned by partners in her work leading technical assistance partnerships. In her article, Skelton considered her unique position to introduce into technical assistance activity systems tensions that simultaneously disrupt existing and marginalizing narratives about students at race/classed/dis/abled intersections and affect educators' development as more inclusive educators. Also central to Skelton's essay are the ways in which she is marginally positioned by educator partners in relation to her embodiment, along with three strategic approaches she takes to mitigating her positionality. I organize these "marginalizing impacts" and "(re)mediating moves" in Table 4.1.

Juxtaposed in relation to each other, Skelton's and my experiences and identities illustrate that there are cumulative and disproportionate impacts of positionality across technical assistance providers and other educational leaders who facilitate professional development and systemic change. In particular, those who are on the receiving end of micro- and macroaggressions are more likely to experience racial battle fatigue and other impacts on physical and mental health. As Skelton (2019a) points out:

> Technical assistance practitioners bear the brunt of the reaction from educators engaged in technical assistance activities and must negotiate through white fragility (DiAngelo, 2011) and various forms of denial that are inevitable when confronting policies and actions which signals their subscription to the dominant ideologies that position minoritized youth as inferior compared to their white, non-disabled, cisgender, middle class peers (Zardoya, 2017). (p. 227)

As Skelton acknowledges elsewhere in her essay, however, the "brunt" is heavier, more violent, and more sustained as enacted upon technical assistance providers of color and those who hold other marginalized identities.

Table 4.1. Marginalizing Impacts and (Re)Mediating Moves of Facilitating Technical Assistance as a Black Woman With a Disability

Marginalizing Impacts	(Re)Mediating Moves
Identity erasure: Educators are reluctant to acknowledge Skelton's dis/ability and race, both ignoring and staring at these aspects of her identity. If and when Skelton's disability is acknowledged, educators and fellow technical assistance providers use euphemisms that contribute to the erasure of, and perpetuation of stigma experienced by people with disabilities (McRuer, 2016). In turn, this present-day treatment triggers memories of the marginalizing impact of schools as predominantly white, nondisabled spaces where Skelton's identity was erased.	*Naming and claiming identities out loud:* Skelton openly identifies as a Black woman with a disability, thus situating her identity as important, as well as relevant to being a technical assistance provider. Here, Skelton points out that naming her identity and detailing her professional background function differently for her compared with technical assistance colleagues who are affirmed and presumed credible based on their identities. She aims to disrupt presumptions of her incompetence; acknowledge a sense of pride, membership, and responsibility to Black, female, and dis/ability communities; and acknowledge power dynamics that marginalize and privilege people based on differences.
Privileging certain identities: Skelton notes that although most educators are somewhat receptive to considering privilege at a conceptual level, they are reluctant to consider how they are personally complicit in dynamics of privilege and oppression through race and disability-neutral practices that impact how, whether, and why technical assistance providers with certain identities are sought.	*Leveraging one's identities to shed light on incongruences between equity rhetoric and marginalizing practices:* By identifying oppressive discourse and actions in the local setting, Skelton shows that equity-focused goals require equity-centric processes. Skelton provides examples of naming her presence as the only person with one or more of her identities in a given space, and the incongruence of this exclusion with the equity-focused goals the agency or organization claims to desire.
Deficit thinking: Skelton shares directly about microaggressions she has experienced in the course of her work with partners. In doing so, she illustrates how educators' belief systems and biases sustain systems of oppression. To do so, she points out instances in which educators assign blame to families and communities to which students belong, and express pity for students, while ignoring systemic inequities as a result of race-based processes, practices, and policies (Fergus, 2017), and in turn the impact on her as a Black woman with a disability.	*Personal storytelling:* Skelton intentionally tells stories about how deficit thinking like that expressed by educators in the present impacted her as a student, thus disrupting dominant discourse associated with individualism and meritocracy that maintains that one's race, class, or gender is irrelevant to one's opportunities. Skelton shared a personal story about how despite her high grades in college prep high school courses, she was discouraged from attending a university by her guidance counselor. Skelton pairs her counselor's actions with a de jure state policy for tracking students with IEPs into vocational programs.

Note. Adapted from Skelton, 2019a, pp. 234–237

The concept of *rightful presence* (Calabrese Barton & Tan, 2020) recognizes that like minoritized students (Tedesco & Bagelman, 2017), minoritized technical assistance providers over time have been positioned through dominant discourses and practices as "out-of-place" within technical assistance as a field and within partnerships, socially, culturally, and historically (Skelton, 2019). According to Calabrese Barton and Tan (2020):

> Rightful presence, as a justice-oriented political project, focuses on the processes of reauthoring rights towards making present the lives of those made missing by the systemic injustices inherent in schooling and the disciplines (Calabrese Barton & Tan, 2019). These processes take shape in political struggles to legitimize the wisdom of lives lived (Delpit, 1988; Tuck, 2009) and the historicized inequities incurred in local practice (Ladson-Billings, 2006), with the goal of making both injustice and social change in the here-and-now visible in classroom practice. (p. 438)

There are two broad strategies I offer for equity expansive technical assistance providers across identity constellations to address and redistribute and/or claim rightful presence in our work. The first is the consideration of a set of questions that account for our professional figured worlds along with our embodiment and associated positionality, as shown in Table 4.2.

The second approach to redistributing and/or claiming rightful presence in our work is the creation of and participation in social organizations that allow us to affiliate with other technical assistance providers and/or educational stakeholders with identities like our own. For those whose identities and experiences are more similar to mine, these spaces and structures support our ongoing accountability for our own enactment and complicity in macro- and microaggressive acts within and outside the context of technical assistance partnerships, including with our own colleagues. Our own center holds white affinity groups on a monthly basis, and all white employees attend. During these meetings, white staff members rotate responsibility for facilitation and typically bring at least one grounding activity or prompt to the group. The central question with which we engage during each session, however, is, "In what ways since our last meeting have I participated in, been complicit in, and/or benefitted from racism?" Concurrently, we consider the same question in relation to other identities and identity-related oppression, such as disability and ableism; how our identities function to maintain our status and privilege is the primary concern. This group meeting is required for all white staff; as white technical assistance providers who facilitate others' engagement with similar forms of critical self-reflection, we must commit to the same for ourselves. Over the past several years as our nation has continued to grapple with state-sanctioned violence against people of color, and as instances of white supremacy and anti-Semitism have continued to rise and intensify, given the sociopolitical climate, our white

Table 4.2. Critical Reflections on Positionality for Technical Assistance Providers

How was I socialized?	What is my embodiment?	What is the impact?
How did I come to this profession of technical assistance (or educational leadership)?	What are my perceivable and imperceivable identity markers (e.g., race, gender identity, disability)?	In what ways does my socialization about students and families position me in relation to them (e.g., helper/helped; in solidarity)?
What are the messages I have received about the students and families with whom I work?	What are my histories of participation in education and as a technical assistance provider with others who share my identity markers?	In what ways does my embodiment position me in relation to the education stakeholders with whom I partner?
What are the predominant views and theories of teaching, learning, and social interaction that undergird my orientation to my work?	What aspects of my identity do I consider as most relevant to my work and why?	In what specific ways am I received, acknowledged, treated, and recognized for who I am and what I do as a technical assistance provider?
What aspects of my professional characteristics and activities are most important to me; which do I hold the most central to who I am and what I do as a technical assistance provider?	What aspects of my identity are less relevant to me in my work, if any, and why?	In what ways do my central professional characteristics and activities facilitate or hinder equitable distribution of power within technical assistance relationships and partnerships?

staff have invited white advisory board members and other center affiliates to join us in these activities.

Simultaneously, our staff of color and at other identity intersections have developed two mechanisms for affiliation, which function quite differently. The first of these is an internal affinity group for people of color within the organization; during their meetings, individuals engage in shared reading, discussion, and reflection on the ways in which their identities mediate their experiences as technical assistance providers and with their white (and otherwise privileged) colleagues. Also central to this group, a Black LGBTQ+ external wellness care provider has led yoga and other forms of healing and restorative practices on a regular basis to promote restoration and healing from the impact of racialized professional experiences. Importantly, this group and these activities are built into, not separate from, the workday, signaling the organization's framing of such activities as part of individuals' professional activities. However, they are also optional, to account for varying desire and bandwidth for participating in what are generally intensive sessions that both restore and also take considerable energy.

As our center opens opportunities to white advisors and affiliates to engage in racial affinity activities, over the past year and a half, the Black women on our staff have developed a formal network of Black, Indigenous, People of Color (BIPOC) technical assistance providers and educational leader partners. Termed the BIPOC Network, and coplanned with select education leaders of color around the MAP Center's 13-state region, along with a few technical assistance providers from sister centers, the purpose of the network is to "fortify individual and collective efforts to further realize wholeness while leading transformative systems change towards educational equity." Since February 2022, a series of BIPOC Network convenings have made space for equity leaders to spend concerted time on healing, self-care, and networking. From the description on our center's website, these sessions

> center on affective domains of learning such as responding to and reflecting on one's racial identity as a mediating factor of their leadership, personhood, and source of pride, joy, and renewal. Additionally, discussion . . . focus[es] on the reflection of status quo values of educational organizations versus a reimagined value set of educational organizations as self-determined from those more proximal to conditions of inequity. Lastly, the BIPOC convening . . . discuss[es] the recognition and examination of internalized values to support healing, harmony, and self-care. (https://greatlakesequity.org/event/bipoc-education-leaders-network-convening-session-1)

The network has grown into a "cohort-structured restorative experience" with education leaders of color from 26 states and two territories, and has been featured at two recent peer-reviewed conferences: those of the Critical Race Studies in Education Association and the American Education Studies Association (Kyser et al., 2022[a or b], n.p.).

Before detailing the next feature of equity expansive technical assistance, I close with two key assertions that I find helpful for holding myself accountable to the critically conscious nature of the technical assistance providers' work and operating frames. The first is that our roles are grounded in histories of participation that place us in powerful positions of expertise and appraisal. The second is that both the personal and professional aspects of our history require our confrontation and remediation of these roles toward those through which we engage in reflections on our personal and professional identities alongside our partners and our colleagues. By acknowledging and en/countering (i.e., facing and resisting [Tan & Thorius, 2018]) these assertions, we can begin to take responsibility for our personal and collective roles in reproducing them.

EXPANDING AND ENHANCING TECHNICAL SOLUTIONS WITH CONTEXTUAL AND CRITICAL ANALYSIS AND SYSTEMIC TRANSFORMATION

This second element of equity expansive technical assistance—enhancing technical solutions with critical and contextual systemic transformation—represents a much-needed expansion of the historical ways in which technical assistance has been conceptualized to address a phenomenon as complex as disproportionality. Woven throughout this explanation, I provide excerpts and adaptations of open source tools developed by our technical assistance center leadership, to illustrate the ways in which we apply this element in practice as a resource for readers wishing to adapt and develop their own tools for doing the same. Previous chapter discussions demonstrate the rationale for why technical solutions to addressing disproportionality are insufficient; inertial, normative, and political forces (Thorius & Maxcy, 2015; Welner, 2001) shape how disproportionality manifests locally, as do ambiguities and limitations of federal policy. Moreover, deeply ingrained ideologies of racism and ableism intersect and may be characterized as normative forces that shape every aspect of schooling, including curriculum, instruction, and assessment, along with routine practices related to determining which students may require additional instructional supports or referral for special education eligibility determination, for example. All these considerations make disproportionality one of the most complex educational inequities of our time, requiring that technical assistance toward eliminating disproportionality offers equally complex solutions.

To build understanding of equitable education systems, equity expansive technical assistance distinguishes between equality and equity because the two concepts are often conflated. Equality is about sameness of access to resources and opportunities, and is a goal of a socially just educational system in which all students, regardless of race, sex, national origin, religion, socioeconomic status, primary language, or dis/ability, should have access to these same resources and accompanying outcomes. Terms like *gaps* or even *disparities* do not go far enough to explain systemic equity issues, as neither term implies an injustice related to the difference of note. Rather, the term *inequities* conveys the argument that the "differences to which the term refers are presumptively unjust" (Goldberg, 2014, p. 61). Major policy and research reports continue to illustrate that educational equality does not exist in structural factors or student achievement and outcomes (Whiteman et al., 2015); accordingly, a *system of equity* is necessitated.

The notion of fairness, a basic tenet of equity, often creates more tensions in educational systems than do notions of equality (Brayboy et al., 2007), especially when fairness is constructed as all students being treated the same, regardless of differences and oppression in relation to group memberships, as Amos (2011) found in a study of Somali refugee high school students' experiences. Across Great Lakes Equity Center technical assistance projects, we draw from Waitoller and Kozleski's (2013) definition of inclusive education:

> a continuous struggle toward (a) redistribution of quality opportunities to learn and participate in educational programs [redistribution dimension], (b) recognition and value of differences as reflected in content, pedagogy, and assessment tools [recognition dimension], and (c) opportunities for marginalized groups to represent themselves in decision-making processes that advance and define claims of exclusion and the respective solutions that affect their children's educational futures [representation dimension]. (p. 35)

In turn, we apply this definition to the Great Lakes Equity Center's (2012) assertion that equitable education systems exist when educational policies, practices, interaction, and resources are representative of, constructed by, and responsive to all people so that each individual has access to, meaningfully participates in, and has positive outcomes from high-quality learning experiences, regardless of individual characteristics and group memberships.

Both Waitoller and Kozleski's definition of inclusive education and the Great Lakes Equity Center's description of equitable education systems apply Nancy Fraser's (2008) dimensions of justice to a broader equity agenda that acknowledges historical justice claims of educational equity movements and expands them with notions of race, sex, national origin, religion, income, language, and disability intersectionality (Sullivan & Thorius, 2013). Because systemic centers and margins are constantly shifting, educational equity efforts always create new forms of benefit and disadvantage, and demand continual examination of how margins and centers are constructed within these systems (Kozleski & Artiles, 2012). This means that beyond fostering equitable learning opportunities, which may be accomplished only in part through the application of evidence-based practices regarding literacy instruction, for example, we must facilitate creation of systems that dismantle deficit thinking about students, families, and communities, particularly given the connection between such deficit thinking and practices that result in disproportionality, as indicated in earlier discussions of the existing research.

These definitions of equity and justice as related to educational systems also inform the second element of equity expansive technical assistance: that it enhances and expands the purpose of the work from discrete, technical improvements to contextual and critical systemic transformation.

Accordingly, understanding how equitable systems operate in relation to policies, practices, beliefs, and relationships is necessary for enacting technical, contextual, and critical analyses and solutions such that solutions are organized as holistically as possible.

A useful heuristic for organizing this expansion draws from work led by Kozleski and Mulligan, the former of whom directed the OSEP-funded National Institute for Urban School Improvement (NIUSI) and served as principal investigator. NIUSI's overarching goal was to promote inclusive education, including addressing disproportionality in educational settings for students receiving special education services in U.S. urban school districts where students of color were disproportionally identified as disabled and placed in more restrictive settings compared with their white counterparts (D. L. Ferguson et al., 2003). NIUSI–LeadScape, an outgrowth of NIUSI that provided direct coaching to the leaders of schools in these districts, developed the following way of organizing the coach's and principal's focus on increasingly complex frames of analysis: technical, contextual, and critical frames. Accordingly, the coach poses associated prompts to the principal within the coaching dialogue. Technical prompts support the coachee in developing solutions to practice issues in their schools, and contextual prompts support the coachee in identifying how cultural belief and practice systems within a school afford and constrain inclusive education (Mulligan, 2010). Finally, critical prompts facilitate the principal in the examination of issues of power and privilege, and marginalization and oppression, that contribute to inequitable educational practices for some students (Mulligan & Kozleski, 2009) while maintaining and securing educational privilege for others.

Equity expansive technical assistance draws from these three domains for conceptualizing the sources of inequities and the innovations possible for addressing them through and beyond the technical assistance partnership. With some modification to account for Kozleski's more recent research on the nature of technical assistance (Kozleski & Artiles, 2012), I conceptualize these three domains in the following ways to account for both the foci of analyses and the forms of solutions that correspond with the issues that originated a partner's request for technical assistance. In all instances, technical assistance providers require deep understandings of the existing research base on the issue(s) to be addressed and bring this research base to bear in local conceptualizations of root causes.

Technical analysis and solutions are those discrete policies, practices, and procedures that have been shown to improve outcomes in other settings. Outcome improvements typically are defined as observable, quantifiable increases in student achievement, and decreases in student discipline referrals, as well as other readily measurable student outcome data. Examples of areas of technical analysis and solution generation in the context of technical assistance related to disproportionality may include identification and selection of less-biased assessments or the development of a list of standard protocol interventions (i.e., those based on reading intervention research and that require implementation fidelity) to increase reading achievement for students who are learning English.

Contextual domains and solutions are focused on locally configured historical patterns of routines, practices, and values that constrain and afford equitable conditions for students across identities, and that help and/or hinder technical solutions. In NIUSI–LeadScape's original work, *critical* analysis and solutions were focused on the principals' own practices and beliefs as units of analysis that afforded and constrained technical and contextual solutions to inequities. Extending this focus to equity expansive technical assistance, critical analysis and solutions require deep and collaborative reflection on individual *and* systemic practices that benefit some and oppress other students, along with individual belief systems and institutional values that contribute to these patterns of benefit and marginalization as related to student (and other stakeholder) race, sex, national origin, disability, and other identity intersections. I conceptualize the relationship between these three domains as nested, in which any technical analysis, including the identification and implementation of evidence-based practices, is situated within contextual and critical analyses, as indicated in Figure 4.2.

Historically within technical assistance partnerships, as well as in the context of coaching relationships that occur within and outside these partnerships, the bulk of time is spent on technical analysis and solution generation. In equity expansive technical assistance, rather, this emphasis is reconfigured such that critical and contextual analyses and related solutions are emphasized, and that any introduction of technical solutions occurs only in those instances when research supporting such solutions has

Figure 4.2. Equity Expansive Technical Assistance Domains for Analyses and Solutions

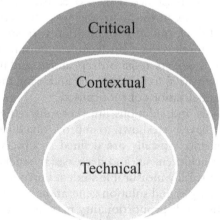

demonstrated their applicability to contexts and students similar to those of and in the current educational setting. Moreover, although such research may be concerned with improvements in student academic outcomes, equity expansive technical assistance providers seek out research concerned with remedying local and global inequities. That is, beyond improvements for improvements' sake, equity expansive technical assistance providers seek out robust research that is simultaneously concerned with remediating patterns of inequitable access, participation, and outcomes for students in relation to identity markers, geographic locale, and other sociocultural factors.

Although broad, I offer examples of prompts that guide partners' analysis and solution focus toward the object of addressing local inequities. These may be adapted by the reader in relation to the specifics of local histories and details.

Another consideration within this second element of equity expansive technical assistance is that, in order to transform systems, we need frameworks for understanding how systems are organized with regard to policy, practice, and personal relationships (see Table 4.3). The Systemic Change Framework (Kozleski et al., 2014) focuses on six interconnected policy and practice arenas across a network of SEAs, LEAs, schools, educators, families, students, policymakers, and community members in a unified educational system of teaching and learning, rather than any one systemic element or level where isolated changes are unlikely to lead to transformation (Kozleski & Thorius, 2014). Each of these systemic elements supports equity expansive technical assistance activities that address the system as a whole and broaden the focus from reactive support strategies toward proactive innovation in culturally responsive and inclusive educational systems where resources are available and used to ensure all students receive high-quality opportunities to learn and experience favorable outcomes.

Kozleski and I (Kozleski & Thorius, 2014) applied the Systemic Change Framework in an edited volume about technical assistance partnerships under the auspices of NIUSI. We demonstrated how attention to these domains across systems can stimulate transformations in people, policy, and practice, and combine to impact student opportunities, learning, and

Table 4.3. Technical, Contextual, and Critical Considerations for Addressing Systemic Education Inequities

Technical	Contextual	Critical
What capacities do educators need to address what is happening; what do people need to know how to do?	What factors about the way things are or always have been done are obstacles and avenues for addressing what is happening?	In what ways are *some* students and educators benefitting from what is happening? Who is not benefitting and why?

achievement (e.g., Hart-Tervalon & Garcia, 2014). The domains were informed by earlier work by NCCRESt, which shaped the development of a rubric widely used for systemically assessing disproportionality in district contexts and as a foundation for planning systemic improvement efforts. The rubric, entitled *Preventing Disproportionality by Strengthening District Policies and Procedures—An Assessment and Strategic Planning Process* (Kozleski & Zion, 2006), can be found archived on many State Department of Education websites, and is open source content. I describe the six domains below, following each description with an example of a technical assistance resource developed in the context of partnerships with school districts and state agencies to improve some aspect of policy or practice that has been linked to disproportionality.

Equitable Resource Development and Distribution

Equity expansive technical assistance facilitates systemic consideration of how financial, material, and human resources are allocated not equally, but equitably, such that all professionals are provided what they need to ensure high-quality services that result in favorable and proportionate access, participation, and outcomes for children across historically underserved groups and that can contribute to disproportionality prevention and remediation. A 2014 "Dear Colleague Letter" by Assistant Secretary of Civil Rights Catherine Lhamon enforced federal statutes related to the requirement that agencies receiving federal financial assistance provide comparable educational resources to all students regardless of race, national origin, socioeconomic status, sex, or disability. This equitable resource distribution includes several resources identified by Secretary Lhamon, including "access to rigorous courses, academic programs, and extracurricular activities; stable workforces of effective teachers, leaders, and support staff; safe and appropriate school buildings and facilities; and modern technology and high-quality instructional materials" (p. 2). The aforementioned NCCRESt rubric (Kozleksi & Zion, 2006) included the equitable distribution of effective educators as one of the core district functions to be assessed in relation to disproportionality as well: "The District has a policy that ensures that monetary, physical, and other resources, including qualified personnel, are distributed to schools according to need. This includes ensuring that all schools have comparable physical facilities in terms of safety and optimal learning environments" (p. 10).

Accordingly, and with application to ensuring all students have access to high-quality opportunities to learn, the Great Lakes Equity Center (2015) designed the Equitable Distribution of Effective Educators Systems Analysis Tool to facilitate local teams' in-depth analysis of their local context and preplanning related to the following domains of teacher efficacy: definition of effective and equitable educators; equitable educator recruitment, induction, and professional development efforts; equitable educator evaluation and retention efforts; and finally, equitable distribution of educators across settings. The tool is offered as a companion resource to the center's research brief entitled *Rethinking Quality: Foregrounding Equity in Definitions of "High Quality" Educators* (Whiteman et al., 2015).

Together, these two resources responded to issues that predicated the USDOE's 2014 reinvestment in equitable distribution of high-quality educators. By requiring Chief State School Officers to submit new State Educator Equity Plans the Department emphasized the importance of stakeholders' input and data analysis (Duncan, 2014) regarding root causes of students from low-income households and racially and linguistically minoritized communities being taught by disproportionally high rates of unqualified teachers (McNeil, 2014). In the above-mentioned brief, we provided educational stakeholders with a set of research-based considerations for policy and practice that extended existing teacher quality frameworks (e.g., Guarino et al., 2006) by foregrounding equity across three key domains: personal qualities, educator practices, and student outcomes. Educators were encouraged to apply these resources together as they critiqued and extended prominent definitions of teacher quality and then applied in their own settings these extensions and critical reflections on how high-quality educators were defined, developed, and distributed.

Inclusive Leadership for Equity and Accountability

The ways in which decisions are made have a strong impact on systemic culture, and the interactions between leaders, educators, families, and students help determine educational equity. Equity expansive technical assistance supports cross-system leaders in building multiple and accessible processes to elicit input and decisions from those with diverse roles, demographics, and perspectives. As reflected in research on distributed leadership, leadership capacity may be greatly enhanced when students, parents, teachers, and administrators act in concert rather than in isolation (Leithwood et al., 2004). But development of such capacity depends heavily on addressing issues of communication, trust, authority, and time (Scribner et al., 2007). These aspects of systems functioning also can be traced to contexts that prevent and address disproportionality. For example, the NCCRESt rubric ties shared governance and decision-making about district and school codes of conduct and associated discipline policies to the prevention and remediation of disproportionality, based on research by Skiba (2002). Each year, the MAP Center hosts an opportunity for education practitioners to engage in 2 full days of intensive collegial study, discussion, and custom planning related to a pressing equity issue. In 2019, our Equity Leaders Institute was concerned with building local and state school boards' and district leadership's capacity to advance educational equity via policymaking and governance. Across these 2 days about 100 educators from all over the United States convened in Indianapolis to achieve the following outcomes:

1. Identify a strong rationale for centering equity in policymaking and governance
2. Showcase state and/or local education agencies leading successful equity efforts in this area
3. Examine the role of school boards and district leadership in facilitating and leading the creation of vision, mission, and policy/systemic goals such that all students benefit regardless of race, sex, national origin, religion, socioeconomic status, and so on
4. Discuss obstacles and avenues for collaboration among school board members, and between school boards and district leaders, in advancing educational equity via policymaking and governance
5. Plan for centering equity in decision-making across policy domains

The institute began with the assertion that equity-centered school governance centers practices and decisions guided by education justice principles. It is exercised by school leaders to provide strategic direction ensuring that historically marginalized voices are centered, resources are equitably distributed throughout the school community, and equitable outcomes are achieved by all (Radd & Macey, 2013; Theoharis, 2007; Thompson, 2007). For one activity, institute participants considered the National School Boards Association's (2017) declaration of the fundamental role of school boards: "to work with their communities to improve student achievement in their local public schools" and acknowledgment that those who embrace the call to serve their communities as school district or county board members face significant opportunities and challenges. Afterward, in diverse stakeholder groups of eight to ten people, they examined three challenges commonly associated with shared governance, and with distinct evidence-based connections to equity: intragroup conflict, pressure to maintain the status quo, and lack of communication and engagement with diverse community stakeholders (Darden & Cavendish, 2012; Dawson & Quinn, 2000; Grissom, 2014; Saatcioglu & Sargut, 2014; Thompson, 2007; Trujillo, 2013). Applying what they learned to a detailed vignette about a fictitious Allearn School District, in which a student shares her concerns at a school board meeting (Skelton, 2019b), participants made decisions about how to respond to the challenges reflected in the vignette.

Culture of Renewal and Improvement

Equity expansive technical assistance supports explicit reform and learning initiatives as informed by the current context of educational inequities and driven by the way things could be if all children had an equitable education.

This requires and supports local use of data on how children and families are served, and with what outcomes, to inform future system and school improvement, including professional development and strategic planning.

Our technical assistance includes guided facilitation of state and district agencies' equity-focused strategic planning. As I mentioned in the opening of this chapter, partners with whom we have entered into a *systemic equity partnership* have the option to select from a set of multisession systemic partnership academies during which center staff facilitate deep learning opportunities related to topics we have determined to be central to systemic change efforts. One such academy, entitled Equity-Oriented Strategic Planning, includes three face-to-face sessions with agency partners. Within this academy, our technical assistance seeks to extend more typical strategic planning with an emphasis on systemic equity, as represented in Table 4.4.

Each of the three sessions has a distinct, but interrelated, connection to strategic planning efforts: *identifying systemic inequities and analyzing learning contexts*; *generating a theory of action and broad equity strategies*; and *creating implementation plans*. During session one, partners learn about how to engage in critical collaborative inquiry cycles (Great Lakes Equity Center, 2018) as part of strategic planning processes that lead to the identification of areas for improvement and framing equity-oriented systemic goals.

Table 4.4. Traditional Versus Equity Expansive Approaches to Strategic Planning

Strategic Planning	MAP Center Equity-Oriented Strategic Planning
A coordinated and systematic way to develop a course and direction for an organization	Critically reflects on who traditionally has benefitted from strategic planning and who has not
Systematic identification of opportunities and obstacles on the path ahead, which combine with other relevant data to create the basis for organizational decision-making	Considers who traditionally has defined, collected, and interpreted data
Setting organizational goals; defining practices, processes, and policies to reach them; and developing detailed plans to ensure such processes and policies are implemented	Collective and continuous ways of being and doing that center perspectives of historically marginalized groups in dialogue intended to (de)construct individual and collective knowledges, use data to identify inequities, and cocreate strategies or actions toward ensuring inclusive, educational practices
References: Allison & Kaye (2005); Steiner (2010)	References: Friere (2000); Rogoff (2003); Waitoller & Kozleski (2013)

With relevance to identifying and remediating disproportionality, partners consider the need to collect and analyze student outcome data along with systems data, rather than outcome data alone. These ways of considering, for example, how student achievement data are mediated by systemic data regarding students' access to curriculum and instruction that is universally designed for learning, support educators in refocusing their concerns from individual student deficits to opportunities for systemic improvement. Figure 4.3 is adapted from a slide that guides partners' consideration of how this expansion of focus from student to system, and also expands goals for transformation.

School (Agency)/Community/Family Connections and Partnerships

Equity expansive technical assistance also provides guidance and supports to systems in the formation of mutually beneficial relationships with community and family members, organizations, and leaders to ensure that the knowledge and resources of all those served are represented and incorporated. Accordingly, many of our open access resources amplify perspectives of historically marginalized families, including *Supporting Student Success Through Authentic Partnerships: Reflection From Parents and Caregivers* (Morton, 2017). With relevance to disproportionality, we intentionally request of our partners that family members be included in many aspects of partnership activities, including as members of the agency's team with whom we engage in partnership academies, and in an advisory capacity to the agency leadership.

Figure 4.3. Expanding Our Consideration of Outcome Data With Systemic Data

Critical Consciousness in Strategic Planning	Individually, Think About (5 Minutes):
There is no such thing as a neutral educational process. Education either functions as an instrument that is used to facilitate the integration of the younger generation into the logic of the present system and bring about conformity to it, or it becomes "the practice of freedom," the means by which men and women deal critically and creatively with reality and discover how to participate in the transformation of their world. (Freire, 2000, p. 34)	The two data sets together: What story can you tell related to students' access to, and representation and meaningful participation in, quality learning opportunities that may have affected student outcomes?
	In Cross-District/Department Groups, Discuss (10 Minutes):
	Whether/how your story changed after systems data were added? Capture your notes.
	Share (5 Minutes):

Infrastructure and Organizational Support

Equity expansive technical assistance supports systemic priorities toward effective use of technology, buildings and grounds, décor, layout, time and structures for planning and communication, and how these create open, safe, accessible student spaces. We have developed a number of environmental assessment tools that enable district leaders, including family members and students, to assess the sufficiency of resources and organizational supports to serve all students. I will expand upon these in subsequent chapters.

Inquiry on Equity

Equity expansive technical assistance supports system stakeholders' inquiry on equity by using multiple forms and sources of real data and making explicit the links between data and inequitable school policy and services to improve these data. Earlier, I described some of the ways in which our center's Equity Context Analysis Process has served as a mediating artifact as we provide partners direct support and facilitation to inclusively, comprehensively assess equitable practices at classroom, school, and district levels. However, it is also important to note that the ECAP is both informed by and extends and revises considerably the 2006 NCCRESt disproportionality rubric (Kozleski & Zion, 2006).

Another of the most robust research-based resources the MAP Center has developed is the Systemic Analysis of Equity and Justice in Education Tool, or the SAEJE. The SAEJE is a set of facilitation training modules, data collection and analysis tools, and collective meaning-making processes developed to enable local education agencies to independently self-assess the extent to which aspects of educational equity are evident in the district and to identify areas that may be opportunities for growth related to advancing educational equity and ensuring educational justice. The SAEJE is built on the premise that effective continuous improvement efforts toward equity must move beyond looking at student outcome (achievement) data alone. Rather, by incorporating both the first and second elements of equity expansive technical assistance, the SAEJE supports districts to develop innovations that disrupt and redress systemic inequities through analyzing the contextual and critical factors that *mediate* student outcomes. In other words, all SAEJE materials support local educators to answer the question: "What is it about our system—people, policies, and practices—that may be contributing to inequitable outcomes for students?" (Skelton et al., 2021, p. 6). To answer this question, the SAEJE assists stakeholders in collecting and analyzing organizational data related to identified areas that may contribute to disparities in student outcomes.

PROCESS-BASED CONCEPTUALIZATION OF SYSTEMIC
TRANSFORMATION INFORMED BY EXPANSIVE LEARNING THEORY

The third element of equity expansive technical assistance is its procedural nature; it is designed and carried out as a formative intervention process (Engeström, 2011). As introduced in Chapter 3, formative intervention is a CHAT methodology in which researchers intentionally introduce artifacts into the research context to stimulate innovations that support participants to resolve contradictions beyond the research setting. Unlike the construct of intervention typical in (special) education research (e.g., Haager et al., 2007) and technical assistance approaches (Blase, 2009), formative intervention refers to "purposeful action by a human agent to create change" (Midgley, 2000, p. 113). In the case of equity expansive technical assistance, the technical assistance provider's role is akin to that of the researcher across generational CHAT studies in which providers "provoke and support" participants by applying their own intentions to the initial process of learners' reconceptualization and expansion of the object of shared work activity, along with learners' leadership and ownership of the process (Sannino et al., 2016).

One of the first and most well-known formative intervention research approaches is the Change Laboratory (Engeström et al., 1996), which has been used across countries, work and education settings, and communities (see, for example, Bal and colleagues' work [2014, 2018] with culturally responsive behavior interventions and supports in a formative intervention process Bal calls Learning Lab). According to Sannino and colleagues (2016), Change Laboratories typically consist of six to 12 weekly sessions of about 2 hours each, with one or more follow-up sessions in which participants and researcher-interventionists use a set of representational devices designed for jointly analyzing disturbances and contradictions in their activities and for developing new solutions. Formative intervention approaches also have been applied to a limited number of teacher professional development studies. For example, Turner and colleagues (2017) examined a 2-year professional development program wherein educational leaders developed their identities and responsibilities as change agents. In another instance, Teräs and Lasonen (2013) applied Change Laboratory methodology to develop educators' intercultural competence.

As a characteristic of our approach, equity expansive technical assistance providers aim to stimulate "historically accumulated contradictions" (Sannino & Engeström, 2017, p. 84) in the partnership stakeholders' activities and shared efforts to understand and face these contradictions and the problems they create. Vygotsky located contradictions as emerging within individuals in response to external change; however, Leontiev identified the process of shared labor as the unit of analysis for the emergence of contradictions; that is, contradictions appear as tensions within systems of workplace activity.

More generally, contradictions are theorized as the motivating forces of changes and development within activity systems (Engeström, 1999), and there are four types of contradictions that mediate such development. Foot and Groleau (2011) inferred from Engeström's works that *primary contradictions*, or dilemmas, are expressions or exchanges of incompatible perspectives between people or in an individual's discourse, and that they precipitate the epistemic action of questioning by participants in the activity system. As dilemmas intensify, they stimulate other contradictions. *Secondary contradictions*, or double binds, are traps of equally unacceptable options that require practical systemic changes (Ellis et al., 2010) as a result of analyzing and modeling possible resolutions (i.e., new activity models). *Tertiary contradictions*, or conflicts, are resistance, arguments, disagreements, and criticisms, usually resolved through compromise, that emerge during implementation, examination, and evaluation of new activity models. Lastly, *quaternary contradictions* typically emerge as participants refine and adapt new practices, and provoke a new round of questioning (Engeström & Sannino, 2011).

In equity expansive approaches, technical assistance providers reflect back to partners an analysis of their systemic status quo in order to stimulate engagement with primary contradictions that prevent participants' efforts to accomplish the collective object of activity that motivates their work: at this point, the initial reason for the partnership. As I have illustrated in other publications (e.g., Tan & Thorius, 2018; Thorius, 2016, 2019), by evoking these primary contradictions in partners' consciousness, secondary contradictions become the motivation for the partnership stakeholders to work together to develop new possibilities for meeting the object of the partnership, during which tertiary contradictions often arise. Importantly, unlike more traditional approaches to technical assistance, and as reflected in my description of the role of critical friends, there is no expectation that the technical assistance provider will recommend practical fixes to the issues at hand; rather, it is our role to foster our partners' development of agency in order to more deeply and clearly analyze the system, past and present, and envision what is possible in a more equitable future, during which quaternary contradictions will emerge in the process of revising and adapting new practices, and motivate a new round of systemic questioning.

Engagement in *expansive learning cycles* (Engeström & Sannino, 2010) is central to our approach (Tan & Thorius, 2018) in stimulating and resolving these contradictions with our partners through a process of double stimulation. Vygotsky described this process in which a researcher presents to a participant a problem that is beyond their current competency to resolve, which is the first stimulus. However, while the participant is attempting to solve the problem, the researcher introduces a second stimulus, or mediating artifact. Then, the researcher observes whether and how the participant applies the mediating artifact to develop an innovative way of solving the problem. According to Daniels (2010), "The crucial element in a Vygotskian dual stimulation event is the co-occurrence of both the problem and tools with which to engage with that problem" (p. 382). Engeström (2001) first applied the term *expansive learning* to the process of evoking and resolving contradictions through the development of new practices that both expand the objects of those engaged in collective workplace improvement effort and lead to systemic transformation. It is through cycles of technical assistance partnership activities that our goals of partners' expansive learning are accomplished.

In the expansive learning cycles characteristic of equity expansive technical assistance and as a departure from the dissemination of interventions typical of top-down technical assistance, providers deliberately select, develop, and introduce into each partnership specific artifacts (i.e., tools [Cole, 1996]) to (a) mediate educators' examination of local contexts for in/equities; (b) stimulate contradictions between the status quo and partners' desired outcome of the partnership; and (c) support partners' selection, development, and refinement of innovations that support equity-focused systemic changes in policy, practice, and belief systems (Thorius, 2019). The expansive learning process involves a seven-step learning cycle that we apply in partnership design and facilitation. I introduce these steps below and expand on them further in the next chapter as applied to equity expansive technical assistance partnerships to eliminate disproportionality.

In step 1 of expansive learning cycles, participants analyze their current activity system, with an emphasis on problematic situations and contributing forces. Applying this step, equity expansive technical assistance engages three overlapping activities: (1) preliminary mapping of the partners' historical and current systemic contexts through holistic data collection and analysis activities; (2) more deeply and descriptively defining the equity issues to be addressed through the partnership; and (3) identifying policy, practice, relational, and other contextual factors that appear to contribute to these issues. Working in collaboration with our partners, step 1 of equity expansive technical assistance involves several data collection activities that range from individual interviews and focus groups with local education leaders, educators, students, and families to scans of publicly available data. Depending on the intensity of the partnership, we either guide partners to center-developed resources that facilitate their engagement in such activities in their own settings, or facilitate these processes in close collaboration.

Step 2 of expansive learning cycles is geared toward uncovering and evoking contradictions and tensions within the system. Here, the technical assistance providers synthesize, probe more deeply, and often reframe and extend available data and initial conclusions about the status quo within historical and cultural contexts.

In step 3 of expansive learning cycles, participants work on transforming the problematic systemic structure toward an expansive way of resolving the contradictions within it. Here, the equity expansive technical assistance provider introduces mediating artifacts into shared activities, which participants may choose to take up as they begin to develop solutions toward addressing the reason they reached out for technical assistance.

Step 4 is about expanding the purpose, or *object*, of the activity system through determining a new model of activity. Here, the technical assistance provider supports partners in developing next steps for addressing inequities, but in ways that support participants in determining that their original conceptualizations of these inequities, including contributing factors, manifestations, and impacts, inadequately account for the systemic nature of the work to be done. Thus, the partnership takes on new and more systemically oriented goals that reflect an expanded focus, alongside an expanded understanding of what equity must look and feel like in the future.

In step 5, participants implement the new activity model while solidifying and testing out innovations, putting initial steps into action, and developing and implementing new tools for doing so. Here, the technical assistance provider is what we colloquially call a "thought partner," reflecting with stakeholders on the relevance, usefulness, viability, and strength of the innovations in process.

Step 6 involves reflecting on the implementation of the new activity model (Engeström, 1987). Here, the technical assistance provider supports all of these processes, bringing to bear new mediating artifacts such as strategic planning protocols, professional development resources, policy review and revision rubrics, and, as applicable, lessons learned from partnering with other agencies with similar goals. Finally, in step 7, partners consolidate and generalize the new activity model by building into it processes and efficiencies and then disseminating the model throughout connected activity systems. Here, the partnership may continue as activities lead to new lines of questioning regarding which students are benefitting and not benefitting from the ways things are, reflecting Vygotsky's theorizing of the spiraling, elevating, and reorganizational nature of human development (Engeström & Sannino, 2010).

CRITICAL TOOLS FOR ENCOUNTERING AND EXPANDING POLICIES AND PRACTICES

The fourth element of equity expansive technical assistance is embedded within the third, but warrants emphasis given the intentionality required in designing, selecting, and cocreating artifacts useful for stimulating and resolving systemic contradictions with technical assistance partners. Equity expansive technical assistance purposefully applies critical theories and practice-based interventions informed by research, as both primary and secondary stimuli (i.e., mediating artifacts), given the usefulness of such tools for illuminating and resolving complex systemic inequities. That is, contradictions are stimulated and resolved through partners' mediated examination of inequities and identification of possibilities for equity-focused systemic improvements that have been shown to be effective with multiply marginalized students. Over time, we have found that the mediating artifacts that most effectively engage partners with examination and resolution of historical and current sociocultural beliefs, relationships, practices, policies, and other contextual factors related to manifestations of inequities in local settings are informed by critical theory and its outgrowths.

Broadly, critical theory seeks to reveal, critique, and confront the social, historical, and ideological forces and structures that afford and constrain access to power. In other words, critical theory critiques and challenges power structures that keep the rules and functions of society from benefitting all toward realizing a more just, equitable, and democratic world (Horkheimer, 1993). Critical theory emerged in the Frankfurt School during the rise of fascism, and its initial goals were tied closely to critiquing that form of government along with the exploitative functions of capitalism. Contrary to much of today's disinformation about one particular "next-gen" version of critical theory (i.e., critical race theory), however, the purpose was not to transform society into communist or socialist forms of government. Rather, it was to transform capitalism to a more consensus-based democracy in which systems of domination and exploitation (Horkheimer, 1972) were dismantled. Critical theory also critiqued the role of media in promoting passive consumption of content and thus the intellectual and political passivity of the masses rather than democratic engagement (C. Fuchs, 2011). This facet of the theory is particularly relevant to the ways in which today's mass disinformation campaign about critical race theory being taught in pre-K–12 schools is a tactical approach in current political culture conflicts. People who have never read an original source document on critical race theory, or indeed any seminal work on race and structural racism, or experienced oppression because of their own identities claim expertise and make accusations that seek to squash any systemic critique of the role of systemic racism and other forms of oppression in structuring (in)opportunity.

Second-generation critical theorist Habermas grew up in post–World War I Germany in the context of the failed system of national socialism. As a graduate student, he grew interested in and then critical of Heidegger's (1959) claim of the "inner truth and greatness" of national socialism (p. 199). This, again, is important because critical theories are not to be equated with national socialism; rather, they emerged as a critique against it. Instead, Habermas (1990) applied American democratic values to his second-generation approach to developing critical theory, at the heart of which was the notion of inclusive critical discussion in which individuals and groups of all social and economic statuses were able to participate as equals in collaborative efforts to address matters of shared concern. Noting that his approach was more than an ideology, but acknowledging the challenges in a full realization of such collaboration among those with more and less social power, throughout his life he worked toward a theory of rationality in public opinion-forming through a process of democratic deliberation, which he asserted could be accomplished only through "the structural transformation of the public sphere itself and in the dimension of its development" (p. 244).

I provide this brief and incomplete foundation to critical theory because it forms the basis of more contemporary critical theories that have been applied to and developed within the field and practice of education. Two critical theories in particular are central to equity expansive technical assistance and, as I will discuss in the following chapter, to addressing disproportionality. These theories—critical race theory and disability studies in education, along with intersectional versions or outgrowths of these theories (e.g., LatCrit [Valdes, 1998, critical whiteness studies [Leonardo, 2013], and DisCrit [Annamma et al., 2013]), have substantially informed our development of mediating artifacts in line with the fourth and final feature of equity expansive technical assistance. Such artifacts facilitate our partners' explicit engagement with historical and current sociocultural beliefs, relationships, practices, policies, and other contextual factors related to the manifestations of (in)equities in education systems.

Critical Race Theory

Considering that I have made the case for disproportionality as an oppression at the intersection of racism and ableism, and accounting for the pervasiveness of racism in our schools and society, critical race theory is one of the key theoretical constructs that informs equity expansive technical assistance in relation to requests for assistance based on individual acts of or systemic racism. However daunting this overt stance may be or feel in this moment of dis/misinformation about what critical race theory is and is not, including whether and how it is incorporated into curriculum and instruction in schools, our approaches are not deterred from using the most powerful tools at our disposal to understand and dismantle inequities that have been framed, with little disagreement, as connected with systemic racism.

The equity expansive technical assistance provider also must understand the origins of scrutiny regarding CRT, as the anti-CRT movement originated as a way to discredit any and all diversity, equity, inclusion, and justice work. In July 2020, an employee of Seattle Public Schools (SPS) sent details of an antibias training session in which they were required to participate to local journalist Christopher Rufo. The SPS employee sought Rufo out after a political controversy surrounding a 2018 policy paper on causes of and solutions to homelessness Rufo had authored for the conservative Discovery Institute think tank. In the piece, Rufo blamed homelessness on "perverse incentives" (p. 1) (e.g., rent freezes, taxing corporations, increases to the minimum wage) developed by "socialist revolutionaries, once relegated to the margins, [who] have declared open war on the mainstream Democratic establishment and pushed the political center of gravity ever leftward" (p. 2). Citing the perpetuation of "elaborate mythology" to justify policies of "unlimited compassion" (p. 4), but not citing any peer-reviewed research, Rufo had claimed that the policy approaches of Seattle's local politicians, one of whom he labeled as "Socialist Alternative" (p. 2), were misguided and ineffective, and that most people should and could deal effectively with rising rents in cities like Seattle by "moving to a less expensive neighborhood, downsizing to a smaller apartment, taking on a roommate, moving in with family, or leaving the city altogether" (p. 3). Rufo further scoffed at democratic politicians' framing of Seattle's unaffordability as linked to root causes like systemic racism. Running on this platform for city council, Rufo dropped out of the race after 2 months, citing bullying and harassment by homelessness activists who had posted his photograph and home address around his Seattle neighborhood. So, when Rufo received the antibias training materials from the local educator, which included discussion of the systemic racism that he had characterized in his policy report as an elaborate myth, he saw an opportunity to respond. He also saw a much larger political opportunity.

Following Rufo's individual analyses of professional development materials he obtained through public records requests as well as those he was sent by dissatisfied employees of various public and private institutions, he concluded that critical race theory could be positioned as "the perfect villain" and political weapon (Wallace-Wells, 2021) that would exacerbate concerns of even self-identified liberal white Americans that a focus on eliminating inequities through the study of race and gender was replacing a focus on academic context. Indeed, in many ways, it did. Almost any and all diversity, equity, and inclusion efforts immediately came under fire after former president Trump invited Rufo to draft his executive order requiring all federal contractors and their subcontractors, federal agencies, certain federal grant recipients, and the military to halt all trainings on so-called race or sex stereotyping or scapegoating, calling these efforts, "un-American propaganda training" (Exec. Order No. 13950, 2020, p. 60683). My own Indiana University School of Education (IUPUI) responded to this executive order, like other university schools and colleges throughout the United States, asserting two main points of disagreement. I include an excerpt from our public statement:

> First, there is extensive research in education and across the social sciences that documents the existence of substantial racism and intersectional oppressions including sexism in education and in virtually all other U.S. institutions and systems, including law enforcement, the media, health care, employment, banking,

and housing, among other areas. And a considerable portion of that research has shown that "critical race theory" or "white privilege" are productive concepts for understanding racism and racial inequities and for building racial equity training. Thus, the President's Executive Order could be said to abnegate all of that research and its applications. Second, we would adamantly disagree that addressing racism and antiracism is anti-American, and, in response, we would strongly assert that addressing racism and antiracism is the hallmark of U.S. citizenship, public education, social science research, and the research, teaching, and service work of universities in a democracy. In addition, we would recommend that as public educators in a racially and intersectionally-diverse democracy, we have an imperative, a democratic imperative, to address racial inequity in schooling, especially given that research in education and other social sciences has well documented those inequities and their founding in racism. More, as educators, our scholarly inquiries and research on race/racism is valuable as it helps to spotlight more critical examinations of U.S. and world history. This is especially important for current and future generations of young people. Thus, we believe that we have a democratic imperative to do and publish research on racism and racial inequities, along with other forms of oppression; to prepare educators to create educational environments that are free of inequities; and to speak and act publicly to address all forms of oppression. (Faculty of the Indiana University School of Education, 2021)

At the same time, several legal and educational scholars who have contributed to the foundations and outgrowths of critical race theory have responded to set the record straight. For example, the widely renowned legal scholar Kimberlé Crenshaw, who coined the term and concept of "intersectionality," has released dozens of resources to clarify and correct misinformation about the origins and applications of critical race theory. The NAACP's Legal Defense Fund ([LDF], 2022) asserted:

> Critical Race Theory should be embraced as a framework to develop laws and policies that can dismantle structural inequities and systemic racism. Building a more equitable future requires an examination of how the shameful history of slavery, caste, and systemic racism were foundational to laws and institutions that exist today. (https://www.naacpldf.org/critical-race-theory-faq/)

Following the LDF's lead, rather than spending any more time defending critical race theory against what it is not, I make distinct connections between what it is and, briefly, its application for understanding and addressing disproportionality as a systemic and social issue.

Critical race theory originated from critical legal studies, whose central argument was that the law was not objective or apolitical, but rather had been and could be complicit in maintaining social inequality. CRT further posited, however, that the law actually had been leveraged to reproduce and maintain this inequality in relation to race. In a 1989 workshop spearheaded by Crenshaw and co-organized by her, Neil Gotanda, and Stephanie Phillips, a total of 24 participants laid out the tenets of CRT in detail. Participants included Derrick Bell, Richard Delgado, Angela Harris, Mari Matsuda, and Patricia Williams, who along with the others proposed CRT's original tenets. These tenets have been modified and expanded over the past 3 decades by scholars across disciplines. In the field of education, Daniel Solórzano, Tara Yosso, Gloria Ladson-Billings, William Tate, Cleveland Hayes, Robin L. Hughes, and many more have applied and further developed CRT to demonstrate how racism has been perpetuated through education systems. Disproportionality is a powerful example of such systemic racism. I organize and define these tenets of CRT, along with a brief mention of their application in education, and a few associated scholar contributors, in Table 4.5.

Disability Studies in Education

In the bulk of disproportionality research, scholars have centered concerns with educators' and systems' perpetuation of racial hierarchies. Moreover, when interpreted through the lens of critical special education and disability studies in education scholarship, much of the interpretive framing of culture in current disproportionality research and technical assistance conceptualizes disproportionality as creating racialized hierarchies. From a disability studies in education perspective, however, our analysis of hierarchies also must account for how ableism influences special education eligibility processes aimed at confirming students' internal deficits, incapacities, struggles, and pathologies. Moreover, beyond locating and revealing the manifestations of ableism in special education processes, some research tacitly has framed disproportionality as a problem simply because disability is something to be avoided, and because of the premise of the medical model of disability that there are objective ways of determining who is and who is not disabled.

Disability studies in education scholars and disabled activists remind us that disability in and of itself is not something abject. Yet, for some otherwise critical scholars, including those whose own identities have been pathologized by others on the basis of race, sex, national origin, religion, and other minoritized status, disability has remained an uncontested pathology (Erevelles, 2014). In other words, the racism and ableism imbued in cultural practices that contribute to, and the research that frames, disproportionality must be examined in tandem and abolished (Waitoller & Thorius, 2016); ableism has a powerful and limiting impact on the expectations of students' capacities for learning. Indeed, several studies have demonstrated that educators are less likely to perceive students labeled with disabilities, and in particular with significant intellectual disabilities, as capable of generating

Table 4.5. Tenets of Critical Race Theory and Contributing Scholars

Tenet	Description	Contributing Scholars
Permanence of racism	Conscious and unconscious racism is a central, permanent component of American life in that hierarchical structures in relation to race govern all political, economic, and social domains to allocate privilege to white people and marginalization to Black people and other people of color. In education, for example, this tenet is illustrated in systemic segregation.	Bell (1992); DeCuir and Dixson (2004); Ladson-Billings and Tate (1995); Yosso and Solórzano (2005)
Whiteness as property	Under U.S. law, property refers to physical objects as well as to anything to which a person assigns value. Historically, being white defined one's legal status as a free person, while being Black defined one's status as enslaved. In public education, whiteness as property refers to the relationship between who has benefitted most from education through property value; students in white communities have attended schools with more funding and access to multiple forms of capital, including high-quality teachers, curriculum, and instruction, and residents of white communities, by way of property ownership, hold more power over public education policy and law that historically have protected white property through such law. Examples of this in education include the enactment of school choice policies, and white students' disproportionate access to multilingual instruction, advanced placement coursework, and extracurricular activities, as documented in the popular *New York Times* podcast, *Nice white Parents* (Joffe-Walt & Snyder, 2020).	Annamma (2015); Buras (2011); Donnor (2013); Harris (1993); Leonardo (2009)

(continued)

Table 4.5. Tenets of Critical Race Theory and Contributing Scholars *(continued)*

Tenet	Description	Contributing Scholars
Counter-storytelling against dominant narratives	Challenges dominant, accepted narratives about the (in)existence of racism by centering the experiences of people of color as integral to understanding racial inequality. Counter-storytelling serves to expose and critique dominant narratives that perpetuate racial stereotypes, to build community, and to imagine and realize possible futures for marginalized peoples. In education, this concept has been applied to the development of asset pedagogies (e.g., culturally sustaining pedagogies [Paris, 2012]) that seek to center and apply the counter-stories of students of color, and at other marginalized identity intersections, in order to identify and address local to global inequities.	Atwood and López (2014); D. A. Cook and Dixson, (2013); Delgado and Stefancic (2012); Matsuda (1995); Solórzano and Yosso (2001)
Interest convergence	Asserts that racial equality and equity for Black people (and other people of color) will be pursued and advanced when these converge with the interests, needs, desires, and ideologies of white people. Conversely, when the desires of people of color are at odds with those of white people, it is extremely difficult to expose and address racism (Leigh, 2003). This tenet was developed and applied by Bell in analyzing the reasons white families supported integrated schools following *Brown v. Board of Education* in order to better situate the United States in national and world politics and economics during the Cold War.	Bell (1980); Leigh (2003); Milner (2008)

Tenet	Description	Contributing Scholars
Critique of liberalism	CRT challenges dominant liberal claims of neutrality, objectivity, colorblindness, and meritocracy in society, which have functioned to prevent examination of and addressing the manifestations and impact of racism. This tenet has been applied to critiques of the notion of the Black–white "achievement gap" toward developing a more accurate understanding of "opportunity gaps" (Milner, 2012) and "educational debt" (Ladson-Billings, 2006) that contribute to disparate outcomes between student groups on the basis of race and other identity markers.	Bell (1995); Bonilla-Silva (2006); Castagno (2009); Ladson-Billings (1998)
Intersectionality	Refers to a commitment to a social justice activism that seeks to eliminate oppression for all people at subjugated identity intersections. In education, intersectionality has been applied to the development of DisCrit, or disability critical race theory (Annamma et al., 2013) to analyze and illustrate systemic oppressions affecting students/people of color with disabilities in education and other settings.	Collins (2015); Crenshaw (1989, 1991); McCall (2005)

knowledge and engaging in complex learning (Lambert, 2018; Shifrer, 2016; Tan & Thorius, 2018), and more likely to perceive them as requiring instruction that is skill and remediation based (Tan, 2014). Disability studies in education (DSE) is an extension of the interdisciplinary disability studies and disability rights movements (e.g., Connor et al., 2008; Davis, 1997; Linton, 1998), whose central purpose was to critique and assert a just alternative to the U.S. approach to (special) education for students with disabilities: creating and sustaining inclusive and accessible schools (Connor et al., 2019). At the heart of the origins of DSE is a social model of disability (Oliver, 1983, 2013) in which the concept is defined in relation to marginalizing social and environmental contexts that alienate disabled people and deny them basic civil rights (Finkelstein, 1980; Shakespeare & Watson, 2002). This theorization marked the reframing of disability as a contextual failure to recognize and accommodate disabled people—school contexts being a prime example—rather than as the medical pathology of an individual (Acevedo & Roscigno, 2022). This construction of disability as a medical pathology is at the heart of the medical model of disability that is prevalent in schools and society. The medical model situates the professional (e.g., doctor, clinician, priest, speech therapist, special education teacher) as having influence over the disabled individual, and the goal of that influence is to fix, cure, or ameliorate the individual's impairment, which is situated entirely within their body/mind (Thorius, 2016).

Instead, the social model of disability marked the characterization of disability rights as, indeed, civil rights (Baglieri et al., 2011). Although this model acknowledged the impact of impairment on disabled people's individual and collective experiences, the central feature is that society imposes disability upon those with such impairments, along with negative consequences, including those associated with (special) education (Turnbull & Stowe, 2001). Extensions of the social model of disability (Mitra, 2006) and the addition of nuance related to social relational and cultural models of disability further acknowledge that despite people with disabilities accounting for the largest minoritized group across global contexts, their experiences of segregation, exploitation, and other forms of oppression-based violence have been left out of larger civil rights movements (unlike race, ethnicity, sex, and gender). This point underscores my earlier argument that efforts to understand those social, historical, cultural, and political factors contributing to disproportionality must account for disability oppression at the intersections of race-based violence and marginalization.

Tools Informed by Critical Theories

Although discussions of these theories in and of themselves are one type of mediating artifact through which partners examine and grapple with inequities in their educational systems, in addition to those contextual and critical forms of questioning that characterize consultative partnership activities, our center has developed tools that allow partners to focus critical theoretical lenses on their current processes, practices, and relationships. I offer two examples of such tools—one discretely focused on academic curriculum and standards, and the other in the form of a comprehensive process for examining the context for equity in local education settings.

The Assessing Bias in Standards and Curricular Materials Tool enables users to consider the extent to which their local and state standards and curricular materials reflect the features of educational equity as defined by our center, which are informed by Fraser (2008) and others' work framing social justice. The tool also translates into descriptions of standards and curriculum that reflect asset pedagogies; in our recent edited volume (Thorius & Waitoller, 2022) focused on centering disability in existing asset pedagogies, we utilize the phrase "as an umbrella for various pedagogical approaches that privilege, value, and sustain the cultural and linguistic practices of minoritized students" (p. xv), including those with disabilities.

The tool is organized in the form of a rubric that identifies 10 relevant domains in total, followed by more specific descriptors of how standards and curricular materials under each domain may be manifested. I offer brief descriptions of these domains, all of which are adapted from Coomer et al. (2017b); Great Lakes Equity Center (2016b); and Sadker (n.d.).

The three Standards Domains are

1. Build Consciousness: Cultivate understanding of how knowledge is constructed, and that the co-construction of knowledge is the medium through which society defines itself.
2. Reflect Students' Cultural Repertoires and View Them as Worthy of Sustaining: Perpetuate and foster linguistic, literate, and cultural pluralism by sustaining in-group cultural practices and cross-group cultural practices (Paris, 2012).
3. Social Improvement: Encourage social critique and just action toward equitable schools and systems.

One of six more detailed descriptors of the third Standards Domain is that such standards support students to identify and use tools and knowledge resources from multiple communities that empower them to critique current social, economic, and cultural contexts, and to make decisions that will lead to social change and justice (Aronson & Laughter, 2015; Gay, 2010; Stovall, 2006).

The seven Curriculum and Instructional Standards included in the tool are as follows:

1. Invisibility: The complete or relative exclusion of a group.
2. Stereotyping: Widely held but fixed and oversimplified image or idea of a particular type of person or behavior at the cost of individual attributes and differences.
3. Imbalance and Selectivity: Representation of only one interpretation of an issue, situation, or group of people, typically that associated with dominant identity perspectives.
4. Historical Whitewashing (Sleeter, 2005): Minimization of distasteful historical facts and events because they portray realities of prejudice, racism, discrimination, exploitation, oppression, sexism, and intergroup conflict.
5. Fragmentation and Isolation: Physically or visually isolating a group of people in the text.

6. Linguistic Bias: Ways that language and words reproduce stereotypes, bias, and marginalization of certain groups of people.
7. Cosmetic Bias: Although curricular materials may suggest that
they are free from bias and incorporate diverse perspectives and
groups, it is an illusion. Rather, these suggestions are really, a
marketing strategy to give a favorable impression to potential
purchasers.

One of the four more detailed descriptors of the seventh Curriculum Materials
Domain is that those materials feature, beyond the cover or pictures, the stories, histories, and narratives of people of color, people with dis/abilities,
and LGBTQ+ people.

In addition to making these and other tools available through social
media and our website, we use them in the context of systemic equity partnerships. In the case of the aforementioned standards and curriculum review tool, we applied it in our partnership over a period of several months
with the Nebraska Department of Education, which I mentioned briefly
earlier in this chapter. In 2018, NDE announced a revised strategic direction of foregrounding educational equity to realize their Every Student
Succeeds Act plan and operationalize their focus on continuous improvement with local schools and districts via the parallel launch of their
Accountability for a Quality Education System, Today and Tomorrow.
An NDE member had attended our center's 2018 State Equity Leaders
Summit, Equity in Action: Authentically Engaging Stakeholders in Equity-
Focused State Planning, and thereafter submitted a request for a partnership that would support the NDE board in ensuring equity was centered in
the state's operationalization of multitiered systems of support. Our center
provided several of our existing research-based resources in response to
this initial request. About a month later, Nebraska's chief academic of-
ficer reached back out to seek guidance in reviewing NDE's draft social
studies standards for bias before submission to the state board. NDE and
our center finalized an agreement to work toward an overarching partnership goal of developing and refining the NDE's equity plan to ensure
equity-driven outcomes. The first underlying objective was to utilize the
center's standards and curriculum review tool to identify possible bias
in Nebraska's social studies standards and support needed revisions or
refinement via facilitated professional learning and artifact reviews. The
department requested additional support with their capacities to lead the
review of their health standards—to which the MAP Center responded
with a suite of curated resources, and customized facilitation tools so
the department could seize the opportunity to leverage their own assets
and capacities to review state standards moving forward. Finally, technical assistance continued to support department efforts to increase staff's

critical consciousness and capacity to demonstrate equity-oriented leadership skills and decision-making. Community and LEA representatives who contributed to the department's standards review committees included those from the following organizations: Lincoln Public Schools, University of Nebraska-Omaha's Service Learning Academy, Nebraska Centers for Economic Education, Nebraska State Council for Social Studies, Omaha Public Schools, Cooperative Education Service Agency #4, Educational Service Units #3 and #4, Ponca Tribe of Nebraska, UNO Service Learning Academy, and Millard Public Schools.

As described by Waxman (2019) in *Time* magazine:

> Twenty Nebraska educators and community members met in August to evaluate the proposed new standards for bias, using a checklist developed by the Midwest and Plains Equity Assistance Center, in an attempt to make sure perspectives that have often been disregarded were included. Examples of marginalized or underrepresented events and people covered by the state's new curriculum guidelines include the Stonewall Riots; the United Farm Workers; Susan La Flesche Picotte, hailed as the first Native American woman to receive a medical degree; the Tuskegee Airmen, the African American pilots who served in World War II; and Will Brown, who was lynched in Omaha during the Red Summer, a wave of deadly race riots in 1919. (n.p.)

Although the *Time* article described only Nebraska's use of our "checklist," our staff was present, in person and via video conferencing, as this group of diverse stakeholders learned about the center's tool and then considered and reviewed Nebraska's standards. Rich discussion and deep analysis were evident throughout these meetings, and the rubric served as a jumping-off point from which stakeholders reviewed, revised, eliminated, and developed new social studies standards.

I give another example of how critical theory shaped artifacts developed and/or introduced by center staff into the activity system of a 2018 technical assistance partnership. In this instance, Paulo Tan (at the time one of our center's doctoral research assistants) and I aimed to remediate special and general educators' approaches to teaching mathematics to students with significant disabilities by engaging them with critical artifacts informed by DSE and universal design for learning (UDL). UDL is an asset-based pedagogy built on the idea of planning for learners at the margins (Rose & Meyer, 2006), particularly disabled students (Meyer et al., 2014). Central to partnership activities, special and general educators analyzed their beliefs about students' mathematical capacities and how their teaching accounted for student strengths and capabilities, guided by our introduction of DSE and UDL conceptual and practical tools, including a UDL instructional coaching dialogue guide. For example, after learning UDL principles from Tan and me, educators experienced contradictions over the inaccessibility of existing curriculum and instruction. Over time, they used the dialogue guide to plan instruction that would include all students in meaningful, inquiry-based mathematics: "UDL refocuses on designing educational spaces and curriculum to include a wide range of learners from the outset. Instead of locating disability within individual students, disability is in inaccessible classrooms, curriculum, and spaces" (Lambert et al., 2021, p. 57). This contrasts with special education's typical focus: student deficits and teaching as prescriptive interventions (Johnson & Pugach, 1990). In both these examples—the use of the standards and curriculum tool and the application of the UDL dialogue guide—educators engaged with mediating artifacts introduced by us as technical assistance providers, which evoked contradictions in their analysis of current practices. These tools also created opportunities for expanding the object of activity and developing more equitable practices as educators worked to resolve these contradictions through new practices.

REVISITING THE GOAL OF EQUITY EXPANSIVE TECHNICAL ASSISTANCE: SOMETHING FOR EVERYONE

Despite this book's central concern with technical assistance, the approaches I describe in this chapter and thereafter are not limited to facilitation by technical assistance providers. Indeed, Sannino and colleagues (2016) have asserted that formative interventions, such as those that characterize equity expansive technical assistance, need not be facilitated and supported by researcher-interventionists.

Rather, formative intervention is a process that can take place at the initiative of local actors within collectives: what Sannino and colleagues (2016) called *intra*ventions, at the suggestion of Michael Cole. In their article, Sannino et al. described a case of intravention in which a researcher observed and documented—but did not interfere with—such change efforts in a school and surrounding community in São Paulo, Brazil. In this case, repeated flooding of a polluted river running between the school and community served as the primary stimulus causing school educational leaders to encounter a primary contradiction between teaching and addressing the impact of pollution on the school. As a secondary stimulus to resolve this contradiction, these educators applied learning from recent professional development on school management to transform the object of teaching and learning toward one that would and eventually did improve life for the school and community members.

In the next several chapters, I move into deeper connection and description of how equity expansive technical assistance can be and has been leveraged as an approach to remediating racial disproportionality in special education. In the next chapter, I link the steps of expansive learning cycles to technical assistance partnerships focused on surfacing the problematic situations and forces contributing to disproportionality in localized activity systems, and to evoking and resolving contradictions in these contexts.

CHAPTER 5

Equity Expansive Technical Assistance for Reversing Disproportionality

CHAT frameworks, and more specifically, the elements of activity systems, are a helpful way of organizing the factors that contribute to disproportionality and that may be encountered with partners toward its elimination. To begin this chapter, I apply the research I reviewed in Chapter 1, along with the research we have conducted as technical assistance providers on the history and processes of technical assistance, to map two interacting activity systems relevant to equity expansive technical assistance partnerships toward eliminating racial disproportionality in special education. The first of these is the activity system of disproportionality in a given school district, and the second is the activity system of an associated technical assistance partnership.

As a reminder, CHAT includes six elements in systems of human activity: (1) human *subjects*; (2) an *object* (i.e., activity motive, which also influences activity structure and transforms the subject and object in the process); (3) *artifacts* that mediate human activity toward this object; (4) a *community* of social and/or cultural groups of people involved in the activity; (5) a set of *rules*, which are implicit and explicit social norms that afford, constrain, and otherwise inform and influence subjects' behavior; and finally (6) a *division of labor*, which indicates how responsibilities are distributed across community members within the activity (Cole & Engeström, 1993).

Typically, activity systems are depicted in the form of a triangle to demonstrate the relationships between systemic elements; however, this type of diagram is difficult to create in a form that is accessible for a book, given crowding with text and the small size of book pages. Therefore, I include in Figure 5.1 a general depiction of the two activity systems, followed by Tables 5.1 and 5.2 in which I describe the respective elements of each in more detail.

Moreover, although each of these activity systems has unique objects, these objects are connected and overlap. For example, while the district activity system may be concerned with placing students in special education as

Figure 5.1. Elements and Interactions of an Activity System

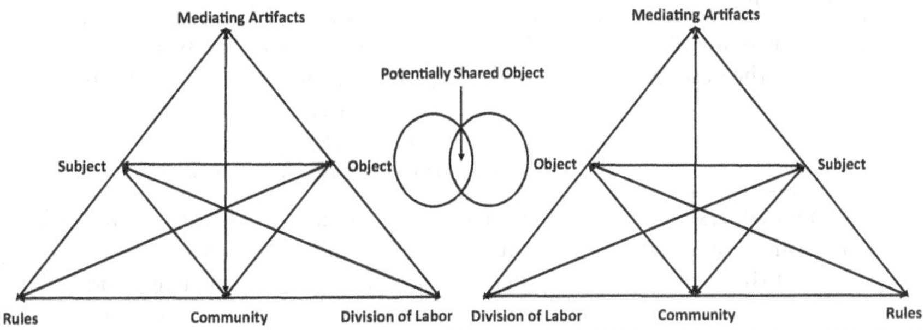

Source: Engeström, 1999.

a way to access resources, the technical assistance partnership activity system may be interested in eliminating disproportionality in order to develop and distribute curriculum and instruction resources prior to prereferral intervention or special education eligibility consideration.

EQUITY EXPANSIVE LEARNING CYCLE(S) OF A TECHNICAL ASSISTANCE PARTNERSHIP TO ELIMINATE DISPROPORTIONALITY

The expansive learning cycles characteristic of equity expansive technical assistance provide a valuable structure for organizing the features and processes for working alongside partners to eliminate disproportionality. Accordingly, I rearticulate a general description of each of the seven steps of a cycle of expansive learning within an equity expansive technical assistance partnership with this general object.

STEP 1: ANALYZING THE "DISPRO STATUS QUO"

In step 1 of expansive learning cycles, participants analyze their current activity system, with an emphasis on problematic situations and contributing forces (see Tables 5.1 and 5.2). Within this step, equity expansive technical assistance providers facilitate partners' preliminary mapping of historical and current systemic contexts that have allowed and reproduced disproportionality, through holistic data collection and analysis activities, which, in turn, allow us to more deeply and descriptively define the equity issues to be addressed through the partnership. This step also involves processes of identifying policy, practice, relational, and other contextual factors that appear to contribute to these issues. We typically start by collecting the most readily available public-facing data connected with the reason for a partner initiating

Table 5.1. Activity System of a School District Within Which Disproportionality Is Occurring

Subjects: Those involved in carrying out the activity	General and special education teachers, school psychologists, school counselors and other related service providers, family members, district administration, including director of special education or similar position
Mediating artifacts: Material and symbolic means for carrying out the activity	State law and guidance related to identification patterns, federal and state law related to identification, educators' knowledge and belief systems and/or theories of disability and race, assessment instruments and procedural documents
Object: Motivation for carrying out the activity	Special education identification as a means to designate children as disabled, allocate additional resources, and remove children from general education setting and accountability
Rules: Local and general norms that define and regulate subjects' activity and relationships with others in the activity	Local prereferral intervention and special education identification processes, federal and state law on identification and eligibility requirements and definitions of disproportionality, local and state accountability requirements, and resources
Community: People who share with subjects an interest in the same object	District administrators, state education agency administrators, general and special educators, school psychologists, school counselors, other related service providers
Division of labor: How the object of activity relates to the community's responsibilities and related recognition or rewards, typically mediated by sociohistorical power structures and relational patterns within and across communities	General education teacher referral practices, school psychologist assessment and analysis procedures, school psychology (and related service provider) professional organization practice and ethics guidelines, teacher labor organization collective bargaining agreements, history and socialization into professional practice, professionals' figured worlds

Note. Two interacting activity systems, with separate and overlapping objects, are the minimum in third-generation activity theory (Engeström, 1987).

contact with our center. I revisit commonly collected disproportionality data regarding risk, risk ratio, and weighted risk ratio to apply these discussions.

As I introduced in Chapter 1 disproportionality risk is calculated by comparing overall enrollment data for student racial groups with the number of students from each group who were identified for a particular disability category (or special education in general). The risk, then, is the likelihood

Table 5.2. Activity System of an Equity Expansive Technical Assistance Partnership to Eliminate Disproportionality

Subjects	Superintendent or designee; director of special education; director or associate superintendent of curriculum and instruction; representative group of general and special education teachers, school psychologists, school counselors, and other related service providers; select family members; technical assistance center personnel
Mediating artifacts	State law and guidance related to identification patterns; federal and state law related to identification; educators' knowledge and belief systems and/or theories of disability and race; assessment instruments and procedural documents; local data including student population, identification patterns, academic participation and outcomes; qualitative data from students and family members on experiences with the processes and impact of special education identification and services; educator discourse regarding student performance and competence; critical theory related to race and disability; protocols for policy and procedure review; asset-based, intersectional curriculum and instruction resources; educator, student, family, and technical assistance providers' embodied and experiential identities
Object	Reduce the number of students of color identified for special education and more restrictive placements as compared with their white counterparts
Rules	Equitable and democratic participation and engagement, critical reflexive practices and consciousness
Community	Superintendent, director of special education, director or associate superintendent of curriculum and instruction; representative group of general and special education teachers, school psychologists, school counselors, and other related service providers; select family members; technical assistance center personnel; technical assistance center project officers and other USDOE administrators; state education agency personnel; disproportionality researchers and other scholars committed to eliminating education inequities
Division of labor	Roles, responsibilities, and recognition associated with each subject's participation in the partnership

that a student belonging to a particular racial group will be identified in a given eligibility category. Disproportionality risk ratio is calculated by comparing one racial group's risk for special education or a particular disability category with another's, to identify inequities between racial groups. The comparison group for calculating risk ratio is usually either white students or all other student racial groups combined, such that the calculation determines how many times more likely students from the specific racial group were to be identified in a disability category than white students. However, it is often necessary to weight risk ratio calculations because while the risk for a racial group may be the same in two districts, the risk ratios will differ unless the racial demographics of the districts are identical. To calculate a weighted risk ratio, the district-level risk for a racial group is the numerator and the weighted risk for all other students is the denominator, which is calculated by using the district-level risks for each racial group in the comparison group, weighted by the racial composition of the state (Losen, 2009). Most of the time in district-level disproportionality analyses, risk and risk ratio are calculated. Figure 5.2 shows an example of district-level disproportionality data from an urban midwestern school district with which we have a partnership, based on real Civil Rights Data Collection data from 2017.

Although the figure does not include the key to interpreting race/ethnicity representation by shaded proportions on the bar graphs, the bottom of each bar represents white students, who make up 23.4% of the district student population overall and 23. 6% of the special education student population. The next-to-bottom bars represent multiracial students, and their special education risk is proportionate to their population, as is the case with white students in this district. However, the population of Black students (middle bars) is 45.3%, and yet they account for 53.8% of the special education population. This means that Black students' special education risk is

Figure 5.2. Student Representation by Race/Ethnicity in General Education, Compared With Special Education Population in an Urban Midwestern District, 2017

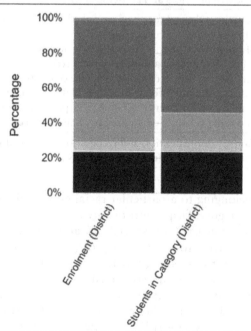

1.2%, and white students' risk is 1.0%: Black students are 1.2% more likely to be identified for special education than white students in this district (risk ratio = 1.2/1.0). In this state, however, disproportionality is determined by comparing the percentage of students with disabilities in an LEA from one particular racial or ethnic group compared with students with disabilities in the LEA in all remaining racial or ethnic groups combined. In this district, Black students are 1.7 times more likely to be identified for special education than all other racial groups combined. Although this risk ratio still does not meet the threshold for significant disproportionality in this state, which is 2.5 or greater for each of the past 3 years, something is going on here. But what *it* is will need to be determined through the data collection and analysis approaches undertaken within this first step of expansive learning cycles. These data cannot and do not tell the full story without further context.

This is where the concept of data triangulation comes into play. Triangulation is a data collection method that typically is defined related to its function in checking and establishing validity by collecting multiple forms of data from multiple sources to investigate the same research question(s). Yet, critical qualitative and mixed-methodology researcher Norman Denzin (2012) offers a different definition:

> The use of multiple methods, or triangulation, reflects an attempt to secure an in-depth understanding of the phenomenon in question. Objective reality can never be captured. We only know a thing through its representations. Triangulation is not a tool or a strategy of validation but an alternative to validation (Flick, 2007). The combination of multiple methodological practices, empirical materials, perspectives, and observers in a single study is best understood as a strategy that adds rigor, breadth complexity, richness, and depth to any inquiry (see Flick, 2002, 2007). (p. 84)

Depending on the partnership, the information relevant to triangulating the existing disproportionality data varies to some degree, although in all instances we aim to further contextualize risk ratio data with information typically overlooked, yet relevant to understanding the issue. This may include any or all of the following data, sources, and relational analyses:

1. Number of students referred to prereferral intervention teams, by school and grade level, analyzed for patterns of concentration or absence of referral
2. Number of special education referrals by school and grade level, as well as month, analyzed for patterns of concentration or absence of referral, as well as in relation to prereferral intervention data (above)
3. Teacher demographics by school, analyzed for patterns in relation to school special education identification

4. Procedural documents guiding prereferral intervention team discussion and student progress monitoring, analyzed for emphasis on student deficit, discussion devoid of instructional context, and degree to which instructional and student progress data are authentically considered

5. Civil Rights Data Collection district equity report (publicly available at https://ocrdata.ed.gov/search/district), analyzed for course-taking patterns and evidence of educational tracking in relation to race, sex, disability, and English learner status

6. Facilitation and analysis of focus group and individual interviews with partnership-involved educators, analyzed for perceptions and perspectives on the adequacy of curriculum and instruction, school and district culture and climate, the function of special education, and belief systems related to students, families, and communities

7. Facilitation and analysis of select student and family interviews regarding special education procedures and experiences (data are scrubbed by technical assistance staff to ensure anonymity and reduce risk), analyzed for experiences of inclusion and marginalization, partnership and shared decision-making, as well as experiences specific to the identification processes and service aspects of special education

Related to the last item, I provide in Table 5.3 a sample protocol for student/family interviews. It includes items from actual interviews our center has facilitated with partnering districts, as well as prompts informed by 10 years of teaching an undergraduate and graduate-level course with educators seeking special education licensure in which I invite parents and family members, typically people of color, to discuss their own and their child's experiences being labeled and receiving special education services. Finally, these prompts were informed by the narratives of four children with disabilities, three of whom were children of color, shared with participants, including me, at a recent meeting convened by the National Center for Systemic Improvement. In this meeting, federal and state agency administrators, scholars, and technical assistance key personnel came together to discuss equity issues related to effective special education services. It is important for the technical assistance providers and district staff to work together to ensure anonymity in recruitment and reporting of interview data. Our center typically asks the district to send out a mass email to families that meet participation criteria, asking interested respondents to contact our center directly, and introducing the reason for the request for their input.

As we prepare for this first step, the pathway by which a particular partner came to request our services provides important information for assembling the right team for the work, which is crucial to collecting and analyzing data that provide the most complete picture of current systemic

Table 5.3. Sample Interview Questions for Family Members of and Students of Color With Disability Labels and Who Receive Special Education

Questions for Parents/Legal Guardians	Questions for Students
How did you come to attend/enroll your child in the district? What brought you here?	Why do you go to the school you go to?
Where and how have you felt valued in the district and your school, and in what ways have you not felt valued?	How do your teachers and your school make you feel important and cared about? Are there things they do or say that make you not feel cared about?
In what ways have educators sought your perspectives on approaches and goals for educating your child?	Have your teachers asked you about what you want to learn and how to best teach you? If they have, will you tell me more about what they've done to find out what you want to learn?
Have you had to seek resources outside of the district setting in order to feel valued and to access high-quality education and services for your child?	Do you think you get everything from your school and your teachers that you need in order to be able to learn?
What has been your experience with assumptions of educators or others about you/your child's competence based on what they know or think they know about you/your child?	Do your teachers think you are smart? Do they think you know how to do things? What about your principal or other adults in your school? What do they think about you?
How have your gender, your sex, your race, and other aspects of your identity shaped how you have been perceived by your child's teachers, and how you/they have been treated? In what ways has this impacted access to general education? In what ways has this impacted the special education process for your child?	Do you think you are treated fairly based on who you are? (on the color of your skin, being a girl, where you are from, your disability label/being in special education?)
What has your experience been like regarding your child being identified for special education services and labeled with a disability? To what extent have you agreed with or differed from educators' decisions along the way?	What do you know about how and why you started going to/getting special education services? How do you feel about it? How does it impact you?
What has been the impact of special education (and, as relevant, separate educational settings like resource room services or self-contained classrooms) on your child's sense of well-being?	In what ways has your disability label and special education affected what others think about you, how they treat you, and how you think about yourself?

(continued)

115

Table 5.3. Sample Interview Questions for Family Members of and Students of Color With Disability Labels and Who Receive Special Education (*continued*)

Questions for Parents/Legal Guardians	Questions for Students
In what ways have you been valued by the IEP team and/or in what ways have you been silenced or unheard in your interactions with the team?	Have you ever joined one of the meetings with your teachers and your parent/caregiver where they talk about your special education? If so, how did you feel about being there? Were you asked to share any ideas during the meeting?
What opportunities have you had to be supported in your advocacy for yourself and others? In what ways have you been supported to develop your advocacy and voice to influence what educators know and how they teach?	Does anyone ever ask you what you like and what you think could be better about your education?
If you had the chance to go back to earlier in your child's education, what would you ask teachers to do differently about how instruction was provided to your child?	What kinds of classrooms, activities, and teachers make you feel the best about school? What do you need to be supported to learn and grow?

functioning. Over time—although with exceptions—we have found that the more earnestly and openly a district seeks our partnership, the more inclusively they convene a diverse team of stakeholders to engage in the partnership activities, including this important initial step of data collection and analysis. However, at times we have found that there are several stakeholder groups whose voices and perspectives are missing from the partnership as the requesting agency personnel have planned it initially. In these instances, planning for data collection activities that center these perspectives also allows the partnership to proceed more inclusively and effectively such that eventual systemic transformation will be informed and engaged by those whom the system has not benefitted. In the case of disproportionality, and as supported by data collection tools and processes like student and parent interviews, we must include students of color with disabilities and their parents and legal guardians in any partnership to reverse disproportionality.

In Chapter 4 I discussed the central role of the technical assistance provider's identity and the importance of critical reflexivity as related to positioning oneself as a partner, as well as considering the ways in which one's embodiment mediates the partnership itself. Drawing from Skelton (2019a) and her application of equity expansive technical assistance framing to explore her own identity as a technical assistance provider, the technical assistance provider's positionality is another important mediating artifact that

supports examination of and stimulation of tensions in relation to participants' analysis of the disproportionality status quo.

Given that the planning for any technical assistance partnership includes
the designation of the key personnel who will be responsible for facilitating
the partnership on behalf of the technical assistance agency, for each partnership our center selects those staff members on the basis of a combination of
embodiment (i.e., personal identity), experience, and knowledge bases. For
partnerships related to disproportionality, to the fullest extent possible, the
key personnel should include those whose racial identities align with those
most impacted by disproportionality, including the students affected and the
educators who are part of and who participate in systems within which disproportionality occurs. In addition, including technical assistance providers
who have firsthand experience with special education is highly desirable, and
in particular firsthand experience as a student who received special education
services. This representation functions in two ways. First, such representation
better ensures that the impacts of disability labeling and special education
placement are understood in explorations of locally unique manifestations
of disproportionality, both from the perspective of the technical assistance
provider and through their actions to understand these impacts in relation to
students. Second, this representation positions a person with a disability in a
role to facilitate the development of remedies, which counters ableist norms
that obscure nondisabled people's recognition of the value and knowledges
of disabled people, including at racial identity intersections. In the absence
of personnel with a disability at a technical assistance center (or district or
state agency, for example), it is preferable that one of the technical assistance
providers be a person of color who has studied deeply and engaged with
disability studies as a way to understand ableism and constructions of disability, and who has a professional history as an educator.

In most instances, the inclusion of a team member who is white and nondisabled also can be a mediating artifact at this stage in expansive learning
cycles to reverse disproportionality, in part because this individual's identity
is most likely to align with the majority of educators in the partnership setting. It is highly preferable that this individual have extensive professional
experience related to special education identification and placement, and be
well versed in the laws, as well as the loopholes in and insufficiencies of these
laws, that hold systems and individuals accountable for identifying and remedying the existence and impact of disproportionality. Within the working
relationship between these two team members, constant critical reflection by
the white, nondisabled technical assistance provider includes goals of power
redistribution in relation to their colleague, and staying vigilant regarding
the ways in which they are positioned by partners as holding (likely, more)
knowledge as compared with their counterpart. Ongoing planning and debriefing sessions about the interpersonal dynamics and impacts of working
in cross-identity teams are necessary beyond interactions with the partner

as well. Considerations like those I provided in Chapter 4, including how each team member is welcomed and received by partners as competent, can be helpful to consider in these sessions, along with corresponding responses to be enacted individually and in tandem during future partnership interactions.

Because the technical assistance provider enters the equity expansive technical assistance partnership as a critical friend, their identities can be leveraged to frame and reframe educators' deficit-based assumptions of students' capacities in relation to race and disability intersections. To become a critical friend, however, requires building trust, particularly in the context of a disproportionality-focused partnership, in part due to legal and other implications of disproportionate representation.

One reason I suggest the technical assistance provider's professional history should relate to the issues to be addressed in the partnership, is that this alignment is a way to establish credibility and trust, but not necessarily because such trust is important in top-down, expert/novice models of technical assistance (i.e., so the partner will be more likely to follow the provider's intervention suggestions with fidelity). Rather, time and time again, I have noticed that our partners are more likely and supported to become vulnerable and self-reflective about the impact of their socialization, belief systems, and practices when they perceive the same in their technical assistance provider. Thus, modeling critical reflexivity in relation to one's prior (and current) practice is a way in which the technical assistance provider can begin to form the critical friendship at the heart of an equity expansive technical assistance partnership and to leverage identity as a mediating artifact.

Within disproportionality-focused partnerships more specifically, I use "corroborating stories" (Thorius, 2019) as mediating artifacts that bring partners into contact with and engage them in critique of the technical assistance providers' participation in white racism and nondisabled ableism in everyday practice. Based on the notion of counter-stories (Delgado, 1989) in critical race scholarship, but mindful of the dangers of white scholars' potential to "take over CRT to promote our own interests or recenter our positions while attempting to 'represent' people of color" (Bergerson, 2003, p. 52), at the beginning of and throughout disproportionality partnerships, personnel introduce to partners our own corroborating stories (Thorius, 2019). Personally, I use many examples of my former practice as a school psychologist to illustrate the ways in which ableism and racism, undergirded by white supremacy, have played out in my own systemically embedded practice. As is the case with historical legacies of eugenics in special education systemic practice, my corroborating stories serve as primary stimuli that mediate participants' mapping of their own systemic practices in order to en/counter the contradictions inherent in their corroboration with racist/ableist practices. The story about José that I shared in Chapter 1 is one such corroborating story, as is another in which I drew a bell curve on a whiteboard as I was explaining intelligence test results to parents of color to explain their children's significant discrepancies between intelligence test and achievement test performance. Paired with such stories, I provide to participants a set of prompts that focus their critique on my beliefs, practices, and inactions related to both egregious and subtle manifestations of racism and ableism.

For my colleagues of color who hold historically marginalized identities, their corroborating stories may reveal the ways in which hegemony functions to cast doubt and self-alienation and oppression (Charlton, 2006), which in turn shape one's beliefs and practices related to student competence: of central importance as an underlying contributor to disproportionality. Sharing these histories with partners who hold similar identities creates space for considering the ways in which internalized oppression impacts their relationship with the issue of disproportionality.

Whether corroborating stories are generated by those technical assistance providers with dominant or with nondominant identities, however, they are an overt example of critical consciousness, which, as a reminder, is defined by Radd and Kramer (2016) as (1) the willingness and ability to attend to manifestations of power and privilege that systematically advantage some while disadvantaging others, and (2) transformation of this attention and related insight into beliefs and actions to "create more just action, processes, structures, and circumstances" (p. 584). From here, although the process is not linear, it repeats throughout the partnership, and additional mediating artifacts may take the form of activities in which the technical assistance providers and partners together critique "arm's-length vignettes" that reflect research-based reasons why disproportionality exists. At times, I use actual transcripts from those Child Study Team and other similarly functioning meetings that schools typically engage in as part of the (pre)referral processes for special education eligibility determination. Other times, we create fictitious, but representative, scenarios upon which we focus our critique. Following Artiles's (2009) conclusion on the basis of existing disproportionality research, we craft these scenarios to allow for critiques of special education referral decisions, along with other eligibility determination practices, as shaped by additional contextual factors of the schools within which these decisions are made, in addition to educators' personal and "cultural beliefs about competence and performance" (p. 26). These vignettes function in the way that qualitative researchers sometimes employ vignettes to provide a "less personal and therefore less threatening way of exploring sensitive topics" (Barter & Reynold, 1999, p. 1).

We pair these types of vignettes with analysis protocols that are applied by participants and technical assistance providers in shared activity. Here, some participants have the opportunity to develop their capacities for critical analysis, while others are validated by both the technical assistance providers and their colleagues, in their critique of the individual and systemic issues raised in the vignette.

STEP 2: EVOKING SYSTEMIC TENSIONS, OR FRAMING AND NAMING THE IMPACT AND RELATIONSHIP OF RACISM AND ABLEISM

Step 2 of expansive learning cycles is geared toward uncovering and evoking contradictions and tensions within the system. These *secondary contradictions*, or double binds, are equally unacceptable options that require practical systemic changes (Ellis et al., 2010). In NIUSI–LeadScape's original work, critical analysis was focused on principals' own practices and beliefs as units of analysis that afforded and constrained technical and contextual solutions to inequities. Extending this focus to equity expansive technical assistance, critical analysis requires deep and collaborative reflection on individual *and* systemic practices that benefit some and oppress other students, along with individual belief systems and institutional values that contribute to these patterns of benefit and marginalization as related to student (and other stakeholder) race, sex, national origin, disability, and other identity intersections. In addition, these analyses are historical and contemporary; in the case of technical assistance focused on addressing disproportionality, they require coming to understandings of how current practices and beliefs are shared across legacies of oppression through social systems of racism, ableism, and their intersection.

In our current work, within this part of the process, technical assistance providers synthesize, probe more deeply, and often reframe and extend available data and initial conclusions about the status quo within historical and cultural contexts. There are several approaches we commonly engage to dig deeper into available data and have found to be effective. I detail two of these approaches, below.

The first approach relates to the ways in which disproportionality typically has been measured and reported through quantitative data, devoid of context, and without processes for meaning-making built into educators' opportunities to engage with the data. Whether it is through the application of our ECAP to synthesize and introduce interpretive statements regarding public-facing, publicly available, and ECAP team–collected local data, or through data synthesis and interpretation separate from this process, this stage of equity expansive learning cycles includes time and space for engaging in shared interpretation of available data, as well as orienting critical discussions on the histories of how education data have functioned and the mythologies of what available data actually reveal. The second approach is that any meaning-making activities are focused on both the self *and* the system, accounting for the sources of disproportionality as situated across individual and institutional planes.

Our center's critical collaborative inquiry process (Skelton et al., 2021) incorporates both approaches. Depicted in Figure 5.3, the process includes four repeating activities that include and condense steps of expansive learning cycles, as signaled in our definition: "Critical collaborative inquiry is a process that engages students, families, community members, educators and policy makers and facilitates the use of perspectives to move toward equitable

Figure 5.3. MAP Center Critical Collaborative Inquiry Cycles

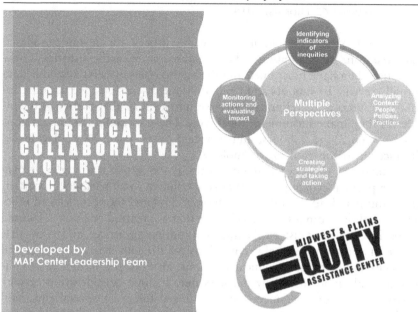

learning environments, and data as a mediating tool within that process"
(Skelton et al., 2021, n.p.)

Starting at the top of the cycle depicted in the figure, the steps "Identifying
Indicators of Inequities" and "Analyzing Context: People, Policies, Practices"
align with this second step of equity expansive learning cycles. As I introduced in Chapter 4, one of the center's most robust tools for engaging in
critical collaborative inquiry cycles is our Equity Context Analysis Process.
More specifically, the ECAP is carried out in three phases (i.e., planning and
preparation, data collection, and rubric analysis co-interpretation and setting equity priorities) and

1. Includes comprehensive tools for data collection and analysis
2. Engages multiple stakeholders in the coordination, collection, and
   interpretation of these data
3. Centers the assessment of equitable practices
4. Is designed to identity opportunities for growth related to
   advancing educational equity systemwide
5. Is organized around domains that have been linked explicitly to
   those policies, practices, belief systems, and relationships that
   contribute to disproportionality, as well as domains for systemic

change derived in part from the Systemic Change Framework
(Kozleski & Thorius, 2014)

Integral to the dedicated time, space, and process for engaging in shared
interpretation, are orientating and critical discussions on the histories of how
education data have functioned and the mythologies of what available data
actually reveal. To support and facilitate these discussions, we organize local data sources and preliminary analysis into a rubric that participants consider as they make meaning of local data. These meaning-making sessions
last between 3 and 4 hours, and in recent years, have taken place using
distance video-conferencing technology.

Sometimes, the second step of an equity expansive learning cycle may
reveal a particular data pattern that is of concern to all partnership participants and may lead to in-depth analysis of a related set of policies of practices. Recalling from a previous chapter that contextual analysis is focused
on locally configured historical patterns of routines, practices, and values that
constrain and afford equitable conditions for students across identities and
that help and/or hinder technical solutions, an example of an area of contextual analysis identified by partners may include consideration of why
a particular set of assessment tools is utilized for every special education
eligibility determination process and whether concerns with efficiency of processes are valued over the individualization and appropriateness of assessment approaches.

Or in a different context, partnership participants may determine it necessary to consider existing policies that may be contributing to disproportionality, as Skiba and colleagues (2006) found in their study of teacher
perspectives on function and purpose of special education referral.

> Despite recent state and federal changes that have mandated the inclusion of
> students with disabilities in high-stakes testing, respondents still believe that
> standardized testing creates pressure on teachers and parents to refer students
> to special education: We've gotten a huge increase in the number of parents
> wanting their child tested. And part of that has to do with our district policy on
> retention and the fear of [the state accountability test] and all that, so, whenever
> a teacher starts talking to a parent about the child being in trouble or probably
> going to be retained, then the parent asks for testing. (school psychologist, WF).
> Our expectations for youngsters have skyrocketed, more and more aren't attain-
> ing the standards the feds and state think should occur. A lot of stressed teachers
> feel tremendous pressure to get kids to a certain level and if I don't then by gosh
> I better . . . find a reason why. (special education director, WM) (p. 1435)

In Table 5.4, I include excerpts from a tool developed by the MAP Center,
based on the critical policy analysis scholarship I referenced in previous
chapters (Thorius & Maxcy, 2015, Welner, 2001), in order to prepare an

Table 5.4. Excerpts and Adaptations From Great Lakes Equity Center's Policy Equity Analysis Toolkit: Critical Policy Review Planning Tool

PART ONE: PLANNING TO CONDUCT THE ANALYSIS

I. Assembling a Representative Team and Establishing Roles

A team that is inclusive, collaborative, and focused on ensuring equitable practices helps to prevent recommendations that may marginalize particular groups (Skelton, 2015). Planners must guard against tokenism and deficit thinking. Teams can be authentic partnerships by establishing cultural reciprocity, drawing on individuals' funds of knowledge (Moll et al., 1992), and negotiating policy and practice with families (Kyser et al., 2015). Consider:

Who will participate, and how will recruitment occur?

How will visibility and awareness of the opportunity for all stakeholders be ensured?

To what extent is the team diverse and representative of the learning community?

Are there members on the team who can adequately address the policy issues?

Who gets to decide on the roles and who will fulfill them?

Key Considerations

Differences should be framed as benefits to the learning community and embrace the rich, intersecting dimensions of diversity each individual brings to the group. Team participants should reflect the population represented in the district and school community. Consider member: race/ethnicity, gender expression, religion (or claimed non-religion), school roles, sexual orientation, socioeconomic status, dis/ability status, national origin, citizenship status, linguistic status, etc. All stakeholder groups who participate in or are affected by policy interpretation, appropriation, and implementation should be included in the review. Possible roles: Facilitator, Timekeeper, Recorder, Reporter, Observer/Critical Friend.

II. Planning Meeting Logistics

The social and physical surroundings should be culturally responsive to participants. Meeting times should accommodate participants' schedules, and space should accommodate everyone (e.g., community members with disabilities, the visually impaired, members who bring children) and provide necessary facilitation tools to host open discussion. Consider arranging the room so that a roundtable discussion can take place.

When, where, and how frequently will you meet?

How will the meeting space be arranged?

What materials and services will be provided for the team meetings?

How will you ensure meeting times, locations, and structure accommodate access for all?

(continued)

Table 5.4. Excerpts and Adaptations From Great Lakes Equity Center's Policy Equity Analysis Toolkit: Critical Policy Review Planning Tool (*continued*)

Key Considerations

Consult with the team to identify times and locations for participants to feel comfortable, safe, and able to contribute. Be responsive to shifting schedules. Include materials and services that encourage inclusivity and participation. It may be important to include interpreters.

III. Orienting and Norming the Team

Establishing clear goals is the next step in conducting a successful equity-oriented policy review. Goals provide clarity about the rationale and intended outcomes of the policy review. Team members should agree on commitments and practices for interaction.

Guiding Questions

Who are the team members, how do they identify or describe themselves, and what aspects of the learning community do they represent?

What is the reason or purpose for conducting a policy equity analysis?

How does the analysis align with district equity goals and improvement plan?

What do you want staff, students, and community members to learn from this process?

How will you know whether you have met your goals and desired outcomes?

Will the team choose policies to review, or will those policies already be selected?

What data or artifacts will be included?

Who gets to decide what to include?

Who gets to decide how the data and artifacts are interpreted?

How have we ensured the voices and perspectives of historically underrepresented groups are central to creating goals and norms?

What are the agreed-upon norms of communication, and through what media (face-to-face, email, phone, etc.) will communication occur?

What are the agreed-upon norms of decision-making (i.e., consensus vs. majority vote, team findings will be implemented vs. team findings are recommendations for another decision-making body, etc.), and through what media will decision-making occur?

IV. Individual Policy Review

Using the Policy Equity Analysis Tool (PEAT), each review team member will independently review the policy documents the team identified for analysis. For productive conversation and authentic exploration of differences, it is important that all team members feel comfortable enough and able to both use the PEAT and to speak their own truths about how they experience or interpret the policy and/or related practice in question.

Guiding Questions

How will team members be oriented to how to use the PEAT?

Is the PEAT accessible to all team participants; are necessary translations, readers, scribes, or other supports needed?

How will shared understanding about procedures, goals, and outputs from the individual review be decided and communicated?

How will individual review findings be summarized and communicated to the team?

Key Considerations

Consider the following key framing questions (Great Lakes Equity Center, 2015; Macey et al., 2012):

1. What is the intent behind the policy being reviewed?

2. What social constructions does this policy embrace?

3. Who benefits from the way things are and who does not (Freire, 1998)?

4. What actions will redress inequities in our policies (Kozleski & Waitoller, 2010)?

When providing evidence or data to support ratings or claims, consider quantitative and numerical data, but also consider qualitative data like the stories from staff, students, and parents/caregivers; open-ended survey questions; and observations (Macey et al., 2012). These data provide valuable insights.

V. Group Discussions

Following the individual reviews using the PEAT, the review team will debrief and discuss individual findings. Group discussions about individual findings provide opportunities to surface assumptions and call attention to issues individuals may not be aware of, based on their positions, roles, and identities in learning communities. When participating in group discussions, team members should expect to experience discomfort, but also to value and appreciate how others experience, and benefit or don't benefit from, the policy in question.

Guiding Questions

Who will facilitate and moderate team discussions? (Consider an outside moderator.)

What process/activities will support team discussions about key questions?

How will tenets of equity (inclusive representation, meaningful access and participation, and positive outcomes for all) be centered in team discussions?

Key Considerations

It is important to follow the norms and roles established by the group in Step III. If those norms or roles are limiting the discussion by preventing viewpoints from entering the conversation, or limiting the potential outcomes or products generated by the discussion, the team may want to revisit those norms.

(continued)

Table 5.4. Excerpts and Adaptations From Great Lakes Equity Center's Policy Equity Analysis Toolkit: Critical Policy Review Planning Tool (*continued*)

VI. Summarizing and Prioritizing Findings and Considerations
After doing the challenging work of establishing a diverse, representative team, having accessible team meetings in which team members determine goals and norms, conduct individual policy reviews, and engage in powerful group discussions, it is now time to summarize the team's work and generate findings and recommendations. Since the process is oriented toward change of policy and practice, findings should be oriented toward actions that members of the learning community can take to make schools equitable for all students.

Guiding Questions

How will individual findings be summarized into recommendations?

What will be the process for prioritizing and selecting the top-level considerations and recommendations for action planning?

What beliefs and attitudes about people, including bias, stereotypes, and prejudices, are influencing priorities, findings, and considerations (Welner, 2001)?

How will findings from the team's review be communicated transparently to others?

What are the next steps, and how will accountability for the next steps be established?

Key Considerations

The team may find it helpful to use prioritization criteria to make decisions. For example:

ROUND 1: Use these criteria to prioritize three or four recommendations.

Urgency—What is most important in terms of impact and timeliness?

Agency—Which recommendations are within the school, district, or agency's purview or power to change or enhance?

Efficacy—Which recommendations would most directly benefit students?

ROUND 2: Use these criteria to pick one or two of Round 1 recommendations.

Feasibility—For which recommendations does the school, district, or agency have the resources to implement in ways that advance desired changes?

Sustainability—For which recommendations does the school or district have the resources to sustain actions over time in light of competing priorities and shifting contexts (e.g., personnel and budget changes, etc.)? (Skelton, 2013)

inclusive team and process for reviewing disproportionality policy. Previous versions of this tool were developed as a response to a Department of Justice–ordered partnership between a school district and the Region V Equity Assistance Center housed at Indiana University School of Education–IUPUI from 2011–2016. The original purpose of the tool was to support the district's ongoing analysis of policies that resulted in discriminatory student treatment, including discipline disproportionality, and the tool could be applied to processes of policy revision and future policy development. The full Policy Equity Analysis Toolkit (Great Lakes Equity Center, 2016c) is open access, available on the Great Lakes Equity Center's website, and archived by the USDOE's Educational Resource and Information Center. The toolkit is highly adaptable to local context, but explicitly guides teams through critical reflection on power, privilege, benefit, and marginalization as they consider policy text and function.

Paired with these locally collected data and initial analysis, the equity expansive technical assistance provider also introduces a different type of mediating artifact into the partnership activity system: critical histories of special education—including stratification of people in ways closely connected with race, immigration status and national origin, language, and disability—and theories that allow for interpretation of these histories. These types of artifacts add cultural–historical lenses through which partners more deeply consider and interpret local system data. Relatedly, these artifacts are aimed at stimulating partners' tensions with the roles and interlocking nature of racist and ableist education contexts in tandem: discriminatory structures and influences that hinder students' affirmation, access, participation, and outcomes, and that on the surface may even appear to be benevolent (Thorius, 2019). Artifacts illustrate how these structures and influences have been perpetuated through education policy and practice. They engage participants in learning about our field's reliance on and failure to challenge medical models of disability, as well as focus on interventions to either prevent disability labels in the first place or remediate students to whom they have been applied, while leaving inequitable, exclusive systems otherwise intact.

In other instances, we have introduced as mediating artifacts counterstories of disabled students, scholars, and activists of color about the stigma and trauma they have experienced, associated with labeling and special education (Hernández-Saca, 2019; Hernández-Saca et al., 2018). Other artifacts have been critiques by disabled scholars of color regarding schools' and society's failure to account for disability identity formation and associated cultural practices of disabled communities, and to provide assets and opportunities for learning and innovation in educational settings (Forber-Pratt et al., 2017).

I cannot overstate the importance of these types of mediating artifacts—those that illuminate cultural–historical practices associated with oppression that have been tied to disproportionality root causes—being introduced in tandem with national, state, and local data resulting in even more triangulated, methodologically and perspective-diverse data analysis than I described in step 1. These cultural–historical mediating artifacts support partners to go from, "These data are problematic!" to "We have to unlearn and remedy the histories of our field that have contributed to these problematic conditions!"

It is the striving toward *un*learning, toward *re*mediation of our historical practices and belief systems that we have found to have the most power to motivate personal and systemic change within disproportionality elimination efforts. I name and briefly describe a few such artifacts in Table 5.5.

Connected to processes and artifacts with which partners engage in critical analysis and (re)framing of available and newly collected data to map the current system of policy, practice, beliefs, and relationships impacting disproportionality, a number of contradictions invariably emerge. I highlight two of the most common, which appear to have the most impact on motivating partners to further critique and seek potential resolutions.

The first contradiction is that of the history of eugenics and the residues of eugenics associated with special education disproportionality. As partners learn more about the distant and more recent past in which children and adults have been sorted along continua of perceived ability and competence as directly related to race and national origin (Annamma et al., 2013; Mitchell & Snyder, 2003; Waitoller & Thorius, 2016) and explore that a central purpose of this sorting was to maintain white supremacy (Stubblefield, 2007) and property (Harris, 1993), they begin to question

Table 5.5. Cultural-Historical Artifacts to Stimulate Disproportionality Partnership Contradictions

Educational Experiences of Students With Multiply-Marginalized Identities: A Qualitative Research Synthesis of Disability Research (Iqtadar et al., 2021)	This MAP Center Equity Spotlight podcast is based on the authors' review of the literature, in which they synthesized 2006–2018 studies of students' experiences. The authors discuss how students made sense of their disability labels within the education system and how they negotiated—and challenged—these labels and their impacts.
"The Intersections of Learning Dis/ability, Ethnicity, and Emotionality in Education: The Voice of Sophia Cruz" (Hernández-Saca, 2020)	This MAP Center *Equity by Design Research Brief* summarizes Hernández-Saca's study with Latina student Sophia Cruz on her experiences of being labeled with a learning disability and associated impact.
We Are Not Technicians: We Are Not Magicians! A Counter-Narrative Framework of Special Educators as Inclusive Education Activists (Thorius, 2016)	This PowerPoint presentation and associated notes authored and delivered by Thorius to a midwestern state education agency introduces the relationship of policies and practices in special education to eugenics, and offers alternative visions for special education and educators' roles vis-à-vis their students, and in particular, students at race and disability intersections.

how individual practices of educators and systemic practices of special education reproduce these practices and purposes (Kliewer & Drake, 1998; Wagner, 2019).

Another common contradiction is that of the figured world of educators who work with disabled students of color or with students of color who are perceived by educators to have disabilities. In some ways related to the first contradiction regarding the relationship between eugenics and special education, educators begin grappling with tensions. These tensions include how they were socialized into their field and profession, their associated cognitive and procedural identities, and how these are connected to maintaining relational binaries in which educators hold a superior helping and even a savior role related to students of color with disabilities, and the impact of these identities on maintaining special education as a tool that can reproduce racist and ableist hierarchies (Thorius, 2019). I will expand on this contradiction in the next chapter, through contextualizing it within a district disproportionality partnership vignette.

STEP 3: INTRODUCING EQUITY RESOURCES AS MEDIATING ARTIFACTS, OR DEFINING THE ELEMENTS OF EQUITABLE (SPECIAL) EDUCATION, CURRICULUM, AND INSTRUCTION

In step 3 of expansive learning cycles, participants work on transforming the problematic systemic structure toward an expansive way of resolving the contradictions within it. Here, the equity expansive technical assistance provider introduces another round of mediating artifacts into shared activities, which participants may choose to take up as they begin to develop solutions toward addressing the reason they reached out for technical assistance and resolving contradictions that have emerged within the partnership thus far. Namely, we introduce specific topical professional learning resources, as well as invite and facilitate participation in our center's systemic partnership academies related to their systemic priorities. Through engagement with these resources, partners critically co-interpret relevant and contextual disproportionality data in ways that begin to offer possibilities for defining equitable education policies and practices that will reverse problematic contributing factors. In Table 5.6, I list and include excerpts from a set of mediating artifacts we have introduced into partnerships to facilitate participants' development of initial ideas for addressing disproportionality. These vary in form, function, depth, and length, and I organize them by universally available equity research and resources, equity learning network resources, and resources introduced within the context of systemic equity partnerships: the three tiers across which we organize our technical assistance services.

Table 5.6. Mediating Artifacts for Resolving Contradictions Related to Disproportionality

"Systemic Approaches to Eliminating Disproportionality in Special Education" (Jackson et al., 2016)	This brief offers strategies in three domains of systemic change intended to address and redress disproportionality.
Creating Brave Spaces for Community Voices in the Fight for Race and Disability-Based Justice in Special Education (Givens et al., 2022)	This Equity Spotlight vodcast centers the voices and stories of students and parents of children with and without disabilities, to learn about the principles of the Individuals With Disabilities Education Act and to develop knowledge, skills, and dispositions against white and ability supremacist ideology in education.
High-Leverage Strategies to Approach Disproportionality (Thorius, 2015)	Organized in relation to the Systemic Change Framework (Kozleski et al., 2014), this interactive PowerPoint archives a session I led with a state education agency in a meeting for districts identified with significant disproportionality convened to discuss technical, critical, and contextual solutions to the issue in their own settings. Solutions included approaches to teacher recruitment and retention, coaching models for educators who are disproportionally referring students of color to special education, and asset-based student interventions paired with systemic improvements to make the need for such interventions less likely, particularly as related to social–emotional well-being.
EquiLearn Focus Session: Creating Caring Classroom Communities Through Culturally Responsive and Sustaining Lesson Planning (Midwest & Plains Equity Assistance Center, 2020)	Educator teams learn and practice how to create learning experiences that include key elements of culturally responsive and sustaining instruction. Participants also discuss how educators leverage equity-focused teaching to create inclusive, responsive, and caring classroom communities for all students. This event engages educator teams across multiple states within each cadre in a 1-day shared learning experience that includes in-depth discussions, individual and group reflection activities, built-in networking opportunities, and individualized, in-person consultation from MAP Center staff to support action planning. During this dynamic and interactive learning experience, participants:

	Examine characteristics of a caring classroom community
	Deconstruct features of culturally responsive teaching practices
	Describe the building blocks of culturally responsive lesson planning
	Practice developing a lesson plan that incorporates the building blocks of culturally responsive teaching
	Initiate development of a district/schoolwide system of support for the design and delivery of culturally responsive and sustaining classroom instruction
"Promoting Socially-Just, Evidence-Based Practices" (Sullivan et al., 2022)	Although specific research-based practices are progressively more frequently practiced by teachers and other school-based professionals, scholars, and practitioners—particularly those from minoritized communities—the authors call attention to the narrow, and often exclusionary, nature of the evidence on which such practices are based. In this *Equity by Design* brief, they first compare conceptualizations of EBP and their limitations. They then challenge common misconceptions about research-based practice to propose an approach to EBP that leverages critical engagement with scholarship and centers community, family, and student voice. They end with key elements of socially just EBP to advance effective prevention, intervention, and systems of support in schools.
Session Three of Equity-Oriented Educator Systemic Partnership Academy (MAP Center), focused on "Ways of Doing" to address disproportionality as one of several "disparities in outcomes among and between groups of people . . . the smoke alerting us to the fires of racism and other systemic inequities"	Equity-oriented educators promote the development of racial and other identity literacy among youth and adults; within this session of this 3-day academy, educators consider the applicability of antiracist practices to developing positive racial and disability identity with youth and adults.

STEP 4: EQUITY EXPANSION OF THE OBJECT THROUGH INNOVATIVE ACTIVITY MODELS, OR EXPANDING THE OBJECT TO A COORDINATED SYSTEM OF EQUITABLE EDUCATION PRACTICE, POLICY, AND CONTRIBUTING BELIEF SYSTEMS

Step 4 is about expanding the purpose, or *object*, of the activity system through determining a new model of activity. Here, the technical assistance provider supports partners in developing next steps for addressing inequities, but in ways that support participants in determining that their original conceptualizations of these inequities, including contributing factors, manifestations, and impacts, may inadequately account for the systemic nature of addressing disproportionality. Here, and in relation to the previous steps of the expansive learning cycle, the partnership takes on new and more systemically oriented goals that reflect an expanded focus, alongside an expanded understanding of what addressing disproportionality must look and feel like in the future.

There are a number of ways in which technical assistance providers may facilitate this process, taking care also to get out of the way and allow collaborative generation of possible solutions. Because of the inclusive and representative team membership of our partnerships, of crucial importance is the development of agency for those whose agency historically has been constrained or stripped away. Although the technical assistance provider is a sounding board whose gentle critiques may be necessary to revisit earlier functions of the expansive learning cycle (e.g., evoke primary contradictions in what is and what is desired), the primary function of technical assistance here is to affirm and support partners in imagining not only what is necessary, but what is possible, to reverse the local manifestations of disproportionality. In doing so, the mark against which the partnership will be measured also expands toward a set of expectations and desired outcomes that reflect a more holistically just system of teaching and learning.

STEP 5: TESTING OUT AND REFINING INNOVATIONS, OR ENGAGING IN CRITICAL PRAXIS

Step 5 includes a continuation of the technical assistance providers' roles in step 4, as partners implement their new model of activity, solidifying and testing out innovations, putting initial steps into action, and developing and implementing new tools for doing so. Here, the technical assistance provider is what we colloquially call a "thought partner," reflecting with stakeholders on the relevance, usefulness, viability, and strength of the innovations in process. *Tertiary contradictions*, or conflicts, typically emerge at this point in the cycle: resistance, arguments, disagreements, and criticisms, usually resolved through compromise. The technical assistance provider supports partners in resolving these contradictions by refining further their ideas for addressing disproportionality.

During a partnership with one district, participants identified concerns with a lack of understanding and implementation of culturally responsive instruction, along with weak school models of MTSS implementation, as contributing heavily to local disproportionality patterns in the special education category of specific learning disability. Although they had identified this earlier in the partnership as an area to be addressed, through ongoing dialogue and engagement with mediating artifacts such as those that applied critical analytic prompts to review policies and procedures, and a MAP Center practitioner brief entitled "Preventing Disproportionality Through Nondiscriminatory Tiered Services" (Sullivan et al., 2018) that included a set of critical recommendations for doing so, the district team members developed an artifact similar to the protocol in Figure 5.4. The purpose of this protocol was to ensure more equitable approaches to ongoing universal screening and progress monitoring within multitiered systems of support at

Figure 5.4. Systemic Analysis and Improvement of Universal and Targeted Supports to Address Disproportionality

Who do the data suggest benefit from our current curriculum and instruction?			
Who do the data suggest do not benefit?			
What changes do we see in the data since last month?			
What do the data suggest about . . .			
. . . consistency of	Teaching and acknowledgment of schoolwide expectations?	Instruction and assessment across grade levels and courses?	Resource distribution across grade levels, classrooms, and content areas?
. . . need for improvements in	Partnerships and dialogue with families?	Curricular resources and materials?	Adult supports in and out of classrooms?
	Professional learning and coaching for teachers?	Improvements to facilities and infrastructure?	Other?

each district school as a means for preventing disproportionality. They applied this protocol to quarterly meetings in which student data on district benchmark assessments were discussed; importantly, this protocol focuses on the *system* as the object of critique, rather than students on the basis of their benchmark performance.

STEPS 6 AND 7: REFLECTING ON AND REFINING THE NEW ACTIVITY MODEL AND DISSEMINATING THE MODEL THROUGH DISTRIBUTED ACTIVITY SYSTEMS, OR DISTRIBUTING EQUITABLE PRACTICE

Step 6 of expansive learning cycles involves partners' reflection on implementation of the new activity model and building into it processes and efficiencies. Here, the technical assistance provider supports all of these processes, often through group and individual consultation with system leaders. In step 7, the partnership may continue as activities lead to new lines of questioning what expansive learning theory denotes as quaternary contradictions, regarding which students are benefitting and not benefitting from the way things are. I describe these steps in the context of the LEA and SEA partnerships that I discuss in detail in the next two chapters, as they are complex processes that involved several iterative subprocesses.

CHAPTER 6

The Florence Unified School District

In this chapter, I present a vignette that represents the types of varying reasons for and contexts within which public education agencies reach out for technical assistance. Importantly, the vignette does not include identifying information that could be linked back to a particular district; it is fictitious, yet representative of the technical assistance partnerships between our Equity Assistance Center and state departments of education and school districts working to redress disproportionality as part of systemic transformation efforts. The vignette details real scenarios that have emerged within such partnerships to illustrate the pervasive nature of disproportionality, and the complexity of technical assistance efforts to address any entrenched and systemic inequity such as disproportionality.

I set the vignette in a suburban university town, surrounded by rural communities and farmland stretching over rolling hills. As a university town, which I will call Florence, there are many international families and students in the public schools, which have a total enrollment of about 12,000 students. Approximately 20% of the population are students of color, and Black and Latina/o students make up about 8% of the population, each. Asian and Pacific Islander students account for about 3.5% of the population, and less than 1% of students are American Indian/Alaskan Native. Florence Unified School District recently experienced an incident in which a doll of color had been hung by a noose in the cafeteria, which prompted the associate superintendent to reach out to our center for assistance. Despite an investigation involving a number of students and staff being questioned, and an anonymous tip line being established, no one had been identified as responsible for the incident. At a recent board meeting, a Black female student spoke to the board, expressing not only her disappointment in the fact that a perpetrator had not been identified, but also an unsafe feeling on the part of Black students, especially due to treatment from some white students and teachers. As a result, the board president requested de-identified data from each of the district's 15 elementary, three middle, and two high schools on office discipline referrals for race-based bullying and harassment, which was shared in the board book provided to members prior to the next meeting. In the data provided, there were a total of 15 investigations of race-based harassment within the current school year, 12 of which had occurred at the middle and high school levels.

In the initial intake interview characteristic of our center's process for receiving new requests for assistance, the associate superintendent shared much of this information. Over the next month, a center leader drafted an MOU and TASS that reflected the initial concern and also accounted for data that staff had located in their review of publicly available district data. These data included Black students' risk ratio of 2.0 in the special education category of specific learning disability (SLD), a 1.6 risk ratio in the emotional disturbance category, and a 1.5 risk ratio for special education overall, although the district was not considered to have significant disproportionality as defined by the SEA's determination that the 2.0 risk ratio for the SLD category was not due to inappropriate special education identification procedures. Risk ratio data related to discipline also revealed that Black students were 2.5 times more likely to be suspended from school than white students. The MOU, signed by the district superintendent and associate superintendent, documented this primary partnership goal:

> Between November 1, 2018 & September 30, 2020, support district staff in increasing their understanding and implementation of culturally responsive and sustaining pedagogy and culturally responsive Positive Behavior Interventions and Supports (PBIS), including utilizing equity-focused tools to eliminate underlying causes of disproportionality (identification, academics, discipline) through the provision of professional learning experiences and research and practice-based tools and resources.

The TASS included monthly consultation calls between the associate superintendent, who among other duties supervised student services (i.e., special education) and monitored district discipline procedures, and a center staff member. The TASS also included support for the district to revitalize a "diversity committee" that had existed several years earlier after community outrage following an incident when a Black 1st-grader had been suspended due to having a box cutter in her winter coat pocket, under a previous "zero-tolerance" discipline policy. The previous committee included a local pastor of an AAME church, four district building leaders (i.e., principals and assistant principals/deans), and a previous associate superintendent. The monthly consultation calls, and monthly committee meetings that two center staff members attended as critical friends, account for the interacting activity systems of this district partnership through which I will illustrate the application of equity expansive technical assistance.

REFRAMING PERCEPTIONS OF ISOLATED INCIDENTS TO UNDERSTAND AND REMEDIATE A PERVASIVE NEGATIVE CLIMATE FOR PEOPLE OF COLOR

My inclusion of this vignette about a technical assistance partnership with Florence schools is meant to illustrate one of the central aspects of equity expansive technical assistance and reflects some of the research findings I included in Chapter 2: that educators can be reticent and avoid talking about race and racism, even in the context of direct evidence of disproportionality. In Florence, this is certainly the case, as it is with many of our partnering agencies, at least initially.

Over time, through conversations with the white woman associate superintendent and through deeper review of news media and other publicly available documents by center staff during the process of finalizing the partnership MOU and TASS, our staff noticed what appeared to be a pattern of racist incidents that had been largely unresolved, including white athletes posting white power hand signals on social media, which had been dismissed as innocuous by white adults in the community who flooded the district office with angry phone calls when two star athletes received 1-day suspensions. After two monthly consultation calls, which also served as a means for center staff to more deeply examine with local educational leaders the context informing their request for assistance, the MAP Center's technical assistance specialist and associate superintendent concluded that there were many missed opportunities to understand the educational and social experiences of students and families of color in the community, and that it was necessary to do so particularly because of these historical patterns of silencing and dismissal. Together, they planned that through the specialist's participation in the revitalized district diversity committee, they could work with members to address this history and its impact on student experiences and outcomes, including disproportionality.

Simultaneously, the specialist suggested to the associate superintendent the importance of having inclusive perspectives on the committee, and that the perspectives of those who had experienced marginalization were of utmost importance, along with the perspective of educational leaders who were at the center of investigating reports of racial harassment and served as points of contact with the larger district community. Through a process of email and written recruitment, a new 10-member committee was formed, following the recommended steps included in the center's Critical Policy Review Planning Tool, excerpted in Table 5.4. The new committee was renamed by the members as the Justice Equity Diversity and Inclusion (JEDI) team and included most of the original members, plus the current associate superintendent, one Black female student, and one white LGBTQ+ student, along with one parent of each of the students. The team members became the core group involved in the technical assistance partnership over the 2 years that followed, meeting monthly and engaging in both the SAEJE assessment process and systemic equity planning, facilitated by center processes and three center staff who constituted the partnership's full technical assistance team. Rather than describe every detail of the partnership, I describe four contradictions and related collective action and development that occurred related to them, emphasizing both the center's role in introducing mediating artifacts to evoke and resolve these contradictions, as well as participants' agency development and action to face their context, and seek and carry out solutions.

THE PRIMARY CONTRADICTION: THE EPISTEMIC QUESTION OF HOW WE CAN HAVE TWO TRUTHS

Among the first actions of the new JEDI team was to begin the SAEJE assessment process. This process can be accessed by the reader by registering for a free online course through Indiana University (https://login.iu.edu/guest /new).

Via the SAEJE process of collecting and considering data, the Florence JEDI team was faced with some powerful and disturbing truths, particularly as related to differences between the perspectives of adults and students of color and those of adults and students who were white. The survey results presented in Figure 6.1, shared and discussed at one of the JEDI team meetings at which two members of the center technical assistance team were present, led team members to experience a primary contradiction that for people of color in the district, there were pervasive feelings and experiences of exclusion, silencing, marginalization, and tokenism.

The Black female student on the team (the same student who had spoken out at the board meeting) shared examples of curriculum that included one person of color, and discussed how slavery was the only connection to African American history that they had experienced in their classes. "And you wonder why we have a noose in our cafeteria," the white LGBTQ+ high school student member responded in validation. white educators remained silent. One Latina physically disabled educator shared her experience being asked to serve on a district curriculum review committee as the "one person of color" and whose critique of the lack of materials dedicated to and from the perspective of people of color and with disabilities was largely ignored by her colleagues. One of the members of the technical assistance team reflected back, "There are two very different versions of how people of color and white people report experiencing the Florence Unified School District," to which the Black student responded, "How can we have two truths? If it's not a good place for some of us, it's not a good place."

Over the next several meetings, the team members examined SAEJE data more closely, as well as publicly available data on special education and discipline introduced into the conversation by the center team members. These

Figure 6.1. Sample SAEJE Student and Adult Survey Results: School Culture and Climate Domain

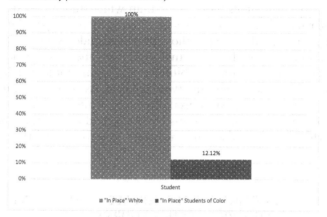

Student Survey (School Culture and Climate)

Interpreting this figure: The graph above summarizes the percentage of respondents who agreed that indicators of Diversity, Equity, and Inclusion were "In Place" in the School Culture and Climate domain. The information is disaggregated by role and by race/ethnicity. A larger percentage means more students agreed the domain is "In Place".

The student respondents who agreed **most** that practices within School Culture and Climate reflect an emphasis on Diversity, Equity, and Inclusion were: <u>White Students</u>.

The student respondents who agreed **least** that practices within School Culture and Climate reflect an emphasis on Diversity, Equity, and Inclusion were: <u>Students of Color</u>.

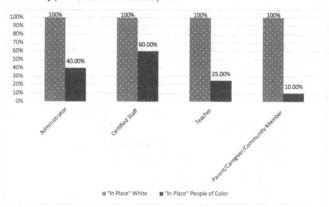

Adult Survey (School Culture and Climate)

Interpreting this figure: The graph above summarizes the percentage of respondents who agreed that indicators of Diversity, Equity, and Inclusion were "In Place" in the School Culture and Climate domain. The information is disaggregated by role and by race/ethnicity. A larger percentage means more people agreed the domain is "In Place".

The adult respondents who agreed **most** that practices within School Culture and Climate reflect an emphasis on Diversity, Equity, and Inclusion were: <u>White Administrators, Certified Staff, Teacher, and Parent/Caregiver/Community Member.</u>

The adult respondents who agreed **least** that practices within School Culture and Climate reflect an emphasis on Diversity, Equity, and Inclusion were: <u>Parent/Caregiver/Community Member of Color.</u>

data showed, for example, that Black students were over three times more likely to be suspended from school for three code of conduct violations: threatening behavior, insubordination, and loitering. Moreover, students of color were over four times more likely than white students to spend over 80% of their school day in the district's 12 self-contained special education classrooms, split equally between those in which students with ED and autism labels and those with intellectual disability labels were placed, than white students with the same disability labels. Within these meetings, tensions were thick. Accordingly, the two technical assistance team members (a Black woman with a physical disability and a white nondisabled lesbian woman), met in racial affinity groups for the second half of three meetings in which white team members and members of color shared their feelings and perspectives.

THE DOUBLE BIND: WE ARE HERE BECAUSE WE WANT TO HELP/WE ARE NOT YOUR CHARITY

As a reminder, secondary contradictions, or double binds, are traps of equally unacceptable options that require practical systemic changes (Ellis et al., 2010) as a result of analyzing and modeling possible resolutions (i.e., new activity models). Within the white affinity group, in response to the technical assistance provider's comment that it must be hard to hear these perspectives from students and colleagues of color, a white female principal exclaimed, "This is not who I am! I came here to help these kids!" To plan for the next session, the technical assistance providers worked together with the associate superintendent during a consultation call to create conversation prompts for the JEDI team around a slide, shown in Figure 6.2. The slide was based on a 2016 study that drew from the concept of figured worlds, to examine the ways in which special education teachers had figured their identities in relation to students with significant disabilities in an urban school district serving a majority of students of color (Thorius, 2016). The associate superintendent introduced the conversation prompts in the next session.

Through ongoing discussion, the JEDI team members took on these tensions with white educators, sharing some of their reactions and reflections that they indeed held these beliefs about themselves and were struggling to see this framing as a problem. One educator shared, "I have always seen my teaching as a calling from God. I *am* his missionary," to which the Latina educator with a disability responded, "We are not your charity!"

In more detail, double binds occur when a demand is imposed upon an individual or group of individuals within an activity system, but the demand is impossible to fulfil because of a limiting broader context. These individuals, therefore, "repeatedly face pressing and equally unacceptable alternatives

Figure 6.2. Dominant Figured Worlds of White Special Educators Who Work in Racially, Ethnically, Linguistically, Ability Diverse Communities

COGNITIVE

Patient
Saint/savior
Inspirational
Missionary
Intelligent
Expert
Leader
Gatekeeper

PROCEDURAL

Conduct
Save
Assess
Observe
Diagnose
Sort
Advise
Fix
Decide

"My last principal was really amazing. But our school didn't really need him. He went to (urban district) where he could really make a difference. I could never work there. It'd be too hard: I'd want to take all the kids home with me!"

IT TAKES
SOMEONE
special
TO TEACH
SOMEONE
special

Patient
Saint/savior
Inspirational
Missionary
Intelligent
Expert
Leader
Gatekeeper

Conduct
Save
Assess
Observe
Diagnose
Sort
Advise
Fix
Decide

Retrieved from www.Keepitschool.com/products/special-education-teacher-someone-special?variant=6107737349

OF THESE, WITH WHICH DO YOU IDENTIFY; WHAT TENSIONS DO THEY RAISE FOR YOU, IF ANY?

in an activity system, with no apparent way out" (Martínez-Álvarez et al., 2014). At this point in the partnership, a double bind began to come into focus: People of color had long been experiencing a double bind of hostile treatment with the expectation that they remain silent or risk exclusionary discipline, or even special education eligibility or more restrictive placement, at the hands of white educators who believed they were doing people of color a service. Although the initial concern with the doll and noose did not disappear, the goal of the partnership was beginning to expand: to create new spaces and procedures for understanding the everyday experiences and impacts of this double bind on district stakeholders of color.

THE TERTIARY CONTRADICTION: SEEKING RESOLUTION
THROUGH TRAUMA AND HARM REDUCTION

A new activity model was beginning to emerge, drawing from the perspectives of the educators and students and family members of color, and that centered available data on experiences and outcomes for students of color in the district. At the same time, white educators often remained silent, appearing to be avoiding risks associated with speaking out, for fear they would be perceived as racist. On several occasions, center staff introduced data on the experiences of students of color outside the presence of the student team members and their parents, and in other instances, they reflected together on the ways in which their positionalities as white and Black individuals had disproportionate impact and burden, as the staff member of color often was expected to teach white people about her experiences so that they could learn, which depleted her energy and at times felt exploitative. Moving toward a new model of activity, educators of color suggested that many of the tensions that had been put on the table thus far could be dealt with head on if the district was able to publicly commit to develop action plans with clear accountability that resulted in improved culture and climate for students, educators, and families of color. However, one educator cautioned that this could not be done on the backs of these groups; white people, 100% of whom thought everything was "just hunky dory" until now, needed to take this accountability to heart.

REFINING THE ACTIVITY MODEL: WHO DOES WHAT,
WHEN, AND HOW

At this point, at the recommendation of the JEDI team to the superintendent, members of the JEDI team, along with each building principal, assistant principal, and instructional coaches, as well as members of the superintendent's cabinet, participated in the MAP Center's Equity-Oriented Strategic Planning systemic partnership academy and its associated 3 full-day sessions: Identifying Systemic Inequities and Analyzing Learning Contexts; Generating a Theory of Action and Broad Equity Strategies; and Creating Implementation Plans. A full agenda for these sessions is depicted in Figure 6.3.

As a result of participation and ongoing meetings of the JEDI team, select team members made a presentation to the school board in which they asked the board to direct the superintendent to develop an equity and improvement plan with clear accountability and metrics related to improving culture and climate, and reducing disproportionate discipline, along with special education identification and restrictive placement, especially for Black students. The team members asked that the plan also include fiscal appropriations toward achieving plan goals, action steps that identified

Figure 6.3. Equity-Oriented Strategic Planning Partnership Academy Agenda

Equity-Oriented Strategic Planning Partnership Academy, Cohort 5
Technical Assistance Scope & Sequence (TASS)
2021-2022

INDIANA UNIVERSITY
SCHOOL OF EDUCATION
IUPUI

TRAJECTORY OF PARTNERSHIP ON-SITE AND/OR VIRTUAL SESSIONS

Goal <<X>> <<Month, Year>> at least 75% of participating agency team members surveyed will report moderate to significant increase in their capacity to engage in equity-oriented strategic planning as a result of the partnership academy. Qualitative evidence of impact will include the team's development of at least two broad systemic, agency-specific strategic actions to advance educational education in their local setting.

Each district will bring a district-level planning team (at least 3-8 members) to attend each session. Due to the COVID-19 pandemic, all sessions will occur virtually.

Equity-Oriented Strategic Planning, Sess. 1, Cohort 5: Identifying Systemic Inequities and Analyzing Learning Contexts **Time: 8:30am – 4:30pm EST** **Date: December 9, 2021** **Facilitators: Dr. Tiffany Kyser and Dr. <<TA Specialist>>** **Virtual Event**	Equity-Oriented Strategic Planning, Sess. 2, Cohort 5: Generating a Theory of Action and Broad Equity Strategies **Time: 8:30am – 4:30pm EST** **Date: December 10, 2021** **Facilitators: Dr. Tiffany Kyser and <<TA Specialist>>** **Virtual Event**	Equity-Oriented Strategic Planning, Sess. 3, Cohort 5: Revisiting a Theory of Action and Broad Equity Strategies **Time: 8:30am – 4:30pm EST** **Date: February 17, 2022** **Facilitators: Dr. Tiffany Kyser and <<TA Specialists>>** **Virtual Event**	Equity-Oriented Strategic Planning Session 4, Cohort 5: Creating Implementation Plans **Time: 8:30am – 5:30pm EST** **Date: February 18, 2022** **Facilitators: Dr. Tiffany Kyser and <<TA Specialist>>** **Virtual Event**
Participants will: Examine their specific role in facilitating their organization equity efforts.	**Participants will:** Discuss ways to analyze the extent to which equitable systemic practices are currently in place, to inform their strategic actions.	**Participants will:** Review and refine practices for analyzing equitable systemic practices are currently in place, to inform their strategic actions.	**Participants will:** Explore strategies for leveraging internal (personal and organizational) assets to facilitate and sustain equity efforts.
Agenda Welcome & Overview Engaging the *Critical Collaborative Inquiry Cycle* in strategic planning Identifying areas for improvement Framing Equity-Oriented Systemic Goals Analyzing the context analysis Developing hypotheses Wrap up and next steps	**Agenda** Welcome back and review previous session Reviewing systemic hypotheses for change Generating a theory of action Developing broad equity goals Wrap up and next steps	**Agenda** Welcome back and review previous sessions Review plan progress -Improvement Areas -Systemic Goals -Hypothesis Statements -Theory of Action -Goals Plan refinement Wrap up and next steps	**Agenda** Welcome back and review previous sessions Examining the foundations for successful plan implementation Developing implementation plans Preparing to be a critical consumer of equity-oriented professional Learning Developing a monitoring and evaluation plan Wrap up and next steps

specific individuals who would serve as leadership on all elements of the work, and mechanisms to publicly share disproportionality data regularly. They also asked that the plan seek to establish more objective and clear school discipline procedures, and enact hiring and new educator orientation plans to ensure equitable discipline and special education referrals. The board agreed, setting a 3-month timeline for the superintendent to present the board with a plan and requiring the superintendent to report to the board on progress toward these goals at least twice a year and to revise and re-present the action plan annually. In the months that followed, team members and other members of the Florence community engaged in more meetings, dialogue, and review of policy and practice that led to the development of this plan and the beginning of its enactment. Along the way, they experienced more contradictions, as this work is never complete and new tensions emerge as old ones are resolved; thus is the nature of equity expansive technical assistance as well.

CHAPTER 7

Representative SEA Center Partnership

Several of the state education agencies with which our center has partnered over the past 11 years have committed to the goal of eliminating race as a factor that predicts a student's eligibility for special education. SEAs have approached these commitments in various ways, with some stating this goal explicitly and designing vast systems of direct technical assistance for significantly disproportionate districts, while also developing and offering guidance and resources to districts seeking to realize equitable education access, participation, and outcomes across student representation. Other SEAs have homed in on a particular aspect of district and state data patterns related to student demographics, such as prioritizing Black male student achievement, in part due to this group of students experiencing disproportionate discipline, special education identification, and restrictive educational placement. In what follows, I present a representative case of a longstanding partnership with a midwestern SEA to illustrate the nature of equity expansive technical assistance partnerships and to demonstrate the iterative and nonlinear nature of systemic change: akin to how Vygotsky (1978b) defined human development as "a spiral, passing through the same point at each revolution while advancing to a higher level" (p. 56). In doing so, however, I obscure and change some of the partnership details to maintain the anonymity of the SEA. What follows are details and findings from a study on this partnership I conducted with other center staff alongside three agency administrators, and for which I obtained Indiana University Institutional Review Board approval.

BACKGROUND FOR THE PARTNERSHIP

Between 2002 and 2009, NCCRESt partnered with dozens of SEAs on addressing new requirements that were included in 2001's No Child Left Behind and 2004 amendments to IDEA. Following new requirements that all states address disproportionality, included in the 2004 amendments to IDEA, the SEA pursued several new initiatives that included a discretionary

grant program to districts with significant disproportionality, and an investment in partnerships and professional development that would contribute
to the creation of an SEA staff group who would hold expertise in reversing
disproportionality and serve as a resource to disproportionate districts. Finally, representative of the understanding that addressing disproportionality
goes beyond special education data and requires consideration of general education curriculum and instruction, as well as policies and other practices,
the SEA initiated a robust annual multiday professional learning event to provide direct technical assistance to disproportionate districts. The SEA also
initiated a direct partnership with NCCRESt to leverage resources toward
these initiatives.

In 2008, toward the close of this partnership due to NCCRESt's project
end date drawing near, the state enrolled over 600,000 students in their public school system, with 20% students of color or Indigenous students, and
7% identified as English language learners. More specifically, the student
population, based on census categories, was approximately 75% white,
13% Black, 7% Hispanic, 3% Asian/Pacific Islander, and 1% American
Indian. Approximately 97% of teachers and 93% of administrators were
white. In 2008, nearly 15% of all students were identified as having a disability, over the national average of 12%.

Over the previous 5 years, about one in every five Black or American
Indian children was identified as having a disability and receiving special education. In the 2006–2007 academic year, as part of their Annual Performance Report under IDEA, Part B, the SEA determined that 12 of a total
of 325 school districts met the criteria for significant overrepresentation of
American Indian or Black students in special education *due to inappropriate identification.* More broadly, the SEA determined that 30 districts had
overrepresentation in one or more disability categories, and 10 had significant underrepresentation in relation to the state-determined risk ratio of 2.0
as the threshold for significant disproportionality.

As a former graduate assistant with NCCRESt, and then as co-director
of professional learning for the Equity Alliance at Arizona State, led by
Kozleski, Artiles, and Dr. JoEtta Gonzales, I had the opportunity to continue
working with this SEA. After moving to Indiana in 2010 and receiving funding for the Region V EAC in 2011, we revitalized this relationship in the
form of a multiyear technical assistance partnership.

In 2016, administrators from this midwestern SEA began to develop
approaches for addressing low performance of students with disabilities
on statewide assessments. As introduced in the previous paragraphs, the
SEA's attention to disproportionate representation of students of color in
special education and discipline had been codified in 10 years of coordinated approaches to increase culturally responsive policies and practices,
and to address racial inequities in educational opportunities, achievement,

and special education eligibility. So, when the federal requirements shifted from special education compliance to accountability in 2015–2016, the SEA identified a statewide goal of improving literacy outcomes for students with disabilities. They deemed this the Keeping Our Promises (KoP), with two desired outcomes: (1) statewide dissemination of a set of instructional strategies that had resulted in positive achievement outcomes for students with disabilities, identified by educators invited to participate in a set of KoP meetings, and (2) scaling-up those practices statewide through professional development and resources to local education agencies (i.e. school districts). The SEA determined they were interested in learning more about the instructional practices occurring in what they deemed to be successful schools; SEA leaders invited staff from higher achieving schools to four meetings to document literacy teaching practices for students with disabilities.

Two interacting methodological approaches informed the study: those associated with partnership design, and those associated with data collection and analysis about partnership processes and outcomes. The former, methods informing project design, were shaped by CHAT and its approaches of formative intervention and expansive learning methodology. Methods associated with data collection were qualitative, involving a convenient and representative case (i.e., readily available and illustrative of a typical case [Yin, 2009]), instrumental (i.e., providing insights on a particular issue and able to be used to refine a theory [Stake, 1995]), illustrative (i.e., descriptive in nature and providing in-depth examples or other information about a program or policy, in this case, technical assistance), and based on an individual case-study approach (Merriam, 1998). All data were textual, observational, and expressed in words, and included artifact content, semistructured interviews, center staff members' written notes, and SEA participants' reflections on partnership activities. Data analysis involved qualitative template and open-coding processes applied to partnership documents, interview transcripts, and written notes (Crabtree & Miller, 1992; King, 1994). Template codes were guided by theoretical constructs of CHAT, formative intervention, and expansive learning.

SITE AND PARTICIPANTS

All partnership activities were on-site, or via phone and video conference. EAC personnel engaged with SEA participants, along with a larger group of 15 SEA administrators, to plan and debrief KoP activities over 4 months. Initially, the SEA had contacted the EAC to request critical observations and feedback on 4 full-day KoP sessions planned for 80 educators from 17 LEAs where students with disabilities had higher reading scores compared with other LEAs.

HOW THE PARTNERSHIP LED TO THE STUDY

An SEA administrator invited me as EAC executive director, along with MAP Center Director of Operations Seena Skelton, to give a keynote that would "center equity concerns" during the first KoP session. The evening after that session, Seena and I facilitated a debriefing meeting with SEA administrators. There, and in smaller group meetings later that evening, administrators shared tensions about the content of our keynote in which we had raised concerns with the form and function of how literacy was being defined in the initiative. For example, we had questioned why disability was being considered in isolation, given that students of color, including those with disabilities, continued to have lower reading scores compared with white students statewide, and noted that racial disproportionality in special education had been a pervasive inequity over many years. Three SEA administrators—Caroline, Fiona, and Korrine—were a part of these conversations. At the time Caroline, a former reading teacher and literacy coach at the elementary and middle school levels, was a literacy specialist with the state whose primary responsibilities were to develop online and face-to-face professional development for state educators. Fiona served as a special education specialist with the SEA's special education team, and Korrine as a consultant to the special education team on universal design for learning related to instruction for students with disabilities.

In response to these tensions, Seena and I, and selected SEA administrators including Fiona and Caroline, shifted the partnership focus from "critical friendship" to collaborative partnership such that Seena and I would facilitate portions of the three remaining KoP sessions. We also cofacilitated planning and meeting debrief sessions with subgroups of the 13-member SEA administration team. Total interactions in the partnership included three planning sessions of 1 hour each, four full-day KoP meetings, and five 1-hour debrief sessions with Fiona, Caroline, and Korrine. Importantly, the partnership initially was not designed as a research study. I approached SEA staff about the research project soon after the KoP sessions concluded, as I had received a university research grant in Summer 2016 to study the process and outcomes of our equity expansive approach to technical assistance partnerships.

DATA COLLECTION AND ANALYSIS PROCESSES

Qualitative methodology informed collection and content analysis of partnership documentation, along with the artifacts developed for and in the context of the recently concluded KoP sessions. Six types of data informed the study: (1) all 12 entries in our MAP Center partnership log, which included date, time, length, and type of interaction (i.e., phone, video conference, face-to-face), people present, deep synthesis of discussion, and next steps, including person(s) responsible; (2) my detailed notes from each planning and KoP session and subsequent debriefing with SEA staff; (3) four MAP Center-created PowerPoints and other resources developed and/or provided by Seena and me; (4) SEA-developed artifacts used in the sessions and/or photos of the artifacts; (5) two 60-minute semistructured interviews, and related transcriptions, between me and Fiona, Caroline, and Korrine regarding their recollection of the nature and outcomes of the partnership; and (6) Fiona's, Caroline's, and Korrine's written responses to a set of my open-ended questions about the partnership and recollections of details and reactions to the partnership as a whole.

To analyze these data, I applied template codes aligned with the steps of expansive learning, including levels of contradictions that may emerge within expansive learning cycles. I also applied open codes, identifying key text relevant to the research questions across partnership artifacts, as well as Fiona's, Caroline's, and Korrine's written responses. I shared interview transcripts and preliminary data analysis, in which I paired key data with template and open codes in written narrative format, with Fiona, Caroline, and Korrine for member checking (Carspecken, 1996).

Three research questions informed data collection, analysis, and the organization of research findings:

1. What was SEA's initial object for the technical assistance partnership, and how did this expand over time?
2. In what ways did partnership activities mediate the expansion of the SEA's initial object, particularly related to equity concerns?
3. In what ways did SEA partners begin to select and develop practice improvements for students with disabilities at other marginalized identity intersections in connection with the partnership activities?

THE INITIAL OBJECT OF COLLECTING AND DISTRIBUTION OF "BEST PRACTICES": SEEKING "CRITICAL FRIENDS" TO LAYER EQUITY ON TECHNICAL ACONTEXTUAL SOLUTIONS

Understanding the process and impact of equity expansive technical assistance begins with examining the initial object of the partnership as defined by the partnering agency. I found that the driving object was to collect from LEA educators those practices believed to account for students' higher reading performance compared with statewide averages for students with disabilities, and then disseminate the practices to less effective teachers statewide. Yet, the request for the EAC to engage as "critical friends" signaled that embedded in this object was the desire to center equity, albeit through technical approaches, in these practices. This object remained relatively intact throughout the first

KoP session, which began with an SEA analyst's presentation on criteria that informed selection of participating schools. The analyst shared that students with disabilities scored over 1.1 standard deviations below nondisabled peers on state assessments. The process of selecting the initiative schools was based on analysis of 2006–2014 state reading scores. The analyst told educators the "good news: High-rank schools for students in specific disability categories show dramatic results in reading score gains. Cumulative effect by 8th grade can be equivalent to multiple extra years of instruction."

Next, a director of another USDOE/OSEP-funded technical assistance center, invited by the SEA to conduct a review of research on instructional and interventional best practices for improving reading performance for students with disabilities, overviewed several studies related to the reading skills framed by the National Reading Panel in 2000 (i.e., phonemic awareness; phonics; vocabulary development; reading fluency, including oral reading skills; reading comprehension strategies). Then, Caroline and Fiona introduced Seena and me to approximately 100 attendees, including SEA staff. Later during her first interview, Fiona explained the history of the EAC/SEA relationship, noting a long partnership with the EAC to support identification of root causes of and policies and practices to eliminate special education disproportionality:

> I understood technical assistance to be about providing "correct" or "compliant" answers to specific questions of a technical or legal nature with a power difference between the parties involved (one person/group has questions and one has answers).

This excerpt from Fiona's interview illustrates aspects of the object of the activity system at the start of the partnership: the EAC's technical consultation on equity.

ARTIFACTS AND CONTRADICTIONS EXPANDING THE INITIAL OBJECT OF ACTIVITY: "OH MY, WHAT ARE WE GOING TO DO NOW?"

The initial partnership object began to expand with Seena's and my introduction of the "critical friend address." This artifact and its relationship to the development of dilemmas, or primary contradictions in the partnership activity systems, led to the epistemic action of questioning by SEA participants. In our address, Seena and I described our roles as critical friends, which I defined in Chapter 4. Then, beginning to enact this role, we shared our "loving critiques" (Paris & Alim, 2014, p. 85) of the partnership goal, framed as three tensions: (1) competing views of reading versus literacy, (2) literacy for whom? and (3) literacy for what purposes? We asked the 100 attendees and SEA staff to reflect on three key questions: (1) What are the goals of literacy development within the state (2) How has literacy been used as a political tool that has both afforded and constrained social access and power historically, and in this state? and (3) What are individuals' and groups' reasons for becoming literate (Ladson-Billings, 1992)? We emphasized the need for such reflection considering a Willis and Harris (2000) quote, projected on a slide:

> Literacy learning and teaching has never been ideologically neutral or culturally unbiased. It has been a series of related political acts of ideological domination and conformity draped under a thin veil of paternalism. Through political acts, powerful elites have pressed others to adopt their points of view and disregard all others. (p. 78)

Next, we added cultural–historical context: Literacy has been withheld from people of color, with disabilities, and at these intersections. We asked everyone to consider the partnership goal in light of these histories and in response to patterns of systemic oppression in which students of color statewide continued to be disproportionally represented in special education despite a series of coordinated and technical supports provided by the SEA to disproportionate LEAs.

Soon thereafter, I introduced content on a slide adapted from Waitoller's and my 2016 (then in-press) manuscript in which we cross-pollinated elements of culturally sustaining pedagogies (Paris, 2012) with universal design for learning (Rose & Meyer, 2002):

> In a CSP/UDL cross-pollination, becoming an expert reader is the means by which students become engaged in literacy curricula that support their contribution to CSP's overarching goal: creation of a socially just world. That is, becoming literate positions students to examine and critique issues that affect them and their local and global communities. And with explicit attention to the intersection of dis/ability and other identity markers such as race, a major goal of a cross-pollinated UDL/CSP curriculum is to debunk and provide alternatives to sorting and tracking people within schools and society. (adapted from Waitoller & Thorius, 2016)

This excerpt, along with others from this article, would resurface later in the partnership as a secondary stimulus for resolving contradictions evoked by the critical friend address.

Primary Contradictions: "Oh My, What Are We Going to Do Now?"

Following our address, SEA staff led several rotating groups of educators to brainstorm and write on poster paper what the SEA framed as "belief statements" about reading instruction related to (a) high-quality instruction, (b) student–teacher relationships, (c) family and community involvement, and (d) school and instructional leadership. However, some LEA educators began to express tensions between the original initiative description and differences between the two technical assistance centers' addresses. Recalling this part of the first KoP session during a semistructured interview, Caroline reflected on this moment: "Right away, I thought, well, 'Oh my, what are we going to do now?'"

Primary Contradictions: Who Is Here and Who Is Not?

Another dilemma emerged related to clarifying with which students the initiative was concerned. A white educator noted that almost all invited educators were white. The educator referenced Seena's and my comments about racial disproportionality in special education and characterized the racial demographics of the room as "disappointing." This dilemma intensified regarding the KoP's focus on disability without acknowledgment of the relationship between student disability and race-based representation, and educational inequities statewide.

From Status Quo to a Need-State: Deepening Contradictions Toward New Conceptualizations of Literacy, for Whom, and for What Purposes?

Following the primary contradictions, a new contradiction began to emerge as partners engaged with artifacts that mediated en/counters with literacy as a sociocultural practice that could transform learning for students with disabilities and at the intersection of race. Deepening contradictions emerged between the status quo of determining promising technical practices versus context-rich explorations of literacy activities and meaning-making of students with disabilities, who in several LEAs were disproportionately students of color.

Reading the Word/Rewriting the World

Korrine pointed out in the second interview, "At times through the course of this project, I have felt that there have been tensions between internal workgroup members . . . primarily due to difference of opinion in practice and beliefs." Caroline recalled in the first interview:

> The first meeting . . . began with a presentation by someone from a TA Center other than the EAC. The lecture promoted a medical view of response to intervention and emphasized technical aspects of implementation, including technical adequacy of screening and progress monitoring tools, fidelity, and the scientific research base for interventions. The EAC engaged participants later in the meeting. Their view of literacy as a way to rewrite the world resonated with me; it was one of the first times I heard an organization from a special education

perspective talk about the transformative nature of literacy [rather than literacy as development of basic skills].

The introduction of critical literacy by the EAC was credited by Caroline with evoking tension between her own orientation to literacy and the way it had been emphasized in the SEA over time: a double bind.

Teaching and Testing/Seeking to Understand

Caroline's comment also indicated another contradiction that had begun to emerge and transform the object of the KoP. As it was formed, the initiative's goal was to increase reading skills measured by statewide assessments. Now, SEA administrators were questioning this goal and considering focused attention to the function of literacy as emancipatory and transformative practice. During a debrief following the second session, Caroline shared concerns with relying on academic data that do not "allow historically marginalized students to demonstrate what they know and are able to do." Korrine connected those concerns to the goal of improving reading scores: "The year we ran the data we shared with stakeholders . . . we had 15% of students with IEPs proficient or advanced on our statewide assessment. [That] is just not acceptable."

Caroline recalled during the semistructured interview:

> I thought what would happen was that people would come together at the first meeting and that—we had identified four buckets—we would bring people together into a single room and we would help them think about those buckets and how things they were changing in their schools or the things that they were doing in their schools fit into one or more of those buckets, and then they'd write up nice little summaries of their practice, and we'd capture some video and we'd put it together in a website or an e-course.

Korrine concurred, signaling how these contradictions were beginning to lead to doubts about the original object of the partnership.

Mediating the Development of New Criteria for Equitable Literacy Instruction With Students With Disabilities at the Intersection of Race

The intensity of tensions continued to grow as the SEA partners and participating educators engaged with artifacts that mediated new ways of understanding how student disability was being identified in schools, and how it was possible that reading instruction played a role. Artifacts included discussion of theoretical constructs drawn from DSE that challenged medical models of disabilities and reframed disproportionality through systemic and individual practices at the intersection of ableism and racism (Annamma et al., 2013). At this point, the object of the KoP began to expand toward deeper and intersectional equity concerns: from curating so-called best practices toward examining practices in light of identified contradictions and, in time, development of new criteria for determining the appropriateness of literacy instruction and intervention—with an intersectional focus on special education eligibility determination.

Before the second session, Seena and I debriefed with several SEA administrators about the lack of acknowledgment of racialized special education patterns and the educator's comment about the majority of invited LEA educators being white. SEA administrators began to question the initiative's relevance and struggled with whether to proceed with the initiative that had been conceived. Demonstrating their agency, they asked Seena and me to start session two by "re-grounding" the initiative. They asked that participants be guided to develop new belief statements about the functions, purposes, and desired outcomes of literacy instruction and supports for students with disabilities at the intersection of race, toward ensuring that students of color were experiencing responsive and relevant literacy instruction in ways that would prevent inappropriate referral to special education in high-incidence disability categories, particularly SLD.

Aggravating Contradictions in Literacy Conceptualizations and Approaches in the Context of Historical and Current Systemic Ableism and Racism

At the start of the next session, Seena and I facilitated critical learning and reflection on DSE's framing of disability and critical race theory, exploring the ways in which racism and ableism interact to create tensions participants would be motivated to resolve. For example, I made connections to special education's reliance on notions of intelligence and its distribution along a normal bell curve with roots in eugenics (Dudley-Marling & Gurn, 2010). Seena asked educators to consider promising practices for literacy instruction with these tensions in mind as the group shifted to an activity asking them to co-develop belief statements about literacy and the ways in which literacy should be approached through curriculum and instruction to sustain, respond to, and otherwise support students of color, even in the event that students had apparent learning or other reading-related disabilities.

In relation to these mediating artifacts, another double bind began to emerge, summarized by Caroline: "It became apparent there was a need for educators to reflect on their local experiences—school culture and personal beliefs around educating students of color and with IEPs—and for us to begin addressing some of the systemic barriers in schools." A growing number of SEA and LEA educators began to reconfigure the desired object of activity toward development of new models for literacy instruction and supports for students with disabilities, students of color, and students at these intersections.

After the conclusion of the second meeting, Seena and I remained with SEA administrators to process all that had been happening; we were all exhausted, but eager to engage. The SEA team grappled with what one administrator called a "bait-and-switch," and several administrators focused on one element of the first "critical friend" commentary—the CSP/UDL cross-pollination—(Waitoller & Thorius, 2016) as holding potential for a new way of framing literacy instruction that would allow educators to bring some existing practices into more critical and equity-focused, asset-based pedagogical approaches that could contribute to reversing disproportionality, as well as ensuring students with disabilities experienced strong literacy instruction.

Expanding the Object and Identifying Initial Solutions: Remediating Literacy to Disrupt Ableism and Racism

Seena and I had another call with Fiona and Caroline prior to session three. Having requested and read the preprint full text of Waitoller's and my (2016) CSP/UDL article, Caroline suggested starting the next session with educators reading and responding to excerpts. After our meeting, SEA administrators chose excerpts they thought would bring participants into contact with contradictions in the activity system. Again, exercising their agency, Fiona and Caroline rewrote an instructional vignette that appeared in the original article, using the original as a model, but writing theirs to illustrate cross-pollinations of UDL and CSP, tying their version to literacy and illustrating the expanding KoP object.

As participants entered session three, they read statements hung around the room excerpted from Waitoller's and my article. Seena asked participants to move around the room to stand or sit near one of the statements, and to engage in discussion on the following prompts with others who chose the same excerpt: (a) Why were you drawn to the statement? (b) What are the key points made by the authors? (c) What information, values, and experiences do you bring to your analysis of the statement? and (d) What questions, thoughts or feelings emerge for you after reading and discussing the statement? Korrine shared in a written reflection:

> [I experienced] key tensions in my understanding of the history of special education/disability studies and the tension of "normal"; fixing the student instead of fixing the system—the medical model of Special Ed (thinking . . . what are we doing??) This reinforced my discomfort with how we have framed Response to Intervention in our state: Wait to fail, intervene with something "separate," intensify "othering"—and it has been so resource heavy! We are all doing our own best work. We've always done that . . . and what have we gotten? I can't unknow what I know, and that is unsettling!

Responding to some of the tensions we heard as we walked around the room listening to the small-group conversations, next we facilitated a large-group discussion about new potential goals for the partnership and educators' own practice, as shown in Figure 7.1.

That afternoon, educators generated ideas about instructional practices guided by these considerations. At Caroline and Korrine's request, I presented more details about literacy instruction informed by a cross-pollination of UDL/CSP, and educators read and discussed a few more excerpts from the article. Over lunch and rather quickly, Seena and I developed a handout that would further support the educators' action given that many of these concepts were new and unsettling for them. I distill key aspects of the handout in Table 7.1.

Throughout the afternoon discussions, educators wrestled with ideas they had engaged over the past two and a half sessions, with some challenging others' suggestions of approaches like preferential seating, small-group "pull-out," and scripted phonics instruction. Yet some suggestions continued to reinforce the initial partnership object of documenting technical practices.

Notably, SEA administrators for the most part had determined that collecting ahistorical, acultural practices, which they had set as an initial

Figure 7.1. Re-Mediated Goals for Literacy Reflective of CSP/UDL Cross-Pollination (adapted from Waitoller & Thorius, 2016)

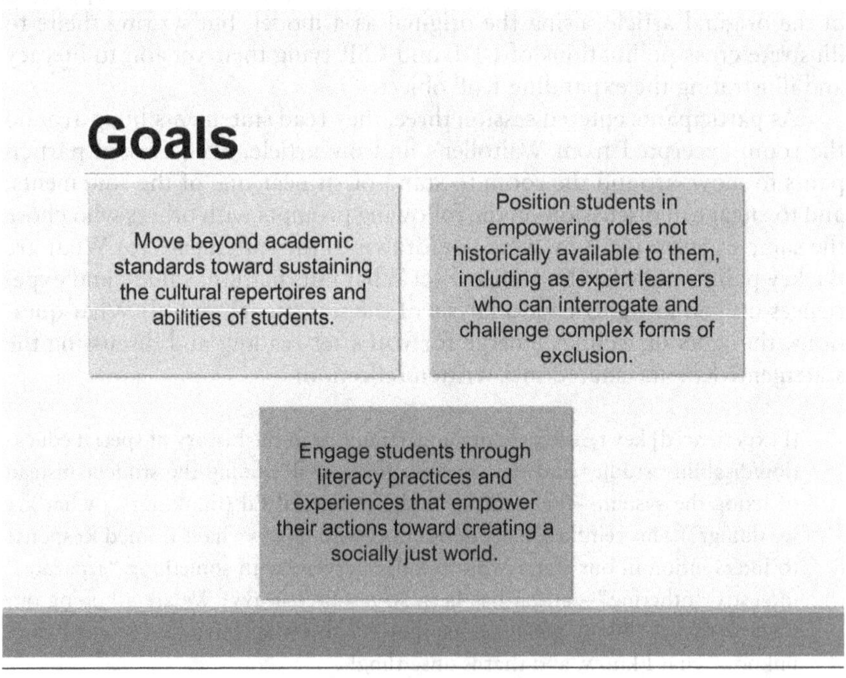

Goals

Move beyond academic standards toward sustaining the cultural repertoires and abilities of students.

Position students in empowering roles not historically available to them, including as expert learners who can interrogate and challenge complex forms of exclusion.

Engage students through literacy practices and experiences that empower their actions toward creating a socially just world.

Table 7.1. A Tool to Guide Educators' Critical Reflection on Culturally Sustaining, Universally Designed Literacy Approaches

Considerations	Critical Reflection Questions	Notes
Goal of Instruction	How do I establish students' ownership of literacy as the overarching goal of the curriculum, while maintaining systematic instruction in the cognitive processes of reading and writing?	
	How do I make literacy personally meaningful and useful for students' own purposes?	
Instructional Materials	How do I increase students' motivation to read, their appreciation and understanding of their own language and cultural heritage, and their valuing of their life experiences as literacy topics?	
Classroom Management and Interaction With Students	How do I create and adjust the classroom environment to allow for genuine literacy activities through which students can feel ownership and learn through collaboration and engage in conversations more like everyday talk rather than for classroom recitation?	
Relationship to the Community	How do I make stronger links to the community; restructure power relationships between school and community; and engage parents, families, and community members?	
Instructional Methods	How do I teach basic literacy skills within authentic, responsive, and culturally sustaining literacy activities?	
Assessment	How do I prepare and analyze my assessments prior to implementation in ways that would help reduce or eliminate sources of bias and more accurately reflect students' literacy knowledge?	

partnership goal, was no longer acceptable. Caroline recalled that at this point in the partnership she was centrally concerned with the need for "deep, critically reflexive thinking" and that the work to address inequities at the intersection of race and disability "should not be done in isolation, especially when we would like to see changes in systems that have historically marginalized groups of students."

MODELING NEW SOLUTIONS: FROM TECHNICAL STRATEGIES
TO TRANSFORMATIVE ASSET PEDAGOGIES

Over time, partners sought to generate *contextual* and *critical* solutions to literacy inequities, although some remained fixed on seeking *technical* solutions, despite a need to focus on all three of these domains simultaneously in teacher learning approaches focused on social justice and equity (Kozleski & Siuty, 2016). Following a fourth session in which educators continued to generate, critique, and expand approaches to engaging in literacy teaching and learning framed through a CSP/UDL cross-pollination, understandings of disability as a social construction, and manifestations of racism/ableism intersections in historical and current education and societal systems that manifested in disproportionality, the SEA extended and reformulated the KoP and began to test solutions to the expanded object of activity. I include excerpts from Caroline and Fiona's vignette to illustrate the new models for literacy that were emerging within the partnership.

> There are five 8th grade students in one of Ms. Zimmerman's classes, three of whom are African American males . . . with dis/abilities labels including specific learning disabilities, speech and language, and autism. All students participate in English language arts (ELA) with their grade-level peers in addition to reading intervention with Ms. Zimmerman. In ELA, students are learning to "determine a theme or central idea of a text and analyze its development over the course of the text" (ELA. RL.8.2). The ELA teacher models her thinking about theme while reading aloud excerpts from a young adult novel about the shooting of an African American teen by a white man in his community. The classroom teacher selected *How It Went Down* to provide students an opportunity to talk about a police involved shooting of a young African American male in their community, as well as similar incidents throughout the county. Students apply the thinking about theme that was modeled for the class to other contemporary young adult novels . . . Students are provided with varied levels of support (including technology) as they annotate texts to bring evidence of how the theme is developed to small group discussions about the text. Eventually, students will create an

argumentative piece (ELA.W.8.1) about teens and systemic violence. Students will select the format and audience for the argument . . . After discussion, Ms. Zimmerman collected five current informational texts in a variety of formats (article from the local newspaper, a piece from Buzz Feed, transcripts from a podcasts, and articles adapted by NEWSELA) . . . Ms. Zimmerman introduced the texts to students, and students voted on the three texts they wanted to study in upcoming classes . . . Students also discuss each text. Discussions focus on accurately understanding the article and applying the standard but also addressing some of the questions and concerns raised in the group's initial discussion of teens and systemic and police violence, connecting students' identities and struggles to reading and writing. Ms. Zimmerman also helps students make connections between informational texts read in intervention and literature read in ELA. Throughout the discussion, Ms. Zimmerman looks for ways to support students in discussing and critiquing oppression, power, and privilege . . . After reading and discussing the three articles and compiling questions . . . Students discuss their interests and concerns in individual conferences with Ms. Zimmerman and peers to solidify what they want to write about. As a large group and with support from Ms. Zimmerman, students brainstorm . . . audiences they might write for along with . . . format.

Thus, a new activity model for framing literacy instruction statewide in relation to the CSP/UDL cross-pollination was underway and led to SEA administrators developing and testing a statewide professional learning module to be made available to all state educators. The MAP Center continued to partner with them throughout this process, and new, connected partnership activity systems emerged, including revisiting the SEA's framing of MTSS and ways in which equity-centered models can support LEAs to prevent and reverse disproportionality. We continued to engage in this process, but with some distance to allow the agency to develop their own approaches to implementation, consolidation, and proliferation of the new model, the next step in a cycle of expansive learning.

The original partnership object had been re-mediated to plan for engaging educators in examining cultural forms such as disabling functions of curriculum in local schools, and disruption through professional development efforts informed by critical historical and current examination of oppression at the intersection of ability and race, and the appropriation of UDL/ CSP cross-pollination as a frame for organizing literacy instruction. This, not selecting acontextual, ahistorical reading interventions, is what was accomplished through the partnership, mediated through technical assistance that disrupted what initially was conceptualized as a compilation and distribution of information about reading instruction. Instead, educators en/countered the complexities of dismantling oppressive educational systems for students with disabilities at the intersection of race. They built understandings of literacy instruction as a political act of liberation, while engaging in messy, critical reflection on existing and historical contradictions between beliefs about literacy, students, and instructional practices within their system that appeared to be related to disproportionality, among other inequities.

CHAPTER 8

Ongoing Cycles and Continued Vigilance

As a result of ongoing cycles of equity expansive learning within our technical assistance partnerships with local and state education agencies, we have observed and been part of mediating several systemic shifts that have impacted quantitative and qualitative indicators of disproportionality. For example, we have seen educators counter local histories of deficit-based language used to describe students at the intersections of race and disability toward identity-affirming language. Within other partnerships, we have observed new practices become codified in the development of new processes and protocols that guide discussion of student capabilities and design of asset-based instruction as part of special education prereferral procedures, as in my 2016 research, which I excerpted in a previous chapter, and which deemphasized student "weaknesses" toward documenting both systemic and individual potentials for growth. Moreover, beyond observations within specific partnerships, the systemic nature of these impacts has been observed through annual partner interviews, postsession questionnaires, an annual Library of Congress survey administered by the USDOE, and annual in-depth case studies of selected partnerships, all part of our center's approach to program evaluation and continuous improvement.

There is not a one-size-fits-all approach to the re-mediation of racism/ableism in educational policies, practices, and belief systems, particularly as related to disproportionality. However, I hope to have demonstrated for the reader that the theory and practice of equity expansive technical assistance have moved us forward on the roadmap originally charted by NCCRESt and other state and national technical assistance centers seeking systemic solutions to addressing racial disproportionality in special education. Of central importance to this approach is the development of systemic solutions to race/disability-related educational injustices, which requires that educators en/counter the histories and status quo of racism and ableism in schools. These en/counters are mediated by artifacts like the ones I have described in this book, which when intentionally introduced, start by shifting conversations, and eventually practices, as partners work to confront their systemic contradictions. Mediating artifacts not only enhance existing structures, policies, and practices, but also contribute to emergent solutions stimulated by educators' and other stakeholders' expanded consciousness of the cultural–historical forces contributing to local inequities.

IMPLICATIONS OF THE APPROACH

Throughout this book, I have aimed to enrich technical assistance theory and research toward systemic change in education practices linked to inequities at the intersection of race and disability. I drew from CHAT and a theory of expansive learning to develop and introduce critical artifacts into the activity system of technical assistance partnerships that were situated within the cultural–historical context of education and special education service provision; historical and current goals and definitions of curriculum, instruction, and reading; and agencies' and educators' own histories of teaching and learning in relation to students with disabilities and students of color. I demonstrated how mediating artifacts can evoke contradictions for stakeholders in a system wherein technical practices are decontextualized from historical and current inequities inherent in education systems poorly designed to teach all students. It is my hope that readers will leverage the theory and practices I have described to inform intersectional technical assistance, professional development, and other partnerships that introduce and develop context-informed, capacity-building interventions and activities to remediate inequitable status quo policies, practice, and belief systems.

I suggest this approach is important for two reasons. First, a prevailing theory informing technical assistance and one that has shaped teacher education is implementation science, with its goal of developing generalizable knowledge that can be universally applied beyond individual systems of concern (Bauer et al., 2015). However, the reasons for which an organization seeks technical assistance are shaped by cultural, social, political, and historical ecologies wherein some students have not benefitted from the way things are. The application of equity expansive learning as a process within which technical assistance providers introduce critical contradiction-evoking and equity-focused artifacts accounts for and addresses these contexts. Second, the field of education has long centered on technical improvements to student or educator *skills*; what is meant by *intervention* is quite different from its meaning within expansive learning cycles. In the latter, *formative* intervention means that participants encounter "a problematic and contradictory object, embedded in their vital life activity agency" and that facilitates their own generation of new concepts they choose to enact "in other settings as frames for the design of locally appropriate new solutions" (Engeström, 2011, p. 606). Partnering agencies' original requests, even though concerned with students' and teachers' capacity development, are often about documenting and disseminating the first kind of interventions, yet even interventions that close such gaps on the surface run the risk of leaving systems intact: systems shaped by racism, ableism, and other intersecting oppressions.

The book provides lessons and concrete resources for the development of new processes and tools for the preparation of educators who are equipped to examine the sociopolitical contexts that surround their concerns with student performance, with emphasis on the remediation of deficit-thinking and disabling systems over the remediation of disabled youth at race and other identity intersections. These lessons may inform, for example, teacher preparation programs' inclusion of artifacts that mediate future educators' examination of the status quo, along with tensions about contextual factors that uphold inequities. Or, these lessons may inform the design of equity-focused professional development opportunities, more broadly. Future research might include studies in which multiple connected activity systems are considered in depth to explore processes and outcomes of equity expansive technical assistance.

I wrap up with an excerpt from a keynote address I gave in the middle of a 2-day professional learning session hosted by an SEA for districts identified as significantly disproportionate. For my remarks, I was asked by the SEA to comment on those sessions that had already occurred and to compel participants to stay engaged in the difficult work ahead.

What more can you do, what more can I do? As Principal Baruti Kefele asked us, asked himself this morning, what more can I do? We are here all here to address disproportionality. This means something similar and different for everyone here together today, shaped by who we are as individuals, members of groups, our collective and individual histories, and current contexts. For those districts that are newly identified as disproportionate, for those who are struggling to see this as something in their control, this question lies at the center of our commitment to be educators, shared Principal Kefele.

In one of the break-out sessions, Anthony Galloway and Dr. Patrick Duffy balanced Kefele's emphasis on adults' personal responsibilities to connect with students to their responsibility to work with students to become and systemically act as antiracists. Facilitating the creation of safe and sacred spaces with students to stimulate exchanges and understandings about race across student groups is central to this work and for redistributing the power of white adults to interracial, antiracist student groups in systems. Even for those with good intentions, like us in this room, unless we strive to work with students rather than on their behalf, in addressing disproportionality, we continue to reinforce a stratified system where people hold more and less power in relation to race, age, dis/ability, religion, ethnicity, and locale.

In doing this work alongside and to mediate students' development
and coming to know themselves, who they were, who they are, and
who they want to be—a theme that cut across Kefele's, Duffy's, and
Galloway's sessions—Wendell Wayku reminded us that knowing our
young people sometimes means that we must investigate ways in
which interactions that show up as "problems" in schools are ways of
expressing trauma. Drawing from notions of trauma-informed care,
it becomes incumbent on a system and the individuals within it to
shift dominant ways of pathologizing students as problems, instead
bringing restorative responses to problematic interactions and actions
into schools. Again, this understanding of students' lived experiences
as a theme continued throughout the day.

At the same time, what these sessions underscore for me is the necessity
of positioning students as critical examiners of how they have been
positioned—as raced, classed, dis/abled bodies and minds. Providing
them access to their test scores in comparison to other districts,
engaging in dialogue about race with other racially nondominant and
dominant students, as well as creating spaces responsive to student
trauma including trauma experienced and reproduced in our schools,
facilitate their roles in determining what is it about who we are that
needs to be acknowledged by adults in our schools and society, what
is it about how I/how we've been positioned that must be disrupted,
and what is it about me/about us that must be sustained through
education in and out of schools. Django Paris, H. Samy Alim, Terri
McCarty, Carol Lee, Gloria Ladson-Billings, and Bryan Brayboy's
work illustrates the importance of culturally sustaining pedagogies as
tools in these efforts. What Professor Brayboy shared with us today
especially highlights the roles students have in teaching us about all of
this and our relationships with students as a necessary condition for
this bidirectional teaching and learning to occur.

Simultaneously, today's sessions collectively call us to critically
examine our own roles in the positioning of students. Isn't that what
disproportionality is? How we physically and ideologically place
students? When we view disproportionality as an act of positioning
students as problematic at the intersection of racism and ableism, the
urgency in our purpose of being here becomes even more glaringly
apparent.

Which is why I am compelled to comment on some things I've
noticed, even here in this space, among us educators, and which
I fall into myself and have fallen into in my past life as a white
school psychologist. Of course, I'm still white. I just used to be a

school psychologist. But the point is, that even gendered, even raced bodies actively and unintentionally distance themselves, ourselves from disability. We still largely buy into the notion that disability is a pathology, as many of us seek to eradicate color "blindness." And we still use special education as a way to sort, separate, and segregate students with disabilities because of the pathological, medical, diagnostic ways we talk about dis/ability in schools. Rather, if disability was dominantly viewed as another form of difference, and this difference was seen as an asset, what would this mean for disproportionality? It's the meaning most commonly assigned to disability in schools and society as the heart of the problem.

As I talked about in my address yesterday morning, a relationship between racism and ableism in the United States continues to be evident in U.S. education policy and practice. Disproportionality is one such way this relationship plays out. As Waitoller and I have discussed, intertwined scientific, political, and economic purposes historically have solidified the relationship between racism and ableism, and simultaneously dis/abled race and racialized dis/ability. At a similar intersection, what Leonardo and Broderick call the relationship between whiteness and smartness, white students continue to be taught their intellectual superiority, and students of color, including Native students, their inferiority, in our schools. This is further aggravated by how whiteness and smartness function as property enjoyed by and that benefits those who own it and which blocks others from such privileges and rights, as Zeus Leonardo and Alicia Broderick propose (2011).

As we go into the afternoon, and back to our local contexts, I'd like to ask us all to reflect on the intellectual and physical resources we've collected today as tools in a comprehensive inclusive education project that aims to eradicate disproportionality and that also seeks to create alternatives to a system that allows us to sort students by all the stratifications we are so good at using and recreating: "intensive," "strategic," "at benchmark," and "exceeding," at-risk, vulnerable, special needs, EBD. This project, drawing from Fraser, Waitoller's, and my own work, is about a continuous struggle toward (a) the redistribution of quality opportunities to learn and participate in educational programs [the redistribution dimension], (b) the recognition and value of differences as reflected in content, pedagogy, and assessment tools [the recognition dimension], and (c) the opportunities for marginalized groups to represent themselves in decision-making processes that advance and define claims of exclusion and the respective solutions that affect their children's

educational futures [the representation dimension]. (Waitoller &
Kozleski, 2013, p. 35)

By knowing ourselves, knowing our students, and creating conditions
for students and ourselves to critically examine positioning in schools
and society, we are well on our way. And we at the Great Lakes
Equity Center, all of our presenters, this SEA's staff, families and
students in districts, schools, and our communities, and indeed, all of
us, are on this journey together.

References

Acevedo, S. M., & Roscigno, R. (2022). Smooth and striated spaces: Autistic (Ill) legibility as a deterritorializing force. In F. R. Waitoller & K. A. K. Thorius (Eds.), *Sustaining disabled youth: Centering disability in asset pedagogies* (pp. 31–45). Teachers College Press.

Ahram, R., Fergus, E., & Noguera, P. (2011). Addressing racial/ethnic disproportionality in special education: Case studies of suburban school districts. *Teachers College Record, 113*(10), 2233–2266.

Albrecht, S. F., Skiba, R. J., Losen, D. J., Chung, C. G., & Middelberg, L. (2011). Federal policy on disproportionality in special education: Is it moving us forward? *Journal of Disability Policy Studies, 23*(1), 14–25.

Algozzine, B. (2017). Toward an acceptable definition of emotional disturbance: Waiting for the change. *Behavioral Disorders, 42*(3), 136–144.

Algozzine, B., & Ysseldyke, J. E. (1981). Special education services for normal children: Better safe than sorry? *Exceptional Children, 48*, 238–243.

Algozzine, B., & Ysseldyke, J. (1983). Learning disabilities as a subset of school failure: The over-sophistication of a concept. *Exceptional Children, 50*(3), 242–246.

Allison, M., & Kaye, J. (2005). *Strategic planning for nonprofit organizations: A practical guide and workbook.* Wiley.

American Civil Liberties Union. (2018). *ACLU comments on IDEA equity compliance delay.* Author. https://www.aclu.org/letter/aclu-comments-equity-idea-compliance-delay

American Psychological Association. (2006). Evidence-based practice in psychology. *American Psychologist, 61*(4), 271–285. https://doi.org/10.1037/0003-066X.61.4.271

Amos, Y. T. (2011). Teacher dispositions for cultural competence: How should we prepare white teacher candidates for moral responsibility? *Action in Teacher Education, 33*(5–6), 481–492.

Annamma, S. A. (2015). Whiteness as property: Innocence and ability in teacher education. *The Urban Review, 47*(2), 293–316.

Annamma, S. A., Connor, D., & Ferri, B. (2013). Dis/ability critical race studies (DisCrit): Theorizing at the intersections of race and dis/ability. *Race Ethnicity and Education, 16*(1), 1–31.

Aronson, B., & Laughter, J. (2015). The theory and practice of culturally relevant education: A synthesis of research across content areas. *Review of Educational Research, 86*(1), 1–44. doi: 10.3102/0034654315582066

Artiles, A. J. (1998). The dilemma of difference: Enriching the disproportionality discourse with theory and context. *The Journal of Special Education, 32*, 32–36.

Artiles, A. J. (2003). Special education's changing identity: Paradoxes and dilemmas in views of culture and space. *Harvard Educational Review, 73*, 164–202.

Artiles, A. J. (2009). Re-framing disproportionality research: Outline of a cultural-historical paradigm. *Multiple Voices for Ethnically Diverse Exceptional Learners, 11*(2), 24–37.

Artiles, A. J., Bal, A., & Thorius, K. A. K. (2010). Back to the future: A critique of response to intervention's social justice views. *Theory Into Practice, 49*(4), 250–257.

Artiles, A. J., & Dyson, A. (2005). Inclusive education in the globalization age: The promise of comparative cultural historical analysis. In D. Mitchell (Ed.), *Contextualizing inclusive education* (pp. 37–62). Routledge.

Artiles, A. J., Kozleski, E. B., Trent, S. C., Osher, D., & Ortiz, A. (2010). Justifying and explaining disproportionality, 1968–2008: A critique of underlying views of culture. *Exceptional Children, 76*(3), 279–299.

Artiles, A. J., Trent, S. C., & Kuan, L. A. (1997). Learning disabilities research on ethnic minority students: An analysis of 22 years of studies published in selected refereed journals. *Learning Disabilities Research & Practice, 12*, 82–91.

Atwood, E., & López, G. R. (2014). Let's be critically honest: Towards a messier counterstory in critical race theory. *International Journal of Qualitative Studies in Education, 27*(9), 1134–1154.

Baglieri, S., Valle, J. W., Connor, D. J., & Gallagher, D. J. (2011). Disability studies in education: The need for a plurality of perspectives on disability. *Remedial and Special Education, 32*(4), 267–278.

Bal, A., Afacan, K., & Cakir, H. I. (2018). Culturally responsive school discipline: Implementing learning lab at a high school for systemic transformation. *American Educational Research Journal, 55*(5), 1007–1050.

Bal, A., Betters-Bubon, J., & Fish, R. E. (2019). A multilevel analysis of statewide disproportionality in exclusionary discipline and the identification of emotional disturbance. *Education and Urban Society, 51*(2), 247–268.

Bal, A., Kozleski, E. B., Schrader, E. M., Rodriguez, E. M., & Pelton, S. (2014). Systemic transformation from the ground-up: Using learning lab to design culturally responsive schoolwide positive behavioral supports. *Remedial and Special Education, 35*(6), 327–339. https://doi.org/10.1177/0741932514536995

Bal, A., Thorius, K.A.K., & Kozleski, E. B. (2012). Culturally responsive positive behavior interventions and supports. *What Matters Series*. Equity Alliance at ASU.

Barter, C., & Reynold, E. (1999). The use of vignettes in qualitative research. *Social Research Update, 25*(9), 1–6.

Batiibwe, M. S. K. (2019). Using cultural historical activity theory to understand how emerging technologies can mediate teaching and learning in a mathematics classroom: A review of literature. *Research and Practice in Technology Enhanced Learning, 14*(1), 1–20.

Bauer, M. S., Damschroder, L., Hagedorn, H., Smith, J., & Kilbourne, A. M. (2015). An introduction to implementation science for the non-specialist. *BMC Psychology, 3*(1), 1–12.

Bauer, M. S., & Kirchner, J. (2020). Implementation science: What is it and why should I care? *Psychiatry Research, 283*, 1–6.

Becker, S. P., Paternite, C. E., & Evans, S. W. (2014). Special educators' conceptualizations of emotional disturbance and educational placement decision making for middle and high school students. *School Mental Health, 6*(3), 163–174.

Bell, D. A. (1980). *Brown v. Board of Education* and the interest-convergence dilemma. *Harvard Law Review, 93*, 518–533.

Bell, D. A. (1992). *Faces at the bottom of the well: The permanence of racism.* Basic Books.

Bell, D. A. (1995). Who's afraid of critical race theory. *University of Illinois Law Review,* 893–910.

Bergerson, A. A. (2003). Critical race theory and white racism: Is there room for white scholars in fighting racism in education?. *International Journal of Qualitative Studies in Education, 16*(1), 51–63.

Berliner, D. C. (2002). Educational research: The hardest science of all. *Educational Researcher, 31*(8), 18–20. https://doi.org/10.3102/0013189X031008018

Blase, K. (2009). *Technical assistance to promote service and system change. Roadmap to effective intervention practices* #4. University of South Florida, Technical Assistance Center on Social Emotional Intervention for Young Children.

Boccio, D. E., Weisz, G., & Lefkowitz, R. (2016). Administrative pressure to practice unethically and burnout within the profession of school psychology. *Psychology in the Schools, 53*(6), 659–672.

Bonilla-Silva, E. (2006). *Racism without racists: Color-blind racism and the persistence of racial inequality in America.* Rowman & Littlefield.

Bradley-Johnson, S., Johnson, C. M., & Jacob-Timm, S. (1995). Where will—and where should—changes in education leave school psychology? *Journal of School Psychology, 33*, 187–200.

Brayboy, B. M. J., Castagno, A. E., & Maughan, E. (2007). Equality and justice for all? Examining race in education scholarship. *Review of Research in Education, 31*, 159–194.

Brookfield, S. D. (2005). *The power of critical theory for adult learning and teaching.* Open University Press.

Brooks, J. S., & Miles, M. T. (2010). Educational leadership and the shaping of school culture: Classic concepts and cutting-edge possibilities. In S. D. Horsford (Ed.), *New perspectives in educational leadership* (pp. 7–28). Peter Lang.

Brooks, J. S., & Witherspoon Arnold, N. (Eds.). (2013). *Anti-racist school leadership: Toward equity in education for America's students.* Information Age Publishers.

Brown v. Board of Education of Topeka, 347 U.S. 483 (1954).

Buras, K. L. (2011). Race, charter schools, and conscious capitalism: On the spatial politics of whiteness as property (and the unconscionable assault on Black New Orleans). *Harvard Educational Review, 81*(2), 296–331.

Calabrese Barton, A., & Tan, E. (2019). Designing for rightful presence in STEM: Community ethnography as pedagogy as an equity-oriented design approach. *Journal of the Learning Sciences, 28*(4–5), 616–658. doi:10.1080/10508406.2019.1591411

Calabrese Barton, A., & Tan, E. (2020). Beyond equity as inclusion: A framework of "rightful presence" for guiding justice-oriented studies in teaching and learning. *Educational Researcher, 49*(6), 433–440. https://doi.org/10.3102/0013189X20927363

Cardona, M. (2022). *Statement from U.S. Secretary of Education Miguel Cardona on "Don't Say Gay" law going into effect today*. https://www.ed.gov/news/press -releases/statement-us-secretary-education-miguel-cardona-dont-say-gay-law -going-effect-today

Carspecken, P. (1996). *Critical ethnography in educational research: A theoretical and practical guide*. Routledge.

Castagno, A. E. (2009). Commonsense understandings of equality and social change: A critical race theory analysis of liberalism at Spruce Middle School. *International Journal of Qualitative Studies in Education, 22*(6), 755–768.

Cavendish, W., Artiles, A. J., & Harry, B. (2014). Tracking inequality 60 years after *Brown*: Does policy legitimize the racialization of disability? *Multiple Voices for Ethnically Diverse Exceptional Learners, 14*(2), 30–40.

Charlton, J. I. (2006). The dimensions of disability oppression: An overview. In L. J. Davis (Ed.), *The disability studies reader* (2nd edition) (pp. 217–227). Routledge.

Chen, K. S., Rogers, J., Le Sesne, J., Bangert, S., Whiteman, R., Skelton, S. M., & Thorius, K. A. K. (2014). Maximizing school improvement efforts through technical assistance. *Equity Dispatch* [Newsletter]. Great Lakes Equity Center.

Chinman, M., Hunter, S. B., Ebener, P., Paddock, S. M., Stillman, L., Imm, P., & Wandersman, A. (2008). The getting to outcomes demonstration and evaluation: An illustration of the prevention support system. *American Journal of Community Psychology, 41*, 206–224.

Clancy, C. (2006). The $1.6 trillion question: If we're spending so much on healthcare, why so little improvement in quality? *Medscape General Medicine, 8*(2), 58.

Cohen, A. M., Stavri, P. Z., & Hersh, W. R. (2004). A categorization and analysis of the criticisms of evidence based medicine. *International Journal of Medical Informatics, 73*(1), 35–43. https://doi.org/10.1016/j.ijmedinf.2003.11.002

Cohen, D. R., Burns, M. K., Riley-Tillman, C., & Hosp, J. L. (2015). Are minority students under-or overrepresented in special education? *NASP Communiqué, 44*(2), 22–23.

Cole, M. (1996). *Cultural psychology: A once and future discipline*. Harvard University Press.

Cole, M., & Engeström, Y. (1993). A cultural-historical approach to distributed cognition. In G. Salomon (Ed.), *Distributed cognitions: Psychological and educational considerations* (pp. 1–46). Cambridge University Press.

Collins, P. H. (2015). Intersectionality's definitional dilemmas. *Annual Review of Sociology, 41*, 1–20.

Connor, D. J., Cavendish, W., Gonzalez, T., & Jean-Pierre, P. (2019). Is a bridge even possible over troubled waters? The field of special education negates the overrepresentation of minority students: A DisCrit analysis. *Race, Ethnicity, and Education, 22*, 723–745. https://doi.org/10.1080/13613324.2019.1599343

Connor, D. J., Gabel, S. L., Gallagher, D. J., & Morton, M. (2008). Disability studies and inclusive education—implications for theory, research, and practice. *International Journal of Inclusive Education, 12*(5–6), 441–457. https://doi.org/10 .1080/13603110802377482

Cook, B. G., Collins, L. W., Cook, S. C., & Cook, L. (2020). Evidence-based reviews: How evidence-based practices are systematically identified. *Learning Disabilities Research & Practice, 35*(1), 6–13. https://doi.org/10.1111/ldrp.12213

Cook, B. G., & Odom, S. L. (2013). Evidence-based practices and implementation science in special education. *Exceptional Children, 79*(2), 135–144.

Cook, B. G., Tankersley, M., & Landrum, T. J. (2009). Determining evidence-based practices in special education. *Exceptional Children, 75*(3), 365–383.

Cook, D. A., & Dixson, A. D. (2013). Writing critical race theory and method: A composite counterstory on the experiences of Black teachers in New Orleans post-Katrina. *International Journal of Qualitative Studies in Education, 26,* 1358–1258. https://doi.org/10.1080/09518398.2012.731531

Coomer, M. N., Pearce, N., Dagli, C., Skelton, S. M., & Thorius, K. A. K. (2017a). The legacy of civil rights in the Every Student Succeeds Act. *Equity Dispatch* [Newsletter]. Great Lakes Equity Center.

Coomer, M. N., Skelton, S. M., Kyser, T. S., Warren, C., & Thorius, K. A. K. (2017b). *Assessing bias in standards and curricular materials.* [Equity tool]. Great Lakes Equity Center.

Crabtree, B. F., & Miller, W. L. (1992). A template approach to text analysis: Developing and using codebooks. In B. F. Crabtree & W. L. Miller (Eds.), *Doing qualitative research* (pp. 93–109). SAGE.

Crandall, D. P., Bauchner, J. E., Loucks, S. F., & Schmidt, W. H. (1982). *Models of the school improvement process: Factors contributing to success. A study of dissemination efforts supporting school improvement.* The Network.

Crenshaw, K. W. (1989). Demarginalizing the intersection of race and sex: A Black feminist critique of antidiscrimination doctrine, feminist theory and antiracist politics. *University of Chicago Legal Forum, 189,* 139–167.

Crenshaw, K. W. (1991). Mapping the margins: Intersectionality, identity politics, and violence against women of color. *Stanford Law Review, 46,* 1241–1299.

Cruz, R. A., & Rodl, J. E. (2018). An integrative synthesis of literature on disproportionality in special education. *The Journal of Special Education, 52*(1), 50–63. https://doi.org/10.1177/0022466918758707

Currie, J. (1996). *Reflection in action: School reform and professional learning through collaborative inquiry. A portrayal evaluation of the innovative links project for teacher professional development.* Murdoch University.

Danforth, S., Taff, S., & Ferguson, P. M. (2006). Place, profession, and program in the history of special education curriculum. In E. Brantlinger (Ed.), *Who benefits from special education? Remediating (fixing) other people's children* (pp. 1–25). Routledge.

Daniels, H. (2010). The mutual shaping of human action and institutional settings: A study of the transformation of children's services and professional work. *British Journal of Sociology of Education, 31*(4), 377–393.

Darden, E. C., & Cavendish, E. (2012). Achieving resource equity within a single school district: Erasing the opportunity gap by examining school board decisions. *Education and Urban Society, 44,* 61–82. doi:10.1177/00131245103 80912

Datnow, A., & Stringfield, S. (2000). Working together for reliable school reform. *Journal of Education for Students Placed at Risk (JESPAR), 5*(1–2), 183–204.

Davis, L. J. (1997). Constructing normalcy: The bell curve, the novel, and the invention of the disabled body in the nineteenth century. In L. J. Davis (Ed.), *The disability studies reader* (pp. 9–28). Routledge.

Dawson, L. J., & Quinn, R. (2000). Clarifying board and superintendent roles. *School Administrator, 57*(3), 12–19.

DeCuir, J. T., & Dixson, A. D. (2004). "So when it comes out, they aren't that surprised that it is there": Using critical race theory as a tool of analysis of race and racism in education. *Educational Researcher, 33*(5), 26–31.

Delgado, R. (1989). Storytelling for oppositionists and others: A plea for narrative. *Michigan Law Review, 87*(8), 2411–2441.

Delgado, R. (2002). White interests and civil rights realism: Rodrigo's bittersweet epiphany. *Michigan Law Review, 101*(5), 1201–1224. https://doi.org/10.2307/3595374

Delgado, R., & Stefancic, J. (2012). *Critical race theory: An introduction* (2nd ed.). New York University Press.

Delgado, R., & Stefancic, J. (2017). *Critical race theory: An introduction* (3rd ed.). New York University Press.

Delpit, L. (1988). The silenced dialogue: Power and pedagogy in educating other people's children. *Harvard Educational Review, 58*, 280–299.

Denzin, N. K. (2012). Triangulation 2.0. *Journal of Mixed Methods Research, 6*(2), 80–88.

DiAngelo, R. (2011). White fragility. *International Journal of Critical Pedagogy, 3*(3), 54–70. Retrieved from http://libjournal.uncg.edu/ijcp/article/view/249/116

Diem, S. (2017). A critical policy analysis of the politics, design, and implementation of student assignment policies. In M. Young & S. Diem (Eds.), *Critical approaches to education policy analysis* (pp. 43–62). Springer.

Diem, S., & Pinto, R. (2017). Promoting racial and socioeconomic integration in public schools. *Equity by Design* [Research brief]. Midwest & Plains Equity Assistance Center.

Donnor, J. (2013). Education as the property of whites: African Americans' continued quest for good schools. In M. Lynn & A. Dixson (Eds.), *Handbook of critical race theory in education* (pp. 195–203). Routledge.

Donovan, S., & Cross, C. (2002). *Minority students in special and gifted education*. National Academy Press.

Dudley-Marling, C., & Gurn, A. (Eds.). (2010). *The myth of the normal curve*. Peter Lang.

Duncan, A. (2014, July 7). Letter to chief state school officers regarding state educator equity plans. Retrieved from http://www2.ed.gov/policy/elsec/guid/secletter/140707.html

Dunn, L. (1968). Special education for the mildly retarded: Is much of it justifiable? *Exceptional Children, 35*, 5–22.

Ellis, V., Edwards, A., & Smagorinsky, P. (Eds.). (2010). *Cultural historical perspectives on teacher education and development*. Routledge.

Engeström, Y. (1987). *Learning by expanding: An activity-theoretical approach to developmental work*. Orienta Konsultit.

Engeström, Y. (1999). Communication, discourse and activity. *Communication Review, 3*, 165–185.

Engeström, Y. (2001). Expansive learning at work: Toward an activity theoretical reconceptualization. *Journal of Education and Work, 14*(1), 133–156.

Engeström, Y. (2011). From design experiments to formative interventions. *Theory & Psychology, 21*(5), 598–628.

Engeström, Y., & Miettinen, R. (1999). Introduction. In R. L. Punamäki, R. Miettinen, & Y. Engeström (Eds.), *Perspectives on activity theory* (pp. 1–16). Cambridge University Press.

Engeström, Y., & Sannino, A. (2010). Studies of expansive learning: Foundations, findings and future challenges. *Educational Research Review, 5*(1), 1–24. https://doi.org/10.1016/j.edurev.2009.12.002

Engeström, Y., & Sannino, A. (2011). Discursive manifestations of contradictions in organizational change efforts. *Journal of Organizational Change Management, 24*(3), 368–387. https://doi.org/10.1108/09534811111132758

Engeström, Y., & Sannino, A. (2021). From mediated actions to heterogenous coalitions: Four generations of activity-theoretical studies of work and learning. *Mind, Culture, and Activity, 28*(1), 4–23.

Engeström, Y., Sannino, A., & Virkkunen, J. (2014). On the methodological demands of formative interventions. *Mind, Culture, and Activity, 21*(2), 118–128.

Engeström, Y., Virkkunen, J., Helle, M., Pihlaja, J., & Poikela, R. (1996). The change laboratory as a tool for transforming work. *Life Long Learning in Europe, 2,* 10–17.

England, K.V.L. (1994). Getting personal: Reflexivity, positionality, and feminist research. *The Professional Geographer, 46*(1), 80–89.

Erevelles, N. (2014). Crippin' Jim Crow: Disability, dis-location, and the school-to-prison pipeline. In L. Ben-Moshe, C. Chapman, & A. C. Carey (Eds.), *Disability incarcerated: Imprisonment and disability in the United States and Canada* (pp. 81–100). Palgrave Macmillan. https://doi.org/10.1057/9781137388476_5

Erickson, F. (2001). Culture in society and in educational practices. In J. Banks & C. M. Banks (Eds.), *Multicultural education: Issues and perspectives* (pp. 31–58). Wiley.

Erickson, F., & Gutiérrez, K. (2002). *Culture, rigor, and science in educational research. Educational Researcher, 31*(8), 21–24. https://doi.org/10.3102/0013189X031008021

Escamilla, K., Hopewell, S., Butvilofsky, S., Sparrow, W., Soltero-González, L., Ruiz-Figueroa, O., & Escamilla, M. (2014). *Biliteracy from the start: Literacy squared in action.* Caslon.

Every Student Succeeds Act, 20 U.S.C. § 6301 (2015). https://www.congress.gov/114/plaws/publ95/PLAW-114publ95.pdf

Exec. Order No. 13950, 85 Fed. Reg. 60683 3 C.F.R. (September 22, 2020). https://trumpwhitehouse.archives.gov/presidential-actions/executive-order-combating-race-sex-stereotyping/

Faculty of the Indiana University School of Education–IUPUI (2021). *Statement in support of antiracist education and research.* Retrieved from https://education.iupui.edu/about/statements/iupui-school-of-education-statement-on-antiracism.pdf

Fergus, E. (2017). The integration project among white teachers and racial/ethnic minority youth: Understanding bias in school practice. *Theory Into Practice, 56*(3), 169–177.

Ferguson, D. L., Kozleski, E. B., & Smith, A. (2003). *Transformed, inclusive schools: A framework to guide fundamental change in urban schools.* National Institute for Urban School Improvement.

Ferguson, P. M. (2008). The doubting dance: Contributions to a history of parent/professional interactions in early 20th century America. *Research and Practice for Persons with Severe Disabilities, 33*(1–2), 48–58.

Ferri, B. A., & Connor, D. J. (2005). Tools of exclusion: Race, disability, and (re) segregated education. *Teachers College Record, 107*(3), 453–474.

Figlio, D. N., & Getzler, L. S. (2002). *Accountability, ability and disability: Gaming the system*. National Bureau of Economic Research. https://www.nber.org/papers/w9307

Finkelstein, V. (1980). *Attitudes and disabled people*. World Rehabilitation Fund.

Fish, R. E. (2017). The racialized construction of exceptionality: Experimental evidence of race/ethnicity effects on teachers' interventions. *Social Science Research, 62*, 317–334.

Fixsen, D. L., & Blase, K. A. (2009). Technical assistance in special education: Past, present, and future. *Topics in Early Childhood Special Education, 29*(1), 62–64.

Fixsen, D. L., Blase, K., Metz, A., & Van Dyke, M. (2013). Statewide implementation of evidence-based programs. *Exceptional Children, 79*(2), 213–230.

Fixsen, D. L., Naoom, S. F., Blase, K. A., Friedman, R. M., & Wallace, F. (2005). *Implementation research: A synthesis of the literature*. University of South Florida, Louis de la Parte Florida Mental Health Institute, The National Implementation Research Network (FMHI Publication No. 231). http://www.fpg.unc.edu/~nirn/resources/publications/Monograph/pdf/Monograph_full.pdf

Flick, U. (2002). *An introduction to qualitative research* (2nd ed.). SAGE.

Flick, U. (2007). *Designing qualitative research*. SAGE.

Foot, K., & Groleau, C. (2011). Contradictions, transitions, and materiality in organizing processes: An activity theory perspective. *First Monday, 16*(6), 1–18.

Forber-Pratt, A. J., Lyew, D. A., Mueller, C., & Samples, L. B. (2017). Disability identity development: A systematic review of the literature. *Rehabilitation Psychology, 62*(2), 198.

Fraser, N. (2008). *Scales of justice: Reimagining political space in a globalizing world*. Polity Press.

Freire, P. (1970). Cultural action and conscientization. *Harvard Educational Review, 40*(3), 452–477.

Freire, P. (1998). *Pedagogy of freedom: Ethics, democracy, and civic courage* (P. Clarke, Trans.). Rowman & Littlefield.

Freire, P. (2000). *Pedagogy of the oppressed*. Continuum.

Fuchs, C. (2011). *Foundations of critical media and information studies*. Routledge.

Fuchs, D., & Fuchs, L. S. (2006). Introduction to response to intervention: What, why, and how valid is it? *Reading Research Quarterly, 41*(1), 93–99.

Fullan, M. G., & Miles, M. B. (1992). Getting reform right: What works and what doesn't. *Phi Delta Kappan, 73*(10), 745–752.

Fullan, M. G. (with Stiegelbauer, S.). (1991). *The new meaning of educational change*. Teachers College Press.

Gabel, S. L., Curcic, S., Powell, J. J., Khader, K., & Albee, L. (2009). Migration and ethnic group disproportionality in special education: An exploratory study. *Disability & Society, 24*(5), 625–639.

Galston, W. A., & Davis, K. (2014). *21st century federalism: Proposals for reform*. Center for Effective Public Management at Brookings. https://www.brookings.edu/wp-content/uploads/2016/06/Galston_Davis_21st-Century-Federalism.pdf

Gamoran, A., & Dibner, K. (Eds.). (2022). *The future of education research at IES: Advancing an equity-oriented science*. The National Academies Press. https://doi.org/10.17226/26428

Garcia, S. B., & Ortiz, A. A. (2004). *Preventing disproportionate representation: Culturally and linguistically responsive prereferral interventions.* National Center for Culturally Responsive Educational Systems.

Gay, G. (2010). *Culturally responsive teaching: Theory, research, practice.* Teachers College Press.

Giffin, J., Lachlan, L., LaTurner, J., & LeVangie, S. (2021). *Generating solutions to COVID-specific educator shortages: A synthesis of insights from a cross-state collaborative.* Region 1 Comprehensive Center.

Givens, V., Ellison, S., Hernández-Saca, D. I., Levingston, J., Mabry, C., Patch Marietta, A., Powell, S., Thompson, K., & Young, J. (2022). *Creating brave spaces for community voices in the fight for race and disability-based justice in special education* [Vodcast]. Midwest and Plains Equity Assistance Center.

Goldberg, D. L. (2014). Racism, the social determinants of health, and health inequities among Black Americans. *Journal of Black Masculinity, 2,* 59–83.

González, T., & Artiles, A. J. (2020). Wrestling with the paradoxes of equity: A cultural-historical reframing of technical assistance interventions. *Multiple Voices: Disability, Race, and Language Intersections in Special Education, 20*(1), 5–15.

Gordon, N. (2017). *Race, poverty, and interpreting overrepresentation in special education.* Brookings Institution. https://www.brookings.edu/research/race-poverty-and-interpreting-overrepresentation-in-special-education/

Government Accountability Office (2013). *Individuals With Disabilities Education Act: Standards needed to improve identification of racial and ethnic over-representation in special education* (GAO 13–137). Author.

Great Lakes Equity Center. (2012). Educational equity. *Equity Dispatch* [Newsletter]. Author. https://greatlakesequity.org/resource/equity-dispatch-classic-edition-educational-equity

Great Lakes Equity Center. (2015). *Equitable distribution of effective educators: Systems analysis tool.* https://greatlakesequity.org/resource/equitable-distribution-effective-educators-systems-analysis-tool

Great Lakes Equity Center. (2016a, September). *Centering equity in curricular and instructional practices: Using universal design for learning and culturally sustaining pedagogy.* Annual Equity Leaders Institute, Indianapolis, IN.

Great Lakes Equity Center. (2016b). *Understanding of institutional racism scale concept framework.* Author.

Great Lakes Equity Center. (2016c). *Policy equity analysis toolkit.* Author. https://greatlakesequity.org/resource/policy-equity-analysis-toolkit-0

Great Lakes Equity Center. (2018). *Engaging in critical collaborative inquiry.* Author.

Greenhalgh, T., Robert, G., MacFarlane, F., Bate, P., & Kyriakidou, O. (2004). Diffusion of innovations in service organizations: Systematic review and recommendations. *The Milbank Quarterly, 82,* 581–629. http://dx.doi.org/10.1111/j.0887-378X.2004.00325.x

Grissom, J. A. (2014). Is discord detrimental? Using institutional variation to identify the impact of public governing board conflict on outcomes. *Journal of Public Administration Research and Theory, 24*(2), 289–315.

Guarino, C. M., Santibañez, L., & Daley, G. A. (2006). Teacher recruitment and retention: A review of the recent empirical literature. *Review of Educational Research, 76*(2), 173–208.

Guskey, T. R., & Huberman, M. (1995). *Professional development in education: New paradigms and practices.* Teachers College Press.

Guyatt, G., Cairns, J., Churchill, D., Cook, C., Haynes, B., Hirsh, J., Irvine, J. Levine, M., Levine, M., Nishikawa, J., Sackett, D., Brill-Edwards, P., Gerstein, H., Gibson, J., Jaeschke, R., Kerigan, A., Neville, A., Panju, A., Detsky, A., . . . Tugwell, P. (1992). Evidence-based medicine: A new approach to teaching the practice of medicine. *JAMA, 268*(17), 2420–2425. https://doi.org/10.1001/jama.1992.03490170092032

Haager, D. E., Klingner, J. E., & Vaughn, S. E. (2007). *Evidence-based reading practices for response to intervention.* Paul H. Brookes.

Habermas, J. (1990). *Moral consciousness and communicative action* (C. Lenhardt & S. W. Nicholsen, Trans.). Polity Press.

Harris, C. (1993). Whiteness as property. *Harvard Law Review, 106,* 1709–1791.

Harris, C. I. (1993). Whiteness as property. In L. Alcoff & E. Mendietta (Eds.) *Identities: Race, class, gender, and nationality* (pp. 75–89). Wiley-Blackwell.

Harry, B. (2017). TMMI: *Dilemmas of knowledge and learning in the age of too much mis-information.* Equity Alliance at Stanford Graduate School of Education.

Harry, B., & Klingner, J. (2006). *Why are so many minority students in special education? Understanding race and disability in schools.* Teachers College Press.

Hart, J. E., Cramer, E. D., Harry, B., Klingner, J. K., & Sturges, K. M. (2010). The continuum of "troubling" to "troubled" behavior: Exploratory case studies of African American students in programs for emotional disturbance. *Remedial and Special Education, 31*(3), 148–162.

Hart-Tervalon, D., & Garcia, D. R. (2014). Educational systems change at the state level. In E. B. Kozleski & K. A. K. Thorius (Eds.), *Ability, equity, and culture: Sustaining inclusive urban education reform* (pp. 199–216). Teachers College Press.

Heidegger, M. (1959). *Introduction to metaphysics.* Translated by Ralph Manheim. Yale University Press.

Hernández-Saca, D. I. (2019). Youth at the intersections of dis/ability, other markers of identity, and emotionality: Toward a critical pedagogy of student knowledge, emotion, feeling, affect, and being. *Teachers College Record, 121*(13), 1–16.

Hernández-Saca, D. I. (2020). The intersections of learning dis/ability, ethnicity, and emotionality in education: The voice of Sophia Cruz. *Equity by design* [Research brief]. Midwest & Plains Equity Assistance Center.

Hernández-Saca, D. I., Gutmann Kahn, L., & Cannon, M. A. (2018). Intersectionality dis/ability research: How dis/ability research in education engages intersectionality to uncover the multidimensional construction of dis/abled experiences. *Review of Research in Education, 42*(1), 286–311.

Holland, D., Lachicotte, W., Skinner, D., & Cain, C. (1998). *Identity and agency in cultural worlds.* Harvard University Press.

Horkheimer, M. (1972). *Critical theory: Selected essays* (Vol. 1). A & C Black.

Horkheimer, M. (1993). *Between philosophy and social science.* MIT Press.

Houtrow, A., Harris, D., Molinero, A., Levin-Decanini, T., & Robichaud, C. (2020). Children with disabilities in the United States and the COVID-19 pandemic. *Journal of Pediatric Rehabilitation Medicine, 13*(3), 415–424.

Huberman, A. M. (1983). Recipes for busy kitchens: A situational analysis of routine knowledge use in schools. *Knowledge: Creation Diffusion, Utilization, 4,* 478–510.

Hughey, M. (2014). *The white savior film: Content, critics, and consumption.* Temple University Press.

Hunter, S. B., Chinman, M., Ebener, P., Imm, P., Wandersman, A., & Ryan, G. W. (2009). Technical assistance as a prevention capacity-building tool: A demonstration using the getting to outcomes® framework. *Health Education & Behavior, 36*(5), 810–828.

Illback, R. J., & Maher, C. A. (1984). The school psychologist as an organizational boundary role professional. *Journal of School Psychology, 22*(1), 63–72.

Individuals With Disabilities Education Act, 20 U.S.C. § 1400 (1997).

Individuals With Disabilities Education Act, 20 U.S.C. § 1400 (2004).

Individuals With Disabilities Education Act of 1990, 20 U.S.C. § 1401–1485.

Individuals With Disabilities Education Act Amendments of 1997, P.L. 105–17, 105th Congress, 1st session.

Institute of Education Sciences. (2010). *Department of Education Institute of Education Sciences fiscal year 2010 request.* Retrieved from http://www2.ed.gov/about/overview/budget/budget10/justifications/y-ies.pdf

Iqtadar, S., Hernández-Saca, D., & Ellison, S. (2021). *Educational experiences of students with multiply-marginalized identities: A qualitative research synthesis of disability research* [Podcast]. Midwest & Plains Equity Assistance Center.

Jackson, R. G., Coomer, M. N., Dagli, C., Skelton, S. M., Kyser, T. S., & Thorius, K.A.K. (2017). Reexamining workforce diversity: Authentic representations of difference. *Equity Dispatch* [Newsletter]. Midwest & Plains Equity Assistance Center.

Jackson, R., Thorius, K. A. K., & Kyser, T. S. (2016). Systemic approaches to eliminating disproportionality in special education. *Equity by Design* [Research brief]. Great Lakes Equity Center.

Joffe-Walt, C. (Host) & Snyder, J. (Producer). (2020). *Nice white parents.* Serial Productions and *The New York Times*, 6 episodes.

Johnson, J. L. (1969). Special education and inner-city: A challenge for the future or another means of cooling the mark out? *Journal of Special Education, 3*, 241–251.

Johnson, L. J., & Pugach, M. C. (1990). Classroom teachers' views of intervention strategies for learning and behavior problems: Which are reasonable and how frequently are they used?. *The Journal of Special Education, 24*(1), 69–84.

Kane, M. B., & Kocher, A. T. (1980, June). The dissemination and use of educational R & D in the United States: An analysis of recent federal attempts to improve educational practice. In *The political realization of social science knowledge and research: Toward new scenarios.* Conference of the Institute for Advanced Studies, Vienna, Austria.

Kaplan, A., Cromley, J., Perez, T., Dai, T., Mara, K., & Balsai, M. (2020). The role of context in educational RCT findings: A call to redefine "evidence-based practice." *Educational Researcher, 49*(4), 285–288. https://doi.org/10.3102/0013189X20921862

Katz, J., & Wandersman, A. (2016). Technical assistance to enhance prevention capacity: A research synthesis of the evidence base. *Prevention Science, 17*, 417–428.

Keith, T. Z. (2008). Best practices in applied research. In A. Thomas & J. Grimes (Eds.), *Best practices in school psychology V* (pp. 91–102). National Association of School Psychologists.

Khalifa, M. A., & Briscoe, F. (2015). A counternarrative autoethnography exploring school districts' role in reproducing racism: Willful blindness to racial inequities. *Teachers College Record, 117*(8), 1–34.

Kincaid, A. P., & Sullivan, A. L. (2017). Parsing the relations of race and socioeconomic status in special education disproportionality. *Remedial and Special Education, 38*(3), 159–170.

King, K. A., Kozleski, E. B., & Artiles, A. J. (with Klingner, J. K., Harry, B., Duran, G. Z., & Sullivan, A. L.). (2008). Culturally responsive response to intervention. *Professional Learning Module Series*. National Center for Culturally Responsive Education Systems.

King, N. (1994). The qualitative research interview. In C. Cassell & G. Symon (Eds), *Qualitative method in organizational research* (pp. 14–36). SAGE

Kliewer, C., & Drake, S. (1998). Disability, eugenics and the current ideology of segregation: A modern moral tale. *Disability & Society, 13*(1), 95–111.

Klingner, J. K., Artiles, A. J., Kozleski, E., Harry, B., Zion, S., Tate, W., Duran, G. Z., & Riley, D. (2005, September 8). Addressing the disproportionate representation of culturally and linguistically diverse students in special education through culturally responsive educational systems. *Education Policy Analysis Archives, 13*(38). Retrieved from https://epaa.asu.edu/index.php/epaa/article/view/143

Klingner, J. K., & Harry, B. (2006). The special education referral and decision-making process for English language learners: Child study team meetings and staffings. *Teachers College Record, 108*, 2247–2281.

Knoff, H. (1983). Investigating disproportionate influence and status in multidisciplinary child study teams. *Exceptional Children, 49*(5), 440–444.

Kostogriz, A., & Veresov, N. (2021). *The zone of proximal development and diversity*. Oxford University Press.

Koszalka, T. A., & Wu, C. P. (2004). A cultural historical activity theory [CHAT] analysis of technology integration: Case study of two teachers. Retrieved from https://files.eric.ed.gov/fulltext/ED485000.pdf

Kozleski, E. B., & Artiles, A. J. (2012). Technical assistance as inquiry: Using activity theory methods to engage equity in educational practice communities. In S. Steinberg & G. Canella (Eds.), *Handbook on critical qualitative research* (pp. 431–445). Peter Lang.

Kozleski, E. B., & Artiles, A. J. (2014). Beyond psychological views of student learning in systemic reform agendas. In E. B. Kozleski & K. A. K. Thorius (Eds.), *Ability, equity, and culture: Sustaining inclusive urban education reform* (pp. 63–79). Teachers College Press.

Kozleski, E. B., & Siuty, M. B. (2016). *The complexities of inclusive education: How cultural histories shape the ways teachers respond to multiple forms of diversity*. Equity-Centered Capacity Building Network. http://capacitybuildingnetwork.org/article6/

Kozleski, E. B., & Thorius, K. A. K. (Eds.). (2014). *Ability, equity and culture: Sustaining inclusive urban education reform*. Teachers College Press.

Kozleski, E. B., Thorius, K. A. K., & Smith, A. (2014). Theorizing systemic reform in urban schools. In E. B. Kozleski & K. A. K. Thorius (Eds.), *Ability, equity, and culture: Sustaining inclusive urban education reform* (pp. 11–31). Teachers College Press.

Kozleski, E. B., & Waitoller, F. R. (2010). Teacher learning for inclusive education: Understanding teaching as a cultural and political practice. *International Journal of Inclusive Education, 14*(7), 655–666.

Kozleski, E. B., & Zion, S. (2006). *Preventing disproportionality by strengthening district policies and procedures—An assessment and strategic planning process.* National Center for Culturally Responsive Educational Systems.

Kuutti, K. (1996). Activity theory as a potential framework for human–computer interaction research. In B. A. Nardi (Ed.), *Context and consciousness: Activity theory and human–computer interaction* (pp. 17–44). MIT Press.

Kyser, T. S., Coomer, N., Moore, T., Cosby, G., Jackson, R. G., & Skelton, S. M. (2015). Parents/caregivers as authentic partners in education. *Equity Dispatch* [Newsletter]. Great Lakes Equity Center. https://greatlakesequity.org/resource/parentscaregivers-authentic-partners-education

Kyser, T. S., Skelton, S. M., Ruiz-Morales, R., Williams, D. (2022a, November 2–6). *Fortifying ourselves and the work: Toward an anti-racist now through equity expansive technical assistance* [Conference presentation]. American Educational Studies Association, Pittsburgh, PA, United States.

Kyser, T. S., Skelton, S. M., Ruiz-Morales, R. (2022b, October 28–29). *Fortifying ourselves and the work: Co-conspiring an unapologetic anti-racist now through equity expansive technical assistance* [Conference presentation]. Critical Race Studies in Education Association, Edwardsville, IL, United States.

Ladson-Billings, G. (1992). Liberatory consequences of literacy: A case of culturally relevant instruction for African American students. *The Journal of Negro Education, 61*(3), 378–391.

Ladson-Billings, G. (1998). Just what is critical race theory and what's it doing in a nice field like education? *International Journal of Qualitative Studies in Education, 11*(1), 7–24.

Ladson-Billings, G. (2006). From the achievement gap to the education debt: Understanding achievement in U.S. schools. *Educational Researcher, 35*(7), 3–12.

Ladson-Billings, G., & Tate, W. F., IV. (1995). Toward a critical race theory of education. *Teachers College Record, 97*(1), 47–68.

Lambert, R. (2018). "Indefensible, illogical, and unsupported": Countering deficit mythologies about the potential of students with learning disabilities in mathematics. *Education Sciences, 8*(2), 1–12. https://doi.org/10.3390/educsci8020072

Lambert, R., Imm, K., Schuck, R., Choi, S., & McNiff, A. (2021). "UDL is the what, design thinking is the how:" Designing for differentiation in mathematics. *Mathematics Teacher Education and Development, 23*(3), 54–77.

Lantolf, J. P. (2000). Introducing sociocultural theory. In J. P. Lantolf (Ed.) *Sociocultural theory and second language learning* (pp. 1–26). Oxford University Press.

Lather, P. (2017). *Future directions of educational change: Social justice, professional capital, and systems change.* Routledge.

Lazzell, D. R., Jackson, R. G., & Skelton, S. M. (2020). Inequities in online classrooms: How do we bridge the distance (learning)? *Equity Digest* [Newsletter]. Midwest & Plains Equity Assistance Center.

Leadership Conference on Civil and Human Rights. (2020). *Trump administration civil and human rights rollbacks*. Retrieved from https://civilrights.org/trump -rollbacks/

Leigh, P. R. (2003). Interest convergence and desegregation in the Ohio Valley. *Journal of Negro Education, 72*(3), 269–296.

Leithwood, K. A., Seashore Louis, K., Anderson, S., & Wahlstrom, K. (2004). *How leadership influences student learning*. Center for Applied Research and Educational Improvement.

Leonardo, Z. (2009). *Race, whiteness, and education*. Routledge.

Leonardo, Z. (2013). *Race frameworks: A multidimensional theory of racism and education*. Teachers College Press.

Leonardo, Z., & Broderick, A. (2011). Smartness as property: A critical exploration of intersections between whiteness and disability studies. *Teachers College Record, 113,* (10), 2206–2232

Leonardo, Z., & Zembylas, M. (2013). Whiteness as technology of affect: Implications for educational praxis. *Equity & Excellence in Education, 46*(1), 150–165. https://doi.org/10.1080/10665684.2013.750539

Lhamon, C. (2014, April 4). Dear colleague letter: Resource comparability. U.S. Department of Education, Office for Civil Rights.

Lilienfeld, S. O., Ritschel, L. A., Lynn, S. J., Cautin, R. L., & Latzman, R. D. (2013). Why many clinical psychologists are resistant to evidence-based practice: Root causes and constructive remedies. *Clinical Psychology Review, 33*(7), 883–900. https://doi.org/10.1016/j.cpr.2012.09.008

Linton, S. (1998). *Claiming disability: Knowledge and identity*. NYU Press.

Little, J. W. (1993). Teachers' professional development in a climate of educational reform. *Educational Evaluation and Policy Analysis, 15*(2), 129–151.

López, S. R. (1989). Patient variable biases in clinical judgment: Conceptual overview and methodological considerations. *Psychological Bulletin, 106*(2), 184–203.

Losen, D. (2009). *Racial disproportionality in special education: District profile workbook*. Wisconsin Department of Public Instruction.

Losen, D. J., & Orfield, G. (Eds.). (2002). *Racial inequity in special education*. Harvard Educational Press.

Loucks-Horsley, S., & Roody, D. S. (1990). Using what is known about change to inform the regular education initiative. *Remedial and Special Education, 11*(3), 51–56.

Louis, K. S., & Rosenblum, S. (1981). *Linking R&D with schools: A program and its implications for dissemination and school improvement policy*. U. S. Department of Education, Office of Education Research and Improvement.

Love, P. (2009). Educational psychologists: The early search for an identity. *Educational Psychology in Practice, 25*(1), 3–8.

Macekura, S. (2013). The point four program and U.S. international development policy. *Political Science Quarterly, 128*(1), 127–160.

Macey, E. M., Thorius, K. A. K., & Skelton, S. M. (2012). *Equity by design: Engaging school communities in critical reflection on policy*. Great Lakes Equity Center. https://greatlakesequity.org/sites/default/files/20120109459_brief.pdf

Mackey, H. J. (2018). Contemporary decolonization: Dismantling policy barriers to systemic equity and self-determination. In R. Papa & S.W. J. Armfield (Eds.), *The Wiley handbook of educational policy* (pp. 267–287). Wiley.

MacLean, N. (2017). *Democracy in chains: The deep history of the radical right's stealth plan for America.* Viking.

Marshall, C., & Olivia, M. (2006). *Leaders for social justice: Making revolutions in education.* Allyn & Bacon.

Martin, D., & Peim, N. (2009). Critical perspectives on activity theory. *Educational Review, 61*(2), 131–138. https://doi.org/10.1080/00131910902844689

Martínez-Álvarez, P., Ghiso, M. P., & Campano, G. (2014). Engaging double binds for critical inquiry with first-grade Latina/o emergent bilinguals. *Darnioji Daugiakalbystė/Sustainable Multilingualism,* No. 5, 62–98.

Matias, C. E. (2016). *Feeling white.* Sense Publishers.

Matias, C. E., & Mackey, J. (2016). Breakin' down whiteness in antiracist teaching: Introducing critical whiteness pedagogy. *The Urban Review, 48*(1), 32–50. https://doi.org10.1007/s11256-015-0344-7

Matsuda, M. (1995). Looking to the bottom: Critical legal studies and reparations. In K. Crenshaw, N. Gotanda, G. Peller, & K. Thomas (Eds.), *Critical race theory: The key writings that formed the movement* (pp. 63–79). The New Press.

McCall, L. (2005). The complexity of intersectionality. *Signs, 30,* 1771–1800.

McDermott, R., Goldman, S., & Varenne, H. (2006). The cultural work of learning disabilities. *Educational Researcher, 35*(6), 18–23.

McDermott, R., & Varenne, H. (1998). *Successful failure: The schools America builds.* Westview Press.

McInerney, M., & Hamilton, J. L. (2007). Elementary and Middle Schools Technical Assistance Center: An approach to support the effective implementation of scientifically based practices in special education. *Exceptional Children, 73*(2), 242–255.

McLaughlin, M. W. (1990). The Rand change agent study revisited: Macro perspectives and micro realities. *Educational Researcher, 19*(9), 11–16.

McNeil, M. (2014), February 19). Scrutiny rises on placement of best teachers. *Education Week.* Retrieved from http://www.edweek.org/ew/articles/2014/02/19/21equity_ep.h33.html

McRuer, R. (2016). Compulsory able-bodiness and queer/disabled existence. In L. J. Davis (Ed.), *The disability studies reader* (4th ed., pp. 412–421). Routledge.

Mehan, H. (1993). Beneath the skin and between the ears: A case study in the politics of representation. In S. Chalklin & J. Lave (Eds.), *Understanding practice: Perspectives on activity and contexts* (pp. 241–268). Cambridge University Press.

Merriam, S. B. (1998). *Qualitative research and case study applications in education. Revised and expanded from "Case study research in education."* Jossey-Bass.

Meyer, A., Rose, D. H., & Gordon, D. (2014). *Universal design for learning: Theory and practice.* CAST.

Midgley, G. (2000). *Systemic intervention: Philosophy, methodology, and practice.* Kluwer.

Midwest & Plains Equity Assistance Center (2020). Creating caring classroom communities through culturally responsive and sustaining lesson planning. Equilearn focus session [professional development session]. Author.

Miles, R. (2020). Making a case for cultural historical activity theory: Examples of CHAT in practice. *Studies in Technology Enhanced Learning, 1*(1), 65–80. https://doi.org/10.21428/8c225f6e.c4feefa5

Milner, H. R. (2008). Critical race theory and interest convergence as analytic tools in teacher education policies and practices. *Journal of Teacher Education, 59*(4), 332–346.

Milner, H. R. (2012). Beyond a test score: Explaining opportunity gaps in educational practice. *Journal of Black Studies, 43*(6), 693–718.

Mitchell, D., & Snyder, S. (2003). The eugenic Atlantic: Race, disability, and the making of an international eugenic science, 1800–1945. *Disability & Society, 18*(7), 843–864.

Mitra, S. (2006). The capability approach and disability. *Journal of Disability Policy Studies, 16*, 236–247. https://doi.org10.1177/10442073060160040501

Moll, L. C., Amati, C., Neff, D., & Gonzalez, N. (1992). Funds of knowledge for teaching: Using a qualitative approach to connect homes and classrooms. *Theory Into Practice, 31*, 132–141.

Morgan, P. L., & Farkas, G. (2015, June 24). Is special education racist? (Opinion pages). *The New York Times.* Retrieved from http://www.nytimes.com/2015/06/24/opinion/is-special-education-racist.html

Morgan, P. L., & Farkas, G. (2016). Evidence of minority under-representation in special education and its implications for school psychologists. *NASP Communique, 44*(6), 30–33.

Morgan, P. L., Farkas, G., Hillemeier, M., Mattison, R., Maczuga, S., Li, H., & Cook, M. (2015). Minorities are disproportionately underrepresented in special education: Longitudinal evidence across five disability conditions. *Educational Researcher, 44*(5), 278–292. https://doi.org10.3102/0013189X15591157

Morton, C. H. (2017). Supporting student success through authentic partnerships: Reflection from parents and caregivers. *Equity by Design* [Research brief]. Midwest & Plains Equity Assistance Center.

Mostert, M. P., & Crockett, J. B. (1999–2000). Reclaiming the history of special education for more effective practice. *Exceptionality, 8*(2), 133–143. http://dx.doi.org/10.1207/S15327035EX0802_4

Mulligan, E. (2010, December). *Culturally responsive cognitive coaching for inclusive practices.* [Paper presentation]. TASH.

Mulligan, E., & Kozleski, E. B. (2009). *NIUSI–LeadScape principal coaching guide.* NIUSI–LeadScape.

NAACP Legal Defense Fund. (2022). Critical Race Theory: Frequently asked questions. https://www.naacpldf.org/critical-race-theory-faq/

Nasir, N., & Saxe, G. B. (2003). Ethnic and academic identities: A cultural practice perspective on emerging tensions and their management in the lives of minority students. *Educational Researcher, 32*(5), 14–18.

National Center for Culturally Responsive Education Systems. (2009). *Final report: How the disproportionality center changed the nature of the conversation about disproportionality in special education.* Author. https://issuu.com/equityallianceatasu/docs/finalreportv4_nccrest

National Council for Learning Disabilities (n.d.). *USED delays the Equity in IDEA Regulation.* Retrieved from https://www.ncld.org/news/policy-and-advocacy/used-delays-the-equity-in-idea-regulation/

National School Boards Association. (2017). *Frequently asked questions: What is the school board's most important responsibility?* Retrieved from https://www.nsba.org/about-us/frequently-asked-questions

Neighbors, H. W., Trierweiler, S. J., Ford, B. C., & Muroff, J. R. (2003). Racial differences in DSM diagnosis using a semi-structured instrument: The importance of clinical judgment in the diagnosis of African Americans. *Journal of Health and Social Behavior, 44*(3), 237–256.

Nord, W. R., & Tucker, S. (1987). *Implementing routine and radical innovations.* Free Press.

Novak, B. (2021). *Persistent barriers to equity: State statutes and state education agency regulations and guidance about specific learning disabilities.* [Doctoral dissertation, University of Wisconsin–Madison]. ProQuest Dissertations.

O'Connor, C., & DeLuca Fernandez, S. (2006). Race, class, and disproportionality: Reevaluating the relationship between poverty and special education placement. *Educational Researcher, 35*(6), 6–11.

Odom, S. L., Brantlinger, E., Gersten, R., Horner, R. H., Thompson, B., & Harris, K. R. (2005). Research in special education: Scientific methods and evidence-based practices. *Exceptional Children, 71*(2), 137–148.

Oliver, M. (1983). *Social work with disabled people.* Macmillan.

Oliver, M. (2013). The social model of disability: Thirty years on. *Disability & Society, 28*(7), 1024–1026.

O'Reilly, C., Northcraft, G. B., & Sabers, D. (1989). The confirmation bias in special education eligibility decisions. *School Psychology Review, 18*(1), 126–135.

Osher, D., & Kane, M. (1993). *Describing and studying innovations in the education of children with attention deficit disorder. A series of papers on the federal role in improving practice in special education.* U. S. Department of Education, Office of Special Education Programs.

Packard, R. (1969). *Sugarcane Island.* Vermont Crossroads Press.

Paris, D. (2012). Culturally sustaining pedagogy: A needed change in stance, terminology, and practice. *Educational Researcher, 41*(3), 93–97. http://doi.org/10.3102/0013189X12441244

Paris, D., & Alim, H. S. (2014). What are we seeking to sustain through culturally sustaining pedagogy? A loving critique forward. *Harvard Educational Review, 84*(1), 85–100.

Parrish, T. (2002). Racial disparities in the identification, funding, and provision of special education. In D. Losen (Ed.), *Minority issues in special education* (pp. 15–38). The Civil Rights Project, Harvard University & Harvard Education Publishing.

Plessy v. Ferguson, 163 U.S. 537 (May 18, 1896).

Radd, S. I. (2019). Avoiding the traps: Identifying and disrupting six paradoxical habits of equity leadership. *Equity by Design* [Research brief]. Midwest & Plains Equity Assistance Center.

Radd, S. I. (2022). Complexities of the self: Inner work for equity leaders. *Equity by Design*. Midwest & Plains Equity Assistance Center.

Radd, S. I., Generett, G. G., Gooden, M. A., & Theoharis, G. (2021). *Five practices for equity-focused school leadership.* Association for Supervision and Curriculum Development.

Radd, S. I., & Kramer, B. H. (2016). Dis eased: Critical consciousness in school leadership for social justice. *Journal of School Leadership, 26*(4), 580–606.

Radd, S. I., & Macey, E. M. (2013). Developing critical consciousness through professional learning. *Equity by Design* [Research brief]. Great Lakes Equity Center.

Rogoff, B. (2003). *The cultural nature of human development*. Oxford University Press.

Rose, D. H., & Meyer, A. (2002). *Teaching every student in the digital age: Universal design for learning*. Association for Supervision and Curriculum Development.

Rose, D. H., & Meyer, A. (2006). *A practical reader in universal design for learning*. Harvard Education Press.

Roth, W. M. (2012). Cultural-historical activity theory: Vygotsky's forgotten and suppressed legacy and its implication for mathematics education. *Mathematics Education Research Journal, 24*, 87–104.

Roth, W. M., Lee, Y. J., & Hsu, P. L. (2009). A tool for changing the world: Possibilities of cultural-historical activity theory to reinvigorate science education. *Studies in Science Education, 45*(2), 131–167.

Rufo, C. (2018, October). *The politics of ruinous compassion: How Seattle's homelessness policy perpetuates the crisis—and how we can fix it* [A Discovery Institute White Paper]. https://www.discovery.org/m/2018/10/The-Politics-of-Ruinous -Compassion.pdf

Rusnak, K. N., Jackson, R. J., Thorius, K. A. K., & Skelton, S. M. (2022). Transgender awareness in sports: A choose your own equitable adventure. *Equity Express, 1*(4). Midwest & Plains Equity Assistance Center.

Saatcioglu, A., & Sargut, G. (2014). Sociology of school boards: A social capital perspective. *Sociological Inquiry, 84*(1), 42–74.

Sachs, J. (2000). The activist professional. *Journal of Educational Change, 1*(1), 77–94.

Sadker, D. (n.d.). Seven forms of bias in instructional materials. http://www.sadker .org/curricularbias.html

Samuels, C. (2016, March 4). Racial bias in special education: Learning about disproportionality. *Education Week*. https://www.edweek.org/teaching-learning /racial-bias-in-special-education-learning-about-disproportionality/2016/03

Sannino, A., & Engeström, Y. (2017). Co-generation of societally impactful knowledge in Change Laboratories. *Management Learning, 48*(1), 80–96.

Sannino, A., Engeström, Y., & Lemos, M. (2016). Formative interventions for expansive learning and transformative agency. *Journal of the Learning Sciences, 25*(4), 599–633.

Santayana, G. (1906). *The life of reason: Reason in science* (Vol. 5). Scribner.

Sashkin, M., & Egermeier, J. (1993). *School change models and processes: A review and synthesis of research and practice*. U.S. Government Printing Office.

Sawyer, R. K. (Ed.). (2005). *The Cambridge handbook of the learning sciences*. Cambridge University Press.

Schalock, M. D., Fredericks, B., Dalke, B. A., & Alberto, P. A. (1994). The house that TRACES built: A conceptual model of service delivery systems and implications for change. *The Journal of Special Education, 28*(2), 203–223.

Schein, E. H. (1992). How can organizations learn faster? The challenge of entering the green room. *Sloan Management Review, 34*, 85–92.

Schiller, E. P., Malouf, D. B., & Danielson, L. C. (1995). Research utilization: A federal perspective. *Remedial and Special Education, 16*(6), 372–375.

Scribner, J. P., Sawyer, K., Watson, S., & Myers, V. (2007). Teacher teams and distributed leadership: A study of group discourse and collaboration. *Educational Administration Quarterly, 43*(1), 67–100.

Senge, P. M. (1990). *The fifth discipline: The art and practice of the learning organization.* Doubleday.

Shakespeare, T., & Watson, N. (2002). The social model of disability: An outdated ideology? *Research in Social Science and Disability, 2,* 9–28.

Shealey, M. W., Lue, M. S., Brooks, M., & McCray, E. (2005). Examining the legacy of "Brown": The impact on special education and teacher practice. *Remedial and Special Education, 26*(2), 113–121.

Shifrer, D. (2016). Stigma and stratification limiting the math course progression of adolescents labeled with a learning disability. *Learning and Instruction, 42,* 47–57. https://doi.org/10.1016/j.learninstruc.2015.12.001

Skelton, S. M. (2013). *Advancing office recommendations: From the critical review of state level operational documents* [PowerPoint slides]. https://greatlakesequity .org/resource/advancing-office-recommendations-critical-review-state-level -operational-documents

Skelton, S. M. (2015). *Beyond diversity day planning guide.* Great Lakes Equity Center. https://greatlakesequity.org/resource/beyond-diversity-day-planning -guide

Skelton, S. M. (2019a). Situating my positionality as a Black woman with a dis/ability in the provision of equity-focused technical assistance: A personal reflection. *International Journal of Qualitative Studies in Education, 32*(3), 225–242.

Skelton, S. M. (2019b). *Allearn County Schools scenario.* Great Lakes Equity Center.

Skelton, S. M., Kyser, T. S., Sehkar, A. A., & Fox, A. (2021). *Systems assessment of equity and justice in education* [Manual]. Midwest & Plains Equity Assistance Center.

Skiba, R. J. (2002). Special education and school discipline: A precarious balance. *Behavioral Disorders, 27*(2), 81–97.

Skiba, R., Albrecht, S., & Losen, D. (2013). CCBD's position summary on federal policy on disproportionality in special education. *Behavioral Disorders, 38*(2) 108–120.

Skiba, R. J., Artiles, A. J., Kozleski, E. B., Losen, D. J., & Harry, E. G. (2016). Risks and consequences of oversimplifying educational inequities: A response to Morgan et al. (2015). *Educational Researcher, 45*(3), 221–225. https://doi.org/10 .3102/0013189X16644606

Skiba, R., Simmons, A., Ritter, S., Kohler, K., Henderson, M., & Wu, T. (2006). The context of minority disproportionality: Practitioner perspectives on special education referral. *Teachers College Record, 108*(7), 1424–1459.

Skiba, R. J., Simmons, A. B., Ritter, S., Gibb, A. C., Rausch, M. K., Cuadrado, J., & Chung, C. G. (2008). Achieving equity in special education: History, status, and current challenges. *Exceptional Children, 74*(3), 264–288.

Skinner, B. F. (1971). Operant conditioning. In J. W. Guthrie (Ed.), *The encyclopedia of education* (Vol. 7, pp. 29–33).

Slavin, R. E. (2002). Evidence-based education policies: Transforming educational practice and research. *Educational Researcher, 31*(7), 15–21.

Sleeter, C. E. (2005). *Un-standardizing curriculum: Multicultural teaching in the standards-based classroom.* Teachers College Press.

Solórzano, D., & Yosso, T. (2001). Critical race and LatCrit theory and method: Counterstorytelling. *International Journal of Qualitative Studies in Education, 14*, 471–495.

Stake, R. E. (1995). *The art of case study research.* SAGE.

Steiner, G. A. (2010). *Strategic planning.* Simon & Schuster.

Strassfeld, N. M. (2017). The future of IDEA: Monitoring disproportionate representation of minority students in special education and intentional discrimination claims. *Case Western Law Review, 67*(4), 1121–1151.

Stovall, D. (2006). Urban poetics: Poetry, social justice, and critical pedagogy in education. *Urban Review, 38*(1), 63–80.

Stubblefield, A. (2007). "Beyond the pale": Tainted whiteness, cognitive disability, and eugenic sterilization. *Hypatia, 22*(2), 162–181.

Sullivan, A. L. (2011). Disproportionality in special education identification and placement of English language learners. *Exceptional Children, 77*(3), 317–334.

Sullivan, A. L., & Artiles, A. J. (2011). Theorizing racial inequity in special education: Applying structural inequity theory to disproportionality. *Urban Education, 46*(6), 1526–1552.

Sullivan, A. L., Li, A., Nguyen, T., & Bose, M. (2022). Promoting socially-just, evidence-based practice. *Equity by Design* [Research brief]. Midwest & Plains Equity Assistance Center.

Sullivan, A. L., & Osher, D. (2019). IDEA's double bind: A synthesis of disproportionality policy interpretations. *Exceptional Children, 85*(4), 395–412. https://doi.org/10.1177/0014402918818047

Sullivan, A. L., Sadeh, S., & Houri, A. K. (2019). Are school psychologists' special education eligibility decisions reliable and unbiased? A multi-study experimental investigation. *Journal of School Psychology, 77*, 90–109.

Sullivan, A. L., & Thorius, K. A. K. (2013). Considering intersections of difference among students identified as disabled and expanding conceptualizations of multicultural education. *Race, Gender & Class, 17*(1/2), 93–109.

Sullivan, A. L., Weeks, M. R., Kulkarni, T., & Goerdt, A. (2018). Preventing disproportionality through nondiscriminatory tiered services. *Equity by Design* [Research brief]. Midwest & Plains Equity Assistance Center.

Swaffield, S., & MacBeath, J. (2005). School self-evaluation and the role of a critical friend. *Cambridge Journal of Education, 35*(2), 239–252.

Tan, P. (2014). *Towards equity in mathematics education for students with severe disabilities: A case study of professional learning.* Indiana University. https://search.proquest.com/openview/1038f01f769432877c6b174ec5c0d04c/1?pq-origsite=gscholar&cbl=18750&diss=y

Tan, P., & Thorius, K. A. K. (2018). En/countering inclusive mathematics education: A case of professional learning. *Mathematics Teacher Educator, 6*(2), 52–67.

Tan, P., & Thorius, K. A. K. (2019). Toward equity in mathematics education for students with dis/abilities: A case study of professional learning. *American Educational Research Journal, 56*(3), 995–1032.

Tedesco, D., & Bagelman, J. (2017). The "missing" politics of whiteness and rightful presence in the settler-colonial city. *Millennium, 45*(3), 380–402. https://doi.org/10.1177/0305829817712075

Tefera, A. A., & Fischman, G. E. (2020). How and why context matters in the study of racial disproportionality in special education: Toward a critical disability education policy approach. *Equity & Excellence in Education, 53*(4), 433–448. https://doi.org/10.1080/10665684.2020.1791284

Tefera, A. A., Thorius, K. A. K., & Artiles, A. J. (2013). Teacher influences in the racialization of disabilities. In R. Milner & K. Lomotey (Eds.). *Handbook of urban education* (pp. 256–270). Routledge.

Teräs, M., & Lasonen, J. (2013). The development of teachers' intercultural competence using a Change Laboratory method. *Vocations and Learning, 6,* 107–134.

Theoharis, G. (2007). Social justice educational leaders and resistance: Toward a theory of social justice leadership. *Educational Administration Quarterly, 43*(2), 221–258.

Thomas, K. G., & Gatz, M. (1997). A tale of two school districts: Lessons to be learned about the impact of relationship building and ecology on consultations. *Journal of Educational and Psychological Consultation, 8*(3), 297–320.

Thompson, R. (2007). *Perceptions of the Texas school board–superintendent working relationship* [Doctoral dissertation]. Stephen F. Austin State University.

Thorius, K. A. K. (2015). *High-leverage strategies for addressing special education disproportionality.* [Keynote address]. Wisconsin Department of Public Instruction. Summer Conference, Madison, WI, United States.

Thorius, K. A. K. (2016). Stimulating artifact-mediated tensions in special education teachers' figured world: An approach toward inclusive education. *International Journal of Inclusive Education, 20,* 1326–1343.

Thorius, K. A. K. (2019). Facilitating en/counters with special education's cloak of benevolence in professional learning to eliminate racial disproportionality in special education. *International Journal of Qualitative Studies in Education, 32*(3), 323–340.

Thorius, K. A. K., & Maxcy, B. D. (2015). Critical practice analysis of special education policy: An RTI example. *Remedial and Special Education, 36*(2), 116–124.

Thorius, K. A. K., Maxcy, B. D., Macey, E., & Cox, A. (2014). A critical practice analysis of response to intervention appropriation in an urban school. *Remedial and Special Education, 35,* 287–299.

Thorius, K. A. K., & Waitoller, F. R. (2022). Disability and asset pedagogies: An introduction to the book. In F. R. Waitoller & K. A. K. Thorius (Eds.) *Sustaining disabled youth: Centering disability in asset pedagogies* (pp. xv–xxxi). Teachers College Press.

Triano, S. (2000). Categorical eligibility for special education: The enshrinement of the medical model in disability policy. *Disability Studies Quarterly, 20*(4).

Trohanis, P. L. (1982). Technical assistance and the improvement of services to exceptional children. *Theory into Practice, 21,* 119–128.

Trujillo, T. M. (2013). The disproportionate erosion of local control: Urban school boards, high-stakes accountability, and democracy. *Educational Policy, 27*(2), 334–359.

Truman, H. S. (1949). Inaugural address, Thursday, 20 January 1949. https://www.trumanlibrary.gov/library/public-papers/19/inaugural-address

Tuck, E. (2009). Suspending damage: A letter to communities. *Harvard Educational Review, 79*(3), 409–428.

Turnbull, H. R., III, & Stowe, M. J. (2001). Five models for thinking about disability: Implications for policy responses. *Journal of Disability Policy Studies, 12*(3), 198–205. https://doi.org/10.1177/104420730101200305

Turner, J. C., Christensen, A., Kackar-Cam, H. Z., Fulmer, S. M., & Trucano, M. (2017). The development of professional learning communities and their teacher leaders: An activity systems analysis. *Journal of the Learning Sciences, 27*, 49–88.

U. S. Department of Education. (2022). *Fiscal year 2022 budget summary*. Author.

U. S. Department of Education, Office of Special Education and Rehabilitative Services, Office of Special Education Programs. (2001). *23rd annual report to Congress on the implementation of the Individuals With Disabilities Education Act*. Author.

U. S. Department of Education, Office of Special Education and Rehabilitative Services, Office of Special Education Programs. (2020). *41st annual report to Congress on the implementation of the Individuals With Disabilities Education Act, 2019*. Author.

U. S. Department of Education, Office of Special Education and Rehabilitative Services, Office of Special Education Programs. (2021). *43rd annual report to Congress on the implementation of the Individuals With Disabilities Act, 2021*. Author.

Valdes, F. (1998). Foreword: Under construction—LatCrit consciousness, community, and theory. *La Raza Law Journal, 10*, 3–53.

VanDerHeyden, A. M., Witt, J. C., & Gilbertson, D. (2007). A multi-year evaluation of the effects of a response to intervention (RTI) model on identification of children for special education. *Journal of School Psychology, 45*(2), 225–256.

Vaughn, S., Gersten, R., Dimino, J., Taylor, M. J., Newman-Gonchar, R., Krowka, S., Kieffer, M. J., McKeown, M., Reed, D., Sanchez, M., St. Martin, K., Wexler, J., Morgan, S., Yañez, A., & Jayanthi, M. (2022). *Providing reading interventions for students in grades 4–9* (WWC 2022007). National Center for Education Evaluation and Regional Assistance, Institute of Education Sciences, U.S. Department of Education. https://ies.ed.gov/ncee/wwc/PracticeGuide/29

Venzant Chambers, T. T. (2019). ROC'ing *Brown*: Understanding the costs of desegregation using a racial opportunity cost framework. *Peabody Journal of Education, 94*(5), 535–544.

Veresov, N. (2020). Perezhivanie (live through) as a phenomenon and a concept: Questions on clarification and methodological meditations. *Main Issues of Pedagogy and Psychology, 17*(1), 46–64.

Vigil-Hayes, M., Joseph, D., Collier, A., & Amerish, A. (2021, April 7). *Using mobile games in rural tribal communities to promote social and emotional resilience in youth* [Short talk]. Smart and Connected Communities Principal Investigators' Meeting, Denver, CO, United States.

Voulgarides, C. K. (2019). Civil rights remedies and persistent inequities: The case of racial disproportionality in special education. In G. Q. Conchas, B. M. Hinga, M. N. Abad, & K. D. Gutiérrez, *The complex web of inequality in North American schools* (pp. 189–201). Routledge.

Voulgarides, C. K., Fergus, E., & Thorius, K.A.K. (2017). Pursuing equity: Disproportionality in special education and the reframing of technical solutions to address systemic inequities. *Review of Research in Education, 41*(1), 61–87.

Vygotsky, L. S. (1978a). Interaction between learning and development. *Readings on the Development of Children, 23*(3), 34–41.

Vygotsky, L. S. (1978b). *Mind in society: The development of higher psychological processes.* Harvard University Press.

Vygotsky, L. S. (1994). The problem of the environment. In R. Van Der Veer & J. Valsiner (Eds.), *The Vygotsky reader* (pp. 338–354). Blackwell.

Vygotsky, L. S. (1997). *The collected works of L.S. Vygotsky: Volume 4—The history of the development of higher mental functions* (M. J. Hall, Trans.). Springer.

Vygotsky, L. S., & Luria, A. R. (1994). Tool and symbol in child development. In R. van der Veer & J. Valsiner (Eds.), *The Vygotsky reader* (pp. 99–175). Blackwell.

Wagner, J. (2019). "Weakness of the soul:" The special education tradition at the intersection of eugenic discourses, race hygiene and education policies. *Conatus–Journal of Philosophy, 4*(2), 83–104.

Waitoller, F. R., Artiles, A. J., & Cheney, D. A. (2010). The miner's canary: A review of overrepresentation research and explanations. *The Journal of Special Education, 44*(1), 29–49.

Waitoller, F. R., & Kozleski, E. B. (2013). Understanding and dismantling barriers for partnerships for inclusive education: A cultural historical activity theory perspective. *International Journal of Whole Schooling, 9*, 23–42.

Waitoller, F. R., & Thorius, K. A. K. (2016). Cross-pollinating culturally sustaining pedagogy and universal design for learning: Toward an inclusive pedagogy that accounts for dis/ability. *Harvard Educational Review, 86*(3), 366–389.

Waitoller, F. R., & Thorius, K. A. K. (Eds.) (2022*). Sustaining disabled youth: Centering disability in asset pedagogies.* Teachers College Press.

Walcott, C. M., Charvat, J., McNamara, K. M., & Hyson, D. M. (2016, February). *School psychology at a glance: 2015 member survey results* [Special session]. Annual meeting of the National Association of School Psychologists, New Orleans, LA, United States.

Wallace-Wells, B. (2021, June). How a conservative activist invented the conflict over critical race theory. *The New Yorker.* https://www.newyorker.com/news/annals-of-inquiry/how-a-conservative-activist-invented-the-conflict-over-critical-race-theory

Wanzek, J., & Vaughn, S. (2011). Is a three-tier reading intervention model associated with reduced placement in special education? *Remedial and Special Education, 32*(2), 167–175.

Watson, J. B. (1913). Psychology as the behaviorist views it. *Psychological Review, 20*(2), 158–177.

Waxman, O. B. (2019, November). Nebraska just approved more inclusive social studies guidelines. They're a window into the changing way kids are learning U.S. history. *TIME Magazine.* https://time.com/5713359/nebraska-social-studies-standards/

Weeks, M. R., & Sullivan, A. L. (2019). Discrimination matters: Relations of perceived discrimination to student mental health. *School Mental Health, 11*(3), 425–437.

Wells, S. J., Merritt, L. M., & Briggs, H. E. (2009). Bias, racism and evidence-based practice: The case for more focused development of the child welfare evidence base. *Children and Youth Services Review, 31*(11), 1160–1171. https://doi.org/10.1016/j.childyouth.2009.09.002

Welner, K. G. (2001). *Legal rights, local wrongs: When community control collides with educational equity.* State University of New York Press.

Wertsch, J. V. (1981). Trends in Soviet cognitive psychology. *Storia a Critica Della Psicologia, 2,* 219–295.

Whiteman, R., Thorius, K. A. K., Skelton, S. M., & Kyser, T. S. (2015). Rethinking quality: Foregrounding equity in definitions of "high quality" educators. *Equity by Design* [Research brief]. Great Lakes Equity Center.

Wilde, J. (2004). *Definitions for the No Child Left Behind Act of 2001: Scientifically-based research.* National Clearinghouse for English Language Acquisition and Language Instruction Educational Programs.

Willis, A. I., & Harris, V. J. (2000). Political acts: Literacy learning and teaching. *Reading Research Quarterly, 35,* 72–88.

Wilson, V. (2014). Examining teacher education through cultural-historical activity theory. *Teacher Education Advancement Network Journal, 6*(1), 20–29.

Yin, R. K. (2009). *Case study research: Design and methods* (Vol. 5). SAGE.

Yoshida, R. K., Fenton, K. S., Maxwell, J. P., & Kaufman, M. J. (1978). Group decision making in the planning team process: Myth or reality? *Journal of School Psychology, 16*(3), 237–244.

Yosso, T. J., & Solórzano, D. G. (2005). Conceptualizing a critical race theory in sociology. In M. Romero & E. Margolis (Eds.), *The Blackwell companion to social inequalities* (pp. 117–146). Wiley.

Ysseldyke, J. E., Algozzine, B., Regan, R., & McGue, M. (1981). The influence of test scores and naturally-occurring pupil characteristics on psychoeducational decision making with children. *Journal of School Psychology, 19*(2), 167–177.

Zardoya, I. (2017). *What school leaders must learn about equity: ESSA offers an opportunity to improve cultural competency.* Retrieved from https://www.edweek.org/policy-politics/opinion-what-school-leaders-must-learn-about-equity/2017/02 Zhang, D., Katsiyannis, A., Ju, S., & Roberts, E. (2014). Minority representation in special education: 5-year trends. *Journal of Child and Family Studies, 23*(1), 118–127. https://doi.org/10.1007/s10826-012-9698-6

Zigmond, N., Kloo, A., & Volonino, V. (2009). What, where, and how? Special education in the climate of full inclusion. *Exceptionality, 17*(4), 189–204.

Index

About the Author

As a professor of special education and founder and executive director of the Great Lakes Equity Center, **Kathleen A. King Thorius** makes explicit her positionality as a white, nondisabled scholar, focusing on theoretical and practical tools for facilitating white, nondisabled educators' critical examination of their own beliefs and practices, particularly in relation to how they construct their roles to their students, and to the function of special education for their students at the intersection of race and disability. Published extensively in practitioner and research outlets, including *Harvard Educational Review*, the *International Journal of Inclusive Education*, *Remedial and Special Education*, and *The International Journal of Qualitative Studies in Education*, Thorius was a school psychologist before earning her Ph.D. from Arizona State University as an USDOE-funded doctoral fellow in an interdisciplinary program to prepare culturally responsive special education professors. During this time, she was the professional learning coordinator for the National Center for Culturally Responsive Education Systems and the National Center for Urban School Improvement—and a co-director of the Equity Alliance at ASU. Thorius presents nationally and internationally on race, language, dis/ability equity, and multitiered systems of support including culturally responsive schoolwide discipline approaches. Her expertise undergirds past and current work with myriad urban, rural, and suburban school districts and state departments of education. She has been awarded over 25 million dollars from the U.S. Department of Education toward her educational equity research and practice. Thorius is professor of special education in Indiana University's School of Education-IUPUI, and co-editor of *Ability, Equity, and Culture: Sustaining Urban Inclusive Education Reform* (with Elizabeth Kozleski, 2014) and *Sustaining Disabled Youth: Centering Disability in Asset Pedagogy* (with Federico Waitoller, 2022), both published by Teachers College Press.